FLAGSTAD

FLAGSTAD

A PERSONAL MEMOIR

by Edwin McArthur

New York: A L F R E D · A · K N O P F

1 9 6 5

L. C. catalog card number: 65—18768

THIS IS A BORZOI BOOK,

PUBLISHED BY ALFRED A. KNOPF, INC.

FIRST EDITION

TO

Dearest Peggy

*Without whose love these years could
not have been lived and without whose
devoted help this book could not have
been written*

INTRODUCTION

Kirsten Flagstad made her debut at the Metropolitan Opera House on February 2, 1935. It was a Saturday afternoon broadcast, and proved to be one of the most exciting occasions in the Metropolitan's entire history. The intermission commentator was Geraldine Farrar, who, in a rare burst of enthusiasm, announced to her audience that "a new star has been born." Press reaction the following day was uniformly ecstatic.

Needless to say, the effect of all this on the musical profession was immediate and profound. Flagstad's name was everywhere, and though I myself had heard only the broadcast, I was as deeply impressed as anyone else. It immediately occurred to me that I might become her accompanist, and that relationship came about in a remarkably simple way.

My old and dear friend, Marks Levine—"Max," as we all call him—was at that time director of the concert division of NBC Artists Service, a division of the National Broadcasting Company. My wife Peggy and I had invited the Levines for bridge on a Sunday evening, the day after that memorable debut. During the course of our game I learned to my delight that the new star was to be under Max Levine's management. I asked for an introduction, but Max had to decline—he had only just met Madame Flagstad and her husband, Henry Johansen. But he was able to give me her address.

Left to myself after the bridge game, I sat down to write Flagstad a letter. Unlike the many letters that were to follow, this first one was in longhand; I have no copy of it. But, after congratulatory words on her triumph, it went something like this: "You may not yet have become aware of this, Madame Flagstad, but the greater part of activity in America is in the concert field. Unlike Europe, we do not have opera houses in every city, and concert tours are by far the best way of creating a nationwide following. I have already been the regular accompanist of many singers— John Charles Thomas, Ezio Pinza, and Gladys Swarthout, among others, and I would consider it a privilege if I could become your accompanist in America. May I have an appointment? If I do not have this good fortune, may I at least make one or two suggestions to you? An artist destined for a big public career in our country must sing programs with great popular appeal. Do not limit yourself to the connoisseurs. You should also be careful in choosing your clothes. In recent years we have had far too many frumpy women singers on our platforms."

Today I must smile at my impudence, but I also remember my excitement at the time. It was a big, ambitious step for a young musician. I sent off my letter by special delivery and this proved to be a very lucky move—mine was the first letter to reach Flagstad. If it had not been, I probably would never have met her. Within a few days she received over twenty-five applications. I was the only person she interviewed, and I have always believed that was because I was the lucky first. The next day I telephoned. Mr. Johansen answered and said only that my letter had been received and that when the time came to settle the matter of an accompanist, I would be considered.

Meanwhile, excitement surrounding the Flagstad career increased daily. It was next to impossible to get into the Metropolitan for her performances. Her first concert season, though not scheduled until the following autumn, was completely booked without benefit of the advice contained in my letter. But, fortunately for me, many business details could not be postponed, and among these was the choice of an accompanist. Max meanwhile had told her something of my background, and must have indicated that she would not be wasting her time in giving me an interview. An appointment was arranged, but before I went to the audition itself, we had one pleasantly informal meeting. NBC Artists Service gave a large cocktail party to present the American musical world to the new Metropolitan Opera prima donna, and that day I met Madame Flagstad and Henry Johansen for the first time.

Both made immediate and vivid impressions on me. Mr. Johansen was tall and good-looking, and even a few moments of casual conversation revealed a worldly poise. He talked like a businessman. He was one. Even though in this world his wife held the center of the stage and he deferred to her with pride, nevertheless he wished to make his own mark, and always did. He had charm, a good sense of humor, and a ready twinkle in his eye. But over all, he seemed stern—even severe—and cautiously aloof. More than Flagstad, he appreciated the income potential of her spectacular success, and he was mightily interested in the return. But he had a certain surprising naïveté, as well. He could brook no criticism of Flagstad's singing and he never hesitated to brag about her, and so extravagantly that at times it was almost childish. In later years I was often surprised at such behavior from so worldly and sophisticated a businessman.

Flagstad herself gave me something of a shock. Naturally, I was excited to meet her. But after having heard her at the Metropolitan in striking costumes and in opulent operatic settings, I was not prepared to meet such a strangely unglamourous woman. She was nothing like most other divas I had known. There is no denying, however, that she attracted attention despite her almost excessive simplicity. Like her husband, she was tall, but she was not beautiful. And at this party of distinguished people gathered to swoon, she gave little if any impression of the glamourous celebrity who had been expected. *Plain* is the only word I can use to describe her. Her dress was unattractive—she wore a hat fit only for a woman to wear to market—and, not yet having learned how to play the role of a famous woman, and obviously feeling self-conscious at meeting so many strangers, she didn't smile at all. I remember standing aside for a few minutes just looking at her, naturally with admiration for what she was, and praying that my ambition to become her accompanist would be realized, but at the same time trying to persuade myself that such a woman could really be a *Flagstad*.

In the interval before the audition I prepared myself down to the last detail. I wanted that assignment more than anything else, and I did everything I could to bring it about. To begin with, I had to have a firsthand impression of her voice—the broadcast had hardly been sufficient for that. After some difficulty, I arranged to hear her in *Tristan und Isolde* at the Metropolitan. I also prepared a number of sample programs as suggested formats, always leaving a space for a group of Scandinavian songs, believing it important for an artist to develop and emphasize a specialty. In addition to these programs I made up several groups of German *Lieder*. Beyond this, for each program I included a group of songs in English, of both British and American composers, and took copies of all of them for her to see.

When the day finally came, I presented myself at her apartment in the Astor Hotel and she greeted me with cordial simplicity. I saw with some surprise that there was nothing in her surroundings of the glamourous prima donna—no secretaries or maids, none of the customary accouterments of stardom. For half an hour we chatted, mostly about herself. Then, with a shyness I was to see later as basic to her personality, she asked me to play. From a pile of music on the piano she chose two songs by the Norwegian composer Eyvind Alnaes: *"Lykken mellem to Mennesker"* and *"Vårlengsler."* The first song is a quiet mood-evocation; the second is dramatic, with a technically demanding piano part. I must have done fairly well, for when we finished she smiled and said: "Now, let's have a cocktail." Shortly after, she thanked me for coming and asked if she might keep the songs in English. And so I left.

Several days went by. I heard nothing. Meanwhile, the musical profession spoke of nothing but Flagstad. Finally, I said to Max: "I'm concerned—can you find out what the decision is?" Shortly after this appeal, Max reported to me that she seemed surprised at the question and said simply: "Didn't I make it clear to Mr. McArthur that I want him? I thought I had. He plays very well. But more important to me, he is tall and I think we will look well together on the stage." Thus began our long association, a remarkable musical collaboration and a close and affectionate friendship that lasted until she died.

CONTENTS

CONTENTS

Appendix

ILLUSTRATIONS

Illustrations

xvi

Illustrations

PART ONE

PART ONE

Chapter I

1895—1935

KIRSTEN FLAGSTAD was born in Hamar, Norway, on July 12, 1895. Her father and mother, both professional musicians, had met while playing together in a small orchestra. They came from sturdy Norwegian peasant stock. After a difficult beginning, her father obtained a post as conductor at the Central Theater in Oslo, where he directed both operas and light works. From her earliest childhood, Flagstad was surrounded by music as both a household pleasure and a regular livelihood. Her two brothers became successful professional musicians and a younger sister had a notable career, principally as an operetta singer.

Very early Flagstad became acquainted with Richard Wagner's music. For her tenth birthday she was given a score of *Lohengrin,* and even at that age she learned the entire role of Elsa, all unaware of what the part had in store for her. Her formal vocal studies began when she was sixteen. Her first teacher, of only three she was ever to have, was Ellen Schytte-Jacobsen, who fortunately recognized the rare talent of her student and began to prepare her systematically for a serious career. The young singer made her professional debut as Nuri in Eugène d'Alberts's *Tiefland* at the Oslo National Theater on December 12, 1913. Curiously, her second role was not in opera. It was a light operetta part—Serpolette in Robert-Jean Planquette's *The Chimes of Normandy*. After those beginnings of her professional career, she spent a year more studying in Norway with Albert Westwang, whose particular specialty was the development of long breath. This phase of her training was undoubtedly the groundwork for her mastery of the great Wagnerian roles that were the staple of her mature style. Her last years of preparation vocally were spent with Dr. Gillis Bratt in the more cosmopolitan atmosphere of Stockholm, where she acquired her standard of genuine professional technique.

Presently, having returned to Norway, Flagstad met and married her first husband, Sigurd Hall, in 1919. She eventually decided to stay in that country, and was soon busy singing new opera roles together with the operetta parts, as opera and operetta alternated in the repertoire at the Opéra-Comique in Oslo. The first interruption in her life as a singer came when she realized that she was about to become a mother. Else, her only child, was born on May 17, 1920. Thereafter, except for singing to her baby girl, Flagstad paid no attention to her voice for some time. Finally her mother, always ambitious for her, talked her into a tentative resumption of her singing. Both women were astonished to find that after the arrival of Else, the Flagstad voice had grown to twice its former size. Without question she now had to begin singing again. Very soon she was doing a great variety of roles, frequently with first-rank guest artists, among them the famous Leo Slezak, whose greatest role was his unforgettable Otello. In Oslo, Flagstad was his Desdemona.

In 1928 she went to Gothenburg, Sweden, to audition and was engaged as a regular member of the opera there. Already in

Norway, in addition to Desdemona, she had sung a great variety of roles, including Nedda (*Pagliacci*), Amelia (*Un Ballo in maschera*), Minnie (*La Fanciulla del West*), Micaëla (*Carmen*), and Marguérite (*Faust*). Now in Gothenburg she had a new and exciting repertoire—Agathe (*Der Freischütz*), Mimi (*La Bohème*), Eva (*Die Meistersinger*), Aïda, and Tosca.

Meanwhile, she had separated from Sigurd Hall and had begun to give her total attention to her career. Not long after, in June 1929, the Norwegian industrialist Henry Johansen saw and heard Flagstad for the first time—Elsa in *Lohengrin*. He was smitten instantly, and a whirlwind romance followed. When divorce from her first husband was finally granted, she married Johansen in Brussels on May 31, 1930. Then she was surrounded by wealth; she did not have to earn a living, and apparently was happy to give up thoughts of a career and the grinding routine of the stage. She went home to Norway to be a good wife to her new husband and a mother to her own daughter and her new stepchildren.

In the spring of 1930, before their marriage, Mr. Johansen had taken Flagstad and his eldest daughter on a vacation trip to Vienna. Curiously enough, it was only then, at the Staatsoper, that she heard *Tristan und Isolde* for the first time. She confessed many times later that she was so bored that she could hardly stay awake. Actually, she would not have stayed through the performance except for Johansen's insistence: he wanted her to know the work, though he kept telling her that "this is one opera you will never be able to sing!"

In the period immediately following her second marriage, Flagstad probably felt more peace and fulfillment than in the years to follow. Even so, she had already become something of a public figure, at least in Scandinavia, and her retirement with her family was still interrupted by pleas from various theaters to

come back. In the end, of course, the performer and artist in her
won out and she accepted the title role in a Gothenburg production of Handel's *Rodelinda*. It is curious that this work should
have been one of the vehicles of her return to the stage. The
world of Handel operas is a world of vocal style, of long, beautifully made lines and brilliant ornamentation. But the dramatic
significance of this world for the modern theater is slight and
certainly has nothing in common with the large Wagnerian
works that Flagstad was later to glorify with the greatest inter-
pretations of her time.

In this particular context it is also a little surprising that after
her *Rodelinda* her husband took back his own words and assured her that now she could sing Isolde. And by chance, the
great part came to her quickly. The directors of the National
Theater in Oslo asked her to undertake the role, and further-
more gave her just six weeks to learn it. Then, as now, there
can have been very few artists equal to such an assignment, but
Flagstad's solid training and matchless musicianship were more
than enough. It was, locally speaking, a glittering success and
by then—it was 1932—the word of her spectacular voice and
remarkable talent had began to spread.

Before Flagstad's spectacular American debut, few outside
Scandinavia had heard her name. To be sure, she had done two
seasons at Bayreuth, but chiefly in secondary roles. In spite of
this relative obscurity, she had, it is true, been approached
tentatively by the Metropolitan Opera. Five or six years before
she finally went there, Otto H. Kahn, then chairman of the
board of the Metropolitan, had heard her in Oslo and had made
inquiries as to her availability. Eric Semon, the agent who
eventually arranged her engagement in America, wrote her at
that time, but she was so completely uninterested that she never
answered his letter. One could call this simple folly. Who in his

right mind would neglect an inquiry from the Metropolitan
Opera Company? But at that time, after what had not been a
good first marriage, she was now very happy in her second—to
a very rich man—and it was easy for a young woman as placid
as Flagstad to pass over even such an inquiry as that. After all,
her second marriage had brought her a security she had never
known before. Henry Johansen, however, continued to press her
forward in her career. More worldly than she, he was also
human enough to revel in her success.

Finally, in 1934, the Metropolitan found itself in even more
urgent need of another Wagnerian soprano. And reports of the
unknown Norwegian singer continued to circulate—the great
basso Alexander Kipnis had been ecstatic in his praise of the
new Isolde in Oslo. And so Mr. Semon wrote her once again.
And she, urged enthusiastically by her husband, finally agreed
to go to St. Moritz, Switzerland, to audition for the Metropolitan's Guilio Gatti-Casazza and Artur Bodanzky. She was engaged immediately.

Gatti-Casazza was one of the most formidable personalities in
the history of opera. Before his long reign as director of the
Metropolitan, he had held the same post at La Scala, Milan,
possibly an even more demanding situation. He was an astute
man, and in Bodanzky he had one of the very great conductors
of the world, particularly in the Wagnerian repertoire. Flagstad's first season at the Metropolitan was Gatti-Casazza's last
before his retirement. But she had the joy of singing under
Bodanzky's direction for several seasons before his untimely
death. His affection for her as well as his tremendous talent
and superb direction played an important part in her life.

Even so, neither of these two brilliant men seemed to realize
completely what he had discovered. They seemed not to understand fully until a few days before her American debut; the

occasion was a dress rehearsal of *Götterdämmerung*. When the first scene was finished, Bodanzky gave his baton to an assistant and went out into the theater, ordering the entire scene to be repeated so that he could himself absorb the wonder of what he heard and saw on the stage.

Earlier in St. Moritz, however, both Gatti-Casazza and Bodanzky had been too cautious and therefore had made the serious error of signing Flagstad for one season only—with no provision for a continuing option. That misstep caused great difficulties first for Gatti-Casazza's successor, Herbert Witherspoon, and later on for Witherspoon's successor, Edward Johnson.

Thus, from an obscure position in the provincial musical world, this woman, relatively late in life, suddenly blazed upon the international scene as the extraordinary singer and artist that she was. Practically overnight, she became the idol of a vast public. Thousands quickly became "dedicated Wagnerites" thanks to her magnificent voice and deep musical instinct. With few exceptions, however, music and intellectual sophisticates accepted her with considerable reservation. That her voice was glorious and beautiful and that she was tremendously musical was evident. But it was equally apparent that she was not in the slightest intellectual. It was often a question whether she really understood the complex characters she played on the stage, and there were those who could accept her as an actress of only minor accomplishment. When a profoundly analytic article about her portrayal of this or that character appeared, she seldom had any idea what the author was talking about. Her understanding was sure, but intuitive—and she knew above all how to use her voice, both musically and dramatically. Therein lay her greatness, and also the paradox of her personality. Despite her protestation to the contrary, she was a complex individual. She was sophisticated in her art. She was completely unsophisticated as a person. Like any prima donna, she feasted upon public adoration, and also found criticism, artistic or personal, either incomprehensible or infuriating. But in her native simplicity, rare sensitivity and wisdom were rooted, the base of her almost universal human and artistic appeal.

After her New York debut in the winter of 1935, Flagstad was not scheduled to return to the Metropolitan until the end of that year. Her first performance that second season at the opera was on December 30 as Isolde. When she arrived from Europe at the end of September, her intention was to devote herself entirely to a heavily booked season of concerts and her first season with the San Francisco Opera. At that point the tug-of-war between her obligations to the Metropolitan and her outside commitments—a conflict familiar to many prima donnas of that institution—began for Flagstad.

When Herbert Witherspoon succeeded Gatti-Casazza as general manager of the Metropolitan in the spring of 1935, he was obliged to consult with the people at the NBC Artists Service in scheduling the heavy season ahead, although they did not at that time represent Flagstad contractually at the Metropolitan. She had become the most sought-after singer before the public and was booked far in advance. Max Levine began a tiresome series of conferences with Witherspoon during which little was accomplished. Witherspoon, for his part, was laboring with a difficulty created by his predecessor—Gatti-Casazza had never established a definite, firm commitment for Flagstad's services. At the same time, while the Metropolitan needed Flagstad, she of course also needed it. Then Witherspoon died suddenly in his office at the Metropolitan after only a few weeks in command. Edward Johnson was immediately chosen as his successor.

All this time Flagstad was in Europe. In Norway, during the

summer of 1935, she had received Paul Cravath, then chairman
of the board of the Metropolitan. Mr. Cravath returned to
America with a report that in his opinion her concert season as
booked was too heavy and that Flagstad would return to the
Metropolitan completely worn out. The conflict began in earnest. Besides these general matters, Johnson had already developed different plans of his own which were to complicate the
situation further. Well knowing the importance of making his
first season as general manager as brilliant as possible, he had
conceived the idea of presenting Flagstad as Norma in a revival
of the Bellini opera—disregarding among other things that her
contract called for performances only of Wagnerian works,
Beethoven's *Fidelio*, and Strauss's *Der Rosenkavalier*. (This last
was soon deleted from her obligations). Further, the part of
Norma was not exactly the most natural one for her talent and
temperament. To be sure, Flagstad had performed in a number
of Italian operas before coming to America, but she had long
since dropped this area of the repertoire from her work. And she
had never sung an opera in Italian. (As a matter of fact, aside
from scattered performances of Wagner in German, she had
sung all her parts in one or another Scandinavian language.)

In his effort to persuade Flagstad, Johnson cited the unusually
rich repertory of Lilli Lehmann. Under that kind of pressure
Flagstad finally agreed. Upon her return to New York, Johnson
arranged for Maestro Riccardo Dellera of the Metropolitan staff
to coach her in *Norma* before she left on her concert tour. I was
present at the sessions Maestro Dellera gave her, and I marked
a score in the greatest detail for myself so that we could work
together while on tour. This was a great privilege for me, as
Maestro Dellera was one of the really great authorities on the
Italian style and was thoroughly familiar with the alterations
that were traditionally made within the work. Flagstad took her

commitment seriously and worked hard on the score. But finally she said to me: "I simply cannot do it. I have always sung an opera the way the composer wrote it. All these changes are foreign to me, and I will never feel at home in the Italian, and I can't sing an entire opera in it." She asked me what I honestly thought. To me, it really did not sound right and I told her so. And I was as eager as anyone that she do only that which would keep her very much at the top. She was in a vulnerable position.

I reminded her that there had been two rather recent and highly successful revivals of *Norma* in America—one in New York with Rosa Ponselle and one in Chicago with Rosa Raïsa. "One day you might sing this part superbly," I went on, "but for now whatever you do will be compared to what they did, and if I were you, I would drop it." Eventually Henry Johansen went to see Mr. Johnson, and after that meeting, Johnson immediately released Flagstad from the special commitment. Of course, jealous tongues wagged. There were stories that she had lost her voice, could not learn a new part, and so on. One of the prices anyone in public life pays is the inevitability of malice and envious criticism. If the pressure from the Metropolitan had continued, I think she would have gone ahead. I am glad she did not. And she continued to decline Italian roles for the rest of her career—wisely, I think.

All this gives an indication of the terrific demands from the Metropolitan upon Flagstad at a time when her only wish was to concentrate entirely on her concerts and the San Francisco season. Also, the heavier dramatic Wagnerian parts were at that point relatively new to her. She had sung Brünnhilde in *Die Walküre* and *Götterdämmerung* for the first time the previous season at the Metropolitan. And ahead of her was still her first *Siegfried* Brünnhilde. The only Wagnerian part of that weight which she had sung before coming to America was Isolde.

Soon after Flagstad's American debut, she had signed a contract to record for RCA Victor and its affiliate in England, His Master's Voice. The first recording session was scheduled for an afternoon soon after her return to America in the autumn of 1935. It was one of the happiest sessions of her long and varied recording career. She was particularly happy with the conductor, Hans Lange. That day, in a single session of three hours, she sang the *"Liebestod"* from *Tristan und Isolde;* both *"Dich teure Halle"* and Elisabeth's "Prayer" from *Tannhäuser;* Elsa's "Dream" from *Lohengrin;* the *"Ho-jo-to-ho"* from *Die Walküre;* and (with myself at the piano) Strauss's *"Allerseelen."* A short time later, Charles O'Connell, who was then in charge of classical recording for the RCA Victor Company, came out to meet us in Chicago so that Flagstad could hear the test pressings. She was pleased and okayed every record for public release.

Flagstad never complained about work or the amount of it as long as its focus was musical. But she did rebel at having to fulfill social obligations, especially when she was under pressure. There was one that autumn of 1935 which caused her particular annoyance. Quite naturally Mr. Cravath, with the other officers of the Metropolitan, wanted to make as much fuss as possible over their prima donna. (She could never understand why they didn't leave her alone to do her job.) They were right and so was she. In any case, one day before we left on tour, Mr. Cravath invited her to a luncheon. She told me before going how unhappy she was at giving her time—she had no interest at all in the event. This surprised me. Most Metropolitan singers would have been delighted to be invited to the home of the chairman of the board. But she did go to the luncheon.

When I saw her afterwards she was furious. Mr. Cravath had smoked cigarettes at the luncheon table! This aversion of hers was almost obsessive, and just then it supplied a convenient way to work off her exasperation. When she had finally delivered her lecture on cigarette smoking and Mr. Cravath's "discourtesy," I laughed aloud and said: "You are a mature woman, a great lady, and also very, very silly. I'm sure Mr. Cravath would never have done anything to make you unhappy if he knew it. The simplest thing would have been for you to ask him not to smoke." But her characteristic shyness had made that impossible, as on many really important later occasions, for her to speak up. She would complain bitterly, but those about whom she was complaining rarely knew of her feelings.

Flagstad's first American concert tour began in Worcester, Massachusetts, on October 4, 1935. Practically the entire staff of NBC Artists Service went to Worcester for the concert. For George Engles, Vice-President of the National Broadcasting Company and head of the Artists Service, there was a personal and sentimental significance in having Flagstad appear in concert the first time under his management in Worcester. (For many years he had been the manager of Paderewski, and he enjoyed recalling that the great pianist's first concert under his management had also been in Worcester.) Flagstad smiled indulgently when she saw the turnout from NBC Artists Service. They had tried to make it appear a gesture of courtesy to a great artist. She was not deceived. It was obvious that they wanted to see for themselves if she could repeat her operatic success on the concert stage. Actually, there was some justification for their fears: many great operatic artists turn out to be miserable flops on the concert stage.

In the first part of the program, Flagstad sang three big Wagnerian pieces with orchestra; in the second part she and I did a group with piano. There was a capacity audience and the reception was tremendous. She looked like and sounded like a queen, and again her musical victory was complete. In nonmusical matters, however, we all made something of a mistake in Worcester. When her part of the program was finished, we should have been prepared to wait until the end of the concert to greet those whom she should have seen. But she balked, to no one's surprise, and on the spur of the moment, Max decided that she could be spared. We all left the hall, only to learn later that the directors of the Worcester Festival were terribly displeased that she had seemed so ungracious. Of course, she was not the first artist to disappear immediately after a performance, but her education in American concert etiquette had got off to a bad beginning.

We went back to the train, and in her drawing room that night Flagstad taught me how to open a champagne bottle. I had never had one in my hands before, and that night I held the first of what was to be hundreds during our years together. After watching me struggle in vain to punch a corkscrew through the metal top, Flagstad with a gay laugh took the bottle out of my hands, removed the wires, and said: "Here, Edwin— this is more important for you to learn than all the songs we will do together." After a few turns, out popped the cork.

Conversely, my own education in Flagstad concert etiquette was also beginning, and it had a rather distressing start. Two days after the Worcester debut, we returned to New York for a broadcast concert sponsored by General Motors, and after the program I handled the backstage amenities with a *gaucherie* forgivable, if at all, only because of my youth. To the artist's room came a number of people, among them my old friend, the American composer A. Walter Kramer. I assumed that we were to follow the pattern established in Worcester of receiving no one, and let this be known with considerable energy. I turned them all away with a loftiness and disdain borrowed from Flagstad herself, and I can still remember the expression on Walter's face. I don't think he ever quite forgave me.

But I was learning. My responsibilities were already spreading beyond those of a mere accompanist. I was in truth the "tour manager," and as such I had to continue acting as a general buffer for Flagstad. It was not always easy. There were many occasions when I had to say "No" even to Edward Johnson, general manager of the Metropolitan, and his assistant, Edward Ziegler. They thought me a most difficult person, but I was simply doing my job as instructed. Similar situations arose in other cities, and after a bit of persuasion I did get Flagstad to receive a few people backstage. But very soon, and with no explanation whatever, she told me that she did not wish to be met at the railroad station when we arrived in a city, did not wish to meet the press unless it was actually forced upon her, and did not wish under any circumstances to receive anyone backstage. These became rules to which few exceptions ever were made.

I presently became aware that Flagstad was reading every motion-picture magazine she could get her hands on. She believed practically everything she read, and I soon came to the conclusion that she had absorbed many of the much-publicized idiosyncrasies of Greta Garbo. She seemed to decide that if Garbo could behave like that, so could she. These unfortunate habits, which Flagstad acquired quickly, I described as her "Greta Garbo complex."

In any case, Flagstad's first American tour was starting in earnest. After two or three more recitals in the neighborhood of New York City, we departed on October 16 for Toronto. As soon as the train had left Grand Central Station, we went into the dining car—the only time I remember that Flagstad ever did such a thing. Thereafter, to keep intact her jealously guarded privacy, she always ordered meals served in her compartment. That first night in the diner, momentarily forgetting the Paul Cravath incident of a few days before, I took out a cigarette. Before it was lit, she said to me: "Edwin, have you ever smoked a cigar?"

I never had. "Please," said she, "let me buy you your first." She called over the steward and ordered the most luxurious cigar to be had. I can still see her face intent, innocent, amused, as she watched me bite off the end and light it up. Presently I managed to admit that I enjoyed it. She gave an exaggerated sigh of relief and asked me for her sake to smoke only cigars. Later, part of her pre-concert ritual in the dressing room would be to have either her husband or me blow cigar smoke in her face. This was really curious. Many singers won't have any smoke around at all. She just happened to love the smell of cigar smoke. Her aversion was only to cigarettes.

We arrived in Toronto the following morning for the first of several concerts in the auditorium of the Eaton Stores, which incidentally is quite exceptional both visually and acoustically. I went to the hall during the day to see that all was in order and found that a fine pipe organ had recently been installed. Remembering long earlier years as a church organist, I asked the management if I might try the new instrument. After playing it for half an hour, I decided to ask Flagstad to sing one song with organ accompaniment. That evening she did so and spoke charmingly of my enthusiasm for the new instrument and of her desire to sing with it. She went back for other recitals in the Eaton Auditorium and always did one song with organ. It is a happy memory of sound, those renditions there of Grieg's "I Love Thee." I often regret that we didn't always use the organ where there was one. In the same way that her voice always sounded so much richer with orchestra, the organ provided her a wonderful accompaniment.

The next concert was in Cleveland the following night. It was impossible to leave Toronto by rail after the concert. Our only way to reach Cleveland was to be driven to Buffalo the next morning and make our train connection there. We decided to take time on the motor trip for a stopover at Niagara Falls. That was an occasion for some snapshots that show Flagstad in her radiant prime and are among my most prized possessions.

The driver of the limousine warned us not to stay too long at the falls. He wanted to make sure of reaching the train in Buffalo on time and knew that we would have to pass through customs at the bridge connecting Canada with the States. Apparently from past experience, he was sure the customs officials would want to open our baggage—not that we had had any chance to buy anything in Canada. When we arrived at the border, a customs official of uncommon geniality appeared. As Flagstad handed him her passport, he looked up and said: "Why, you are Madame Flagstad! I heard you sing last winter on the Metropolitan Opera broadcasts and the General Motors program. I'll never believe you could be a smuggler." And with the promise of an autographed photo, we passed through unexamined.

After the Cleveland concert we left by overnight train for Chicago. The following Sunday, Flagstad was to sing a joint recital with the great tenor Lauritz Melchior. It was the only joint recital the two ever gave. It had been faintly suggested just after her debut at the Metropolitan that a concert combination of Flagstad and Melchior would be a big attraction, and of course it would have been. But Flagstad's career was of such magnitude in its own right that any regular collaboration of this kind would have been a mistake. This particular concert in Chicago had its curious elements. The house was far from sold out despite the announcement of the two great Wagnerian stars in an all-Wagner program. Each of them sang a solo group and they did three big duets. The local manager's only explanation for the poor house was that some two or three years earlier another Wagnerian soprano who had also made a success at her debut at the Metropolitan Opera had sung a recital in Chicago. That recital had been a real failure, and for good reason the public had become skeptical. Despite the very small turnout, the Flagstad-Melchior concert was at least a critical success, and it is worth noting that whenever she sang in Chicago afterwards the houses were packed.

Concerts all over the Midwest followed the appearance in Chicago with Melchior. One of particular note was in Minneapolis, where Flagstad sang for the first time under Eugene Ormandy's direction. It was a cordial meeting and together they gave memorable performances of *"Leise, leise"* from *Der Freischütz* and several Wagnerian excerpts. Ormandy remained one of her favorite conductors.

For me the happiest concert of the tour was in Denver, where I was born and brought up. My mother was still alive then; she was a teacher in the Denver public schools. With other members of the family, many friends, and the late local impresario Arthur Oberfelder, Mother was at the station to meet our train. (Arthur had given me my first professional engagement in 1924, before I went to New York.) All were there to welcome the local boy who now accompanied the greatest singer of the day.

Our schedule called for departure the morning following the concert. Flagstad was due in San Francisco to begin her season at the opera there. But the Denver chapter of the musical sorority, Sigma Alpha Iota, asked her to become an honorary member. We changed our reservations to an afternoon train so that the installation could take place. It all delighted Flagstad, and she wore her sorority pin for years afterwards.

And before we left Denver, Mother simply had to entertain her. That day at home is one of my happiest memories. Flagstad completely forgot that she was a star and seemed content to accept in a simple way the simple hospitality that Mother offered her. "What shall I have to eat for such a famous lady?" she asked.

"She's just a plain human being like everyone else," I replied. "Have whatever you want, but for me, please, the apple pie with American cheese on top like you used to give us."

When the pie with the cheese was served, Flagstad looked at it with some reservation. "Go on—eat it," I told her.

She dug in and from then on—whenever she wasn't worrying about her weight—she would order what she described as "Mc-Arthur's pie." "And remember," she would tell the waiter, "be sure there is a piece of American cheese on top."

We arrived in San Francisco some twelve hours late because of our miniature vacation in Denver. Word came to the hotel that Flagstad was expected immediately at the opera house for rehearsal. (That year the complete *Ring* was scheduled, and Artur Bodanzky was there to conduct the entire cycle.) When we arrived at the War Memorial Opera House, there were warm greetings from her many colleagues out from New York for the occasion. And then a quick run through *Die Walküre* with the faithful Herman Weigert, Bodanzky's assistant. Both wanted to be assured that after the tour Flagstad still had a voice! In the afternoon came the orchestra rehearsal, with Elisabeth Rethberg as the Sieglinde. Everything went well, and as we were going back to the hotel afterward, Flagstad said to me in the taxi: "Never in my life have I heard such a beautiful voice as Elisabeth Rethberg's." The remark was characteristic of her simplicity and generosity; she was too gifted and too innocent to be envious. The two prima donnas eventually became the closest of friends.

Flagstad's San Francisco debut took place on Monday evening, November 4, 1935. She did a stunning Brünnhilde in *Die Walküre*. The spectacular success of her New York debut was at least equaled, and from then on musical San Francisco was at her feet.

Mr. Johansen joined us in San Francisco. Thanks to his desire to meet and know people, Flagstad, Mr. Johansen himself, and I made some friendships which were to last through the years. Most prominent of these friends was the Milton H. Esberg family. The late Mr. Esberg, Sr., was one of the founders of the San Francisco Opera and an important director of the company when we met him and his family. Flagstad had to be persuaded to go to their house, and then went reluctantly. A friendship of indescribable affection was born that first night. Though wealthy and prominent, they were simple and unostentatious in their attentions to Flagstad. Mrs. Esberg became one of Flagstad's very few really close personal friends. A woman of unusual intelligence and warm understanding, she was one to whom Flagstad turned always for comfort and solace and for womanly advice. It is regrettable that Flagstad did not avail herself of such opportunities more often. I used to tell her that "there is an Esberg family in every city." Those few who knew her for the warm person she was find it difficult to believe that she could be very cold and forbidding to outsiders.

One evening during that 1935 season in San Francisco, Artur Bodanzky was invited for dinner and bridge. When the game began, all expected to cut for partners as usual. But as the maestro, accustomed to ordering all things, Bodanzky directed otherwise. In a stern voice he announced: "Flagstad, you will be my partner the entire evening!" And so it was. Bodanzky also decided what the stake was to be. As the game progressed, Flagstad made a bid and played a hand which did not suit her partner. In the tone of a king, Bodanzky started to castigate his soprano.

Flagstad quickly straightened up and replied: "Now look here, Mr. Bodanzky, you are not conducting an opera. We are playing bridge, and already you've made several bids and plays which I think were very bad. Don't you dare to criticize me in this manner." It was startling to hear her speak so to him—but only as a singer would she take his direction. Bodanzky's reaction was a burst of laughter, and the game finished amiably.

In San Francisco, Flagstad indulged her taste for luxurious dressing gowns both for the theater and for home. She had discovered a little shop called Matsuoka's in Chinatown. This establishment was for many years on the corner of California Street and Grant Avenue. One day shortly after our arrival we walked together down the famous hill below the Mark Hopkins Hotel to the shop, enjoying the city on the way. Mrs. Matsuoka was very proud to have the new prima donna of the opera as a customer, and these visits became an annual routine until the Matsuoka family left for Japan just before the war. Mrs. Matsuoka would always have several especially fine robes laid aside for her. When Flagstad became attached to people, places, or things, she would stick with them in a characteristically tenacious way. This made it all the more disturbing in later years when she turned about-face in too many instances, and to our sorrow chose to forget loyal friends of the past.

Flagstad gave just one song recital on the Pacific Coast that season. Just before we started east, she sang in Oakland, and before that concert a little ritual commenced which we carried on through many years. She had become enamored of the way I played popular music. In Oakland that evening I went along to her suite at the hotel, and just before we left for the hall I sat down at the piano and played Jerome Kern's "Lovely to Look At." Then a second time through—and in my frightful voice, I sang her the words. From that night on, she would not leave her apartment or hotel for a performance until I had played and sung that song to her.

On the way back to New York, we had a scheduled stop in Detroit, where on November 24, 1935, Flagstad made her first appearance on the well-remembered Ford Sunday Evening Hour, an excellent series of broadcasts originating in Detroit which became a staple of prewar radio entertainment (who will ever forget the voice of W. J. Cameron?). Flagstad's first engagement on the Ford Hour was in the old Orchestra Hall, long since demolished, but in its day one of the finest in the United States.

Two appearances each season on the Ford Hour became standard for Flagstad, and it is worth a digression to describe some of them; the communications industry was infinitely simpler in those days. One of the most frequent conductors was José Iturbi, whom I had always admired as a pianist. But I was shocked at what seemed to me his inadequacy as a conductor, particularly when he conducted for a soloist. He seemed to lack any grasp of Wagnerian style, and I could hear no evidence of the elementary sense of balance necessary to a satisfactory vocal accompaniment. I was not in a position to speak up about it, and I could not persuade Flagstad to do so. I had been accustomed to other prima donnas—Frances Alda, Anna Case, and Frieda Hempel, for example—who had never hesitated to tell a conductor when things were not right. Flagstad's ungovernable shyness prevented her from demanding adjustments. She found it easier simply to make do. The result too often was that a performance, even from her, was not as good as it should have been.

On occasion we found the scripts for the broadcasts unsatisfactory. In that department I had to be the spokesman. In one such difficult circumstance, I awakened the displeasure of William Reddick, the technical producer of the broadcast series. I had known Bill Reddick casually in New York as a competitive accompanist and organist, and never had had much regard for his talent or ability. He obviously had the same feeling about me. Finally, after we had several wrangles on the subject of scripts, the Ford people made it a regulation that no one in my position with any guest artist would be permitted in the control room, where these controversies usually took place. But I was scarcely the only thorn in their flesh. A good friend of mine, Frank Chapman, the husband of Gladys Swarthout, also had become an annoyance to various producers. Frank had rightfully seen to it that the musical matters for Gladys's broadcasts were properly taken care of. I heard several times that producers were only too willing to bar Frank from the control room as they had barred me.

In contrast, one very happy memory of a Ford Sunday Evening Hour was a program conducted by Fritz Reiner. The season before this particular broadcast, Flagstad had sung Isolde at Covent Garden in London with him as the conductor. She greatly admired him, and they had a cordial professional friendship as well. But shy as she was, she flushed a deep red when upon greeting her backstage in Detroit at the broadcast rehearsal, Mr. Reiner put his arms around her and kissed her on the cheek. This is a habit many of us have, but to Flagstad such a greeting was very strange from a man whom she knew so slightly.

But to return to the 1935 tour, I remember that we spent

Thanksgiving Day that year in Cincinnati. It was Flagstad's first
Thanksgiving in America and Mr. Johansen was there for the
occasion. We were staying at the Gibson Hotel, and after I had
explained to the Johansens the meaning of the holiday, she
agreed that we would go downstairs to the main dining room of
the hotel for dinner. By that time this was an almost unheard-
of breach of routine. The Gibson had a wonderful marbled,
neoclassic old dining room with massive columns. It *looked* like
Thanksgiving. As a genuine connoisseur of wine, Mr. Johansen
asked for the wine card to order the proper vintage as only a
savant could. The elderly waiter was proud to be serving Flagstad, but I think he was even more moved to find someone who
knew wines. With tears in his eyes he said: "Sir, this has been a
real pleasure. It is many years since I have had the privilege of
serving one who knows so well the difference."

Several more concerts on this tour preceded Flagstad's first
Carnegie Hall recital. Right after our return to New York she
sang a special *matinée musicale* at the Junior League. As it
happened, Frances Alda was in the audience. The explosive
Alda was not a person easy to say "No" to, but Max, on orders
from Flagstad, barred her from the green room. Alda was furious and telephoned me the next day to complain about everything, including Flagstad's lack of nail polish. "Tell that Norwegian peasant," she said, "that her singing is great, but she
had better learn how to dress her hair and put some polish on
those rough nails!"

One of the last concerts of the tour was at Yale University.
Flagstad wore one of my favorite concert dresses. It was of a
light crepe material, mauve and very tight-fitting, and had a
long train. We began the program with *"Leise, leise"* from *Der
Freischütz.* I was, as usual, playing from memory. About a third
of the way through the aria, I sensed that something was wrong.

Flagstad's voice wavered as it never had before. I looked up quickly to see what was the matter. She looked perfectly all right, but sounded as though she was about to faint. She was taking much smaller breaths than usual and was cutting her phrases very short. Her face flushed deeply. Offstage after the aria she cried out: "I can't go on!"

"Why?" I asked. "What's the matter?"

"Edwin," she stammered, "the zipper on my corselet has broken. It's in front and they can see! It was creeping up all through the aria—and this dress is so tight. Does it show?"

I looked carefully and could see no evidence of a broken zipper. Then she told me: "For safety, I have another corselet at the hotel. Is there some way we can get it?"

I asked the young attendant backstage to summon two of the student ushers. When they appeared, Flagstad described the corselet and told them where to find it in her hotel room. Key in hand, the laughing young men went off to secure this very private garment for the world-famous prima donna.

I persuaded her to continue with the next group of songs, broken zipper or not. Flagstad changed to the safe corselet at intermission and finished her concert in triumph. I feel sure this story lasted many years for those young men.

Eventually came the day of her first Carnegie Hall recital, focus of all our anticipation. The date was December 11, 1935, and it was the first of many wonderful concerts in that great auditorium. Of all the places in the world, Flagstad often said, she was happiest there. Naturally, the hall was packed with a most distinguished audience. Her New York public had been completely captured the season before at the Metropolitan, and they gave her a shouting ovation. The program was a heavy one. She included the *Freischütz* aria; a group of Beethoven and Brahms; a Scandinavian group; five American songs, including

Elinor Remick Warren's "White Horses of the Sea"—and closed with two big Verdi arias—from *Don Carlos* and *Macbeth*—which she sang in Italian. Of course, enthusiasm ran high—there was a large cluster of encores, ending with a performance of Brünnhilde's "Battle Cry" from *Die Walküre* which brought the house to its feet. They went wild, and I remember how particularly happy Flagstad was.

But the next day she was anything but happy. The critics found much cause for complaint. There was particular comment about her heavy concert schedule, and she was supposed to be returning to the Metropolitan "tired and worn out." Nothing could have been farther from the truth, but there it was in print. I spent a difficult afternoon with her and her husband persuading them that even the greatest must take the bitter with the sweet.

The first three months of that tour of 1935, with the final climax at Carnegie Hall, were possibly the most important period in my long association with Flagstad. In that very short time, she and I came to really know each other. And it was also an opportunity for Henry Johansen and me to broaden the acquaintance between us. We had scarcely seen each other the previous spring. On that tour we began to get used to each other, and the foundation was laid for a close and affectionate relationship that would develop as time went on. And of course the tour gave him an excellent opportunity to see how well I would take care of his wife, understandably a very important matter to him. He said many times in later years that had it not been for his confidence in me, he would never have permitted her long absences from home.

One week after the Carnegie Hall recital, Flagstad was engaged to sing for the first time in Washington, D. C., on December 18, 1935. In those years the late Mrs. Lawrence

Townsend presented a regular series of morning musicales in the ballroom of the Mayflower Hotel. The programs were the equivalent of the more famous Bagby morning musicales in New York, and for years were events of both social and musical importance in Washington.

The principal significance of this visit for Flagstad, however, was an invitation to dinner at the Norwegian legation. At that time Norway's Minister to the United States was the late Honorable Wilhelm M. Morgenstierne, later raised to the rank of Ambassador. Flagstad disliked the Norwegian Minister—I never discovered the reason—and relations between them were never more than frigidly correct, appropriate only to their roles as prominent public figures from Norway. But because in the years immediately following World War II, Mr. Morgenstierne proved to be a formidable enemy of Flagstad, it is important to outline some of their earlier association.

Whether or not Flagstad and Mr. Morgenstierne had any contact during her first season at the Metropolitan, I do not know. But shortly after her arrival from Europe in the autumn of 1935, she received a letter from him welcoming her back to the United States and expressing the desire to entertain her at the legation when she came to Washington to sing the following December. Flagstad should have replied to the letter: Mr. Morgenstierne was the official representative of her government, and a personal letter from him was not one which should have been answered by a secretary. But she asked me to reply and I did so. In my reply I said, under her instructions, that her schedule of travel and singing was extremely heavy and that she did not feel it possible to accept social engagements.

Henry Johansen arrived in America shortly after this, and was appalled at his wife's refusal. He insisted that she herself write Mr. Morgenstierne to accept. She gave in and did so, and after this *volte face* it was arranged that a small dinner would take place at the legation in Washington the evening of the concert at the Mayflower. The affair went well. The guests were among the most distinguished figures of Washington social and political life. All was cordiality except that Mr. Morgenstierne did take the occasion to express a certain mild indignation over the earlier difficulties and to blame me for having tried to prevent Flagstad from accepting his hospitality. We passed it off lightly as the idiosyncrasy of a prima donna.

Flagstad was charming and seemed to enjoy the evening immensely. As we departed, she unbent enough to invite Mr. and Mrs. Morgenstierne to be her guests at the earliest possible date at the Metropolitan. When the time arrived, Mr. Morgenstierne himself could not come to New York, but Mrs. Morgenstierne and a party were guests in a special box at the opera. For the moment at least, relations between Flagstad and official Norway were amiable enough.

Except for one summer concert in 1940, all of Flagstad's Washington appearances after that first morning musicale in 1935 were at Constitution Hall. At her first concert there on February 16, 1937, Mr. Morgenstierne and his party occupied a box, sent a beautiful bouquet of roses to her, and were gracious enough not to visit her backstage. But her dislike persisted nonetheless, and at no time did she ever extend courtesy in the form of tickets to him in Washington.

Flagstad gave another concert in Washington on March 22, 1938, and this time was accompanied by her mother and sister. She was suffering from a severe cold and a cancellation seemed a possibility. Because of that and her desire not to see Mr. Morgenstierne, she gave strict instructions to the stage attendant that no one was to be allowed backstage. Her mother was unhappy about this. Ambitious and star-struck as usual, she would have reveled in a meeting with the Norwegian Minister and in yet another opportunity to brag about her famous daughter. Again a large bouquet of flowers from Morgenstierne was presented over the footlights, and at the intermission the attendant came to report that the Norwegian Minister was outraged at being denied admittance to the green room. I tried to persuade Flagstad to receive him, even if only for a moment, but she adamantly refused. I thought then, and think now, that the refusal was ungracious and unwise on her part. But a prima donna is a prima donna and at such times one does as one is told. When we returned to the hotel that night however, Mr. Morgenstierne did telephone and I distinctly recall the cordiality of the conversation and of his congratulations.

The next time Flagstad had any personal contact with Mr. Morgenstierne was at a concert of the National Symphony in Washington on February 14, 1940, when I was the guest conductor. For some reason, a contradictory whim, she decided this time to receive him and his party backstage at intermission. This proved to be a mistake. No sooner had he and his companions entered her room than three or four of the men lit cigarettes! Flagstad glowered and I was forced to ask them to stop. Mr. Morgenstierne showed his displeasure more than clearly and they left almost at once. Not surprisingly, it came to Flagstad's ear that Mr. Morgenstierne felt her unfriendly! She professed surprise at his lack of understanding of the demands upon her time and strength. It never seemed to occur to her that this was not quite the way to behave toward the official representative of her own government.

That it would have been far better for Flagstad to establish and continue cordial relations with the Norwegian Minister is evident. But this was a clear example of her inability to take a practical view of things. In her own simple, stubborn way she thought of herself as the center of the universe, and if it suited her fancy, she would turn even a Morgenstierne aside.

Many of Flagstad's characteristics were stubbornly methodical. This came out in trivia as well as in important matters. She was an avid player of solitaire. Most of the games she played took two decks of cards. I have watched her play more than twenty different, very involved games. For years she carried a special little book with her in which she carefully put down the number of times each of these intricate bouts came out. On many occasions she would become so absorbed in a particular game that she would take the cards with her to a performance. If by chance some visitor had been admitted during the intermission, he might very well have found her completely oblivious, lost in a match with herself. Five minutes later she could be on stage singing a great scene.

She also kept a complete record of autographed photographs sent out. Dozens of letters came from disappointed fans who accused her of sending out photographs supposedly signed by her, but actually signed by a secretary. In the beginning we could not understand these complaints. Then we realized the reason. The handwriting of the address on the outside envelope was the same as on the photograph itself. She never sent out an autographed photo that she did not sign herself, but she took the greatest delight in addressing the envelope as well. And, in alphabetical order, she kept the names of those to whom she sent her picture, as well as the date of sending.

This woman was no different from dozens of other stars who are convinced that the world literally revolves around them. Early in her concert career she went to sing a concert at Wellesley College. The gentleman who was head of the music department came to me before the concert and said that the dean of the college, a lady, would like to come backstage to greet

Madame Flagstad. I told the gentleman that Flagstad had a rule not to receive anyone backstage, but if it had to be done, the dean should come during intermission so that we could make a quick getaway when the concert was finished. The man looked at me sternly and said: "Now see here, Mr. McArthur, Madame Flagstad may think she is important, but I want you to know our dean is *just* as important. She will come when it suits her convenience." This rather surprised me, and when I told the story to Flagstad later she was furious, principally at me for having allowed the dean to appear at all. She also said she would never sing again at Wellesley, and didn't—she was never invited back!

Chapter II

1936–1937

THE WINTER and spring of 1936 pinpoint a time of trouble in Flagstad's negotiations with the Metropolitan, and this particular time seemed to form a pattern for all her subsequent seasons there. I was thrown into the middle of it and there is no doubt that irreparable harm was done to my relationship with Edward Johnson. And, of course, this in time had a great effect on all his dealings with Flagstad.

NBC Artists Service of necessity wanted to know what the plans were for the 1936–7 Metropolitan season; the concert demands for Flagstad were increasing steadily. Eric Semon, who should have been on hand to negotiate her Metropolitan contract, was in Europe. But Mr. Johansen was in America until the early days of February, and he undertook to negotiate himself. Effective as he was in his own business, it quickly became apparent that he did not know how to arrange contracts in the music profession.

Around the first of January 1936, Mr. Johansen had a conference with George Engles and Max Levine regarding the following season. At the time no one seemed able to find out from the Metropolitan just what the plans were or even the dates and length of the following season. Reasonably enough, Mr. Johansen went ahead and instructed NBC Artists Service to book as many concerts as they chose, leaving only a general provision for Flagstad's Metropolitan appearances. At about that time Mr. Johansen called on the management of the Metropolitan. He immediately reported to Mr. Engles that his meeting had been most unsatisfactory. He was angry enough to tell Mr. Engles that he had no intention of seeing the management of the Metropolitan again, even when he went to the opera to hear his wife sing. All personal contact with Messrs. Johnson and Ziegler was to be avoided.

Apparently the Metropolitan management gave the matter a quick second thought. Two days before Mr. Johansen's sailing for Europe in the early part of February, Edward Johnson telephoned and asked to see Flagstad and her husband. Together they called at his office at the Metropolitan and discussed the following season. The result of this conference was a letter from Edward Johnson to Mr. Johansen which was supposed to cover the terms of this discussion and agreement. But according to

Flagstad and Mr. Johansen, the Metropolitan's letter did not cover everything that had been verbally agreed upon. However, Flagstad did sign the letter, which had been addressed to her husband. In returning it to Mr. Johnson, her husband wrote a supplementary letter incorporating the additional terms. The letter from the Metropolitan was in lieu of the formal contract that would have been drawn up when the dates of the season had been determined. The Metropolitan chose not to accept the terms of Mr. Johansen's supplementary letter.

The point is that Mr. Johansen had conducted a discussion and a correspondence with the Metropolitan without once advising either Mr. Engles or Max about any of it. The first they knew of it was on February 4, 1936, when Mr. Johansen called at Max's office, handed him copies of the letters in question, and told him what he had done. This was a typical Flagstad-Johansen procedure with which we were to become ruefully familiar in years to come. I am sorry to say that they were quite willing to have their chestnuts pulled out of the fire when necessary, but were just as willing to go off on their own, making agreements that only confused issues and embarrassed everyone, as happened many times later.

The letters proved to be bones of contention. Flagstad claimed that she had signed agreement to the Metropolitan's letter only on the basis of the supplementary letter written by her husband. The Metropolitan refused to accept this version. Mr. Johansen had meantime gone to Europe, and the situation worsened because there was still no formal contract with specific dates.

Flagstad had a heavy spring tour of concerts, and Mr. Engles kept her advised constantly of the slow progress of negotiations. Her anger at the Metropolitan was increasing daily, and although she wanted to sing there more than anything else, she stood her ground and insisted that either a formal agreement incorporating the terms as understood by her and her husband would be presented her for signing, or she would sail for Europe on May 2 without a Metropolitan contract.

Rightly or wrongly, George Engles put me in the middle and sent me on behalf of Flagstad to the Metropolitan to iron out the difficulties and secure the contract. To be sure, he did have conferences and correspondence with the management of the Metropolitan, but when it came to the personal contact, the disagreeable task fell to me. At the time I went at it full speed in my enthusiasm and desire to be part of everything. The two meetings I had with Edward Johnson in his office on May 1 and 2, 1936, are not among my happiest memories, but eventually the contract was drawn up to suit Flagstad and she sang all the performances the Metropolitan wanted of her as well as the full schedule of concert and radio engagements booked by NBC Artists Service. Everyone should have been willing to forget the unpleasant past. But Flagstad herself did not easily forget, and although she and Edward Johnson were officially cordial there-after, the feeling was never really warm. The unfortunate episode sowed seeds of an unhappy harvest years later.

After her New York season, Flagstad went directly to London, where she made a spectacular debut as Isolde at Covent Garden. The English press accepted her with some reservation, somewhat amusing to us in America. Some of the critics wrote that she was really "quite unusual," as the Americans had said. It is difficult for the British when some other nation makes the first discovery. Peggy and I were to sail for Europe the end of that May (1936). Before we left, however, there was a bad scare. Our newspapers carried a story that Flagstad had been injured by a severe blow on the head at Covent Garden. What happened was that she was sitting in a section directly beneath the loge. A lady in the seat above had placed a heavy metal compact on the loge railing. It had slipped off and had struck Flagstad. Several stitches had to be taken in her head, but by the time we met her in London, she was quite recovered.

The only casualty of that summer turned out to be me. Five days after arriving in London, to our distress and very much to hers, I came down with scarlet fever. Thereafter, I languished for some six weeks in the London Fever Hospital. This prevented my playing for Flagstad's London recital debut at Queen's Hall. That wonderfully historic hall was destroyed by bombing during World War II, and I never did have the opportunity to play there.

Later in the summer Peggy and I went to Denmark, our journey there having a double purpose. Not only did we have a happy reunion with Flagstad and her husband, but she had agreed to record a number of songs with piano if the Gramophone Company could arrange to do it in Copenhagen. Rex Palmer, the chief of recordings for His Master's Voice in England, made a special trip with his top engineer and portable equipment, and a temporary studio was set up. We spent several days on the project, recording many of the more popular songs of Grieg and other Scandinavian composers and several songs in English which had already become favorites with her recital public. Among these were Cyril Scott's "Lullaby"; Ernest Charles's "When I Have Sung My Songs"; James H. Rogers's "At Parting"; and Frank Bridge's rollicking "Love Went A-riding."

That summer Flagstad did not go home to Norway at all. Except for our days together in Copenhagen, she spent the entire time at a spot by the sea in Sweden where she could rest and study. Ahead of her was her debut at the Vienna Opera, where she was to do the entire *Ring* cycle and, for the first time in her life, the role of Isolde without cuts.

The Metropolitan's Herman Weigert went to Sweden to work with her on the role. That period of study is one of the few in which I ever heard her discuss dramatic characterization in concrete terms. Except at Bayreuth, *Tristan und Isolde* is usually given with big cuts. The one that particularly affects Isolde comes in the second act, where there is traditionally a cut of many pages. This section was completely new to Flagstad, and it baffled her. All of Wagner's operas are full of symbolisms and their meanings are sometimes obscure. The long duet of Tristan and Isolde is deeply involved with a play on words which only the most profound student of the German language and of Wagnerian tradition could possibly understand. Herman Weigert was just such a student and had had the additional experience of coaching innumerable great artists in the parts. Musically these particular pages would not have presented any problem to Flagstad. But interpretatively she very much needed the guidance of Weigert, who had lived with the score for so many years and gave her such good insight and training.

Her success in Vienna was somewhat qualified. As usual, she did not engage a claque—considered by most prima donnas as of first importance in the operatic world—and there were suspicions too that other prima donnas had perhaps intrigued against her. She told me that it wasn't really until the performance of *Götterdämmerung* that she conquered. Although she took personal satisfaction in singing Isolde in the opera house in which only a very few years before she had heard *Tristan und Isolde* for the first time, she was glad when that short Vienna season was finished.

The Magic Key was a radio program sponsored by the Radio Corporation of America specifically for the promotion of RCA Victor records. Most, if not all, artists who appeared on the program were under contract to Victor. I also remember that the fees paid on the program were not as large as those on other commercial broadcasts. Victor could evidently have them for less; every artist was interested in promoting his own product. Flagstad was no exception. The program directors of The Magic Key were unusually imaginative. They learned that Flagstad was in Vienna and that her final performance at the Staatsoper was coming almost immediately. They also discovered that she and her husband planned to motor to Paris and eventually to sail for New York on the S.S. *Normandie*. They decided to pick up her singing from some spot in Europe. It was found that she could reach Stuttgart in time for a broadcast. She arrived only a few hours before air time, rehearsed with an accompanist, and delivered her customary brilliant performance. Transmission to America was superb—we heard the broadcast at home in New York—and the unique concert was a complete success.

Just a few days after Flagstad's arrival in New York the following week, she appeared as a special surprise artist at a dinner in the ballroom of the old Ritz-Carlton Hotel. The affair was in honor of the chief of the Radio Corporation of America, David Sarnoff. I played for her that evening. When Milton Cross introduced her, he told the story of her broadcast only a few days earlier from Stuttgart. When Flagstad came on the stage, she described some of the details of her excitement in having been asked to do such a broadcast, her pleasure in having honored the RCA "family" from across the sea, and the privilege she felt that evening in personally honoring Mr. Sarnoff himself. She went on to perform a short program for the guests, and her list for the evening included *"Dich teure Halle"* from *Tannhäuser*. As we were performing, I began to hear a text that was completely unrecognizable and realized that her memory had failed. It was not a series of "scat syllables" as originated by Louis Armstrong, the customary resource of

singers in this situation. The phrases appeared to have some
meaning, to Flagstad, at least. When we finished, she colored
and, raising her hand to her face, said: "Forgive me—it was in
Swedish. I simply forgot the German words." She had often
sung that work in Sweden in the language of that country.

This episode and the Stuttgart broadcast give some hint of
Flagstad's complete adaptability to professional emergencies of
all sorts. There was a later incident of this kind during her
second tour of the United States, which began a few days after
the RCA evening. She was scheduled for a recital in Pasadena,
California, just one night before a posted dress rehearsal of
Tristan at the San Francisco Opera, which, by the way, was as
upset as the Metropolitan over her heavy concert bookings. The
rehearsal could have very well gone on without her. She and
Melchior, the Tristan, had by then sung *Tristan* together many
times, and she had also recently sung Isolde at Covent Garden
under the same conductor, Fritz Reiner. But the Opera insisted
that she be there. We appealed to the manager of the Pasadena
concert, who graciously permitted it to begin fifteen minutes
early so that we could get to the overnight train. We were given
a police escort, sirens and all, to the railroad station. Flagstad
took an almost childish delight in this very special attention.

Next morning on our arrival in San Francisco another police
escort was waiting for us and we raced directly to the Opera
House—no time even to stop at the hotel. Mr. Reiner had purposely started the rehearsal with Act III, in which Tristan, bat-
tling off death, sings for a full hour before the final meeting with
Isolde. As we rushed in the stage door, Flagstad could hear that
her first cue was only a few seconds away. Quickly giving me
her handbag, she ran out on the stage and, just in time, sent
forth in full voice her line *"Tristan, Geliebter!"* Of course everyone was absolutely stunned—not least, Mr. Reiner. Then she

sang the whole rehearsal, as usual, in full voice—this after a concert the evening before and a sleepless night of travel. At times capricious and willful, Flagstad nonetheless never failed in her obligations to her colleagues or to her public.

The late James M. Speyer, a New York banker of prominence, had a custom of presenting a musicale each year in his house on upper Fifth Avenue. These were for the benefit of the Ellen Prince Speyer Hospital for Animals in New York City. (Mrs. Speyer had died many years before Flagstad came to America.) Mr. Speyer was a close friend of Arthur Bodanzky, and through him many of the leading artists of the Metropolitan were asked to sing at the programs. The Speyer musicales usually took place as matinées in the spring of the year.

Mr. Speyer had the charming custom of presenting to each female singer some piece of jewelry which had belonged to his wife. I do not know how he expressed his appreciation to male artists, but I am sure it must have been in an equally generous and personal manner. During her career in America, Flagstad sang three times for Mr. Speyer. After her first appearance at Mr. Speyer's house, he gave her a beautiful emerald ring. The history of that ring is in itself a revealing indicator of her personality. She had enough feminine vanity to love jewelry and had a number of pieces that were really very beautiful, though none was so spectacular as some I have seen worn by stars like Geraldine Farrar, Mary Garden, and Anna Case Mackay.

The decorative value of such a thing as the emerald ring was not enough for Flagstad, however. Her peasant side was also intensely interested in how much money it could bring. She waited some time before satisfying her curiosity; eventually, on a trip to Norway, she had it appraised, and the answer was 4,000 Kroner, at that time about $1,000. When she returned to America, she told me of this and petulantly said that she would never wear it again—it wasn't worth enough. I told her I could not believe that Mr. Speyer would have given her anything cheaper than the best, and persuaded her to let me take it to a Fifth Avenue jeweler for an American appraisal. The valuation this time was $4,000, and Flagstad immediately became intensely fond of it. She wore it almost constantly until some years later, when she gave it to her daughter Else, who has it now.

At a later musicale for which I accompanied her, Mr. Speyer gave her a beautiful pin in the shape of a bowknot with rather long tassels, all of diamonds. This piece became another favorite of hers. One evening after the war Flagstad, Peggy, and I were dinner guests at the home of J. Cheever Cowdin, at that time head of Universal Pictures. Flagstad wore the pin that night. Much after midnight Peggy and I took her home, and although it was very late she insisted that we come up for a nightcap. It was better to accept than argue. We were no sooner in her apartment than she took off this beautiful pin and with a kiss pinned it on my Peggy, saying, "Now this is yours."

A great many stories were told about Flagstad's drinking habits, which I think were about the same as those of most Scandinavians I have known. Those rugged people simply like their liquor. In any case, I prefer to think of it as their concern. Flagstad's favorite cocktail was a dry, eventually a very dry, martini. In the beginning we used to make them of three parts of gin to one of vermouth, but she soon came to find that rather tame. Frances Alda, among others, insisted noisily that this made no cocktail at all. On her instructions, we changed to a ratio of six to one. Flagstad already detested the weak cocktails of commercial places, particularly those served on trains. Very soon on tour we carried a large leather case that she had had made in Europe. The case contained four heavy glass bottles. In two of these we carried our own martinis; another was filled with cognac, the fourth with plain, and delicious, Scotch, which I always preferred to the champagne Flagstad usually had in the evening. Wherever we were, it was always my task to see that the four bottles were full.

Cocktail drinking on transcontinental train trips became a particular ritual. There is a tradition among Scandinavians, so I have been told, which forbids a drink before noon. Once one has started, it is perfectly permissible to drink around the clock until the next noon. But if there is any break, one never begins again until twelve the following day. We often used to travel on the *Overland Limited* from Chicago to San Francisco, a trip of three nights and two days across the West. Usually in the morning, around eleven o'clock, the porter would notify me that the lady in Drawing Room A was ready to receive me. Flagstad would be all comfortably fixed for the day and already would be glancing impatiently at her watch. Five minutes would slip by, and still another five, with more and more fidgeting from the star. Finally, at about quarter to twelve, I would say: "Oh, for heaven's sake, in New York it's already nearly two—we can start." Then we would ask the porter to bring two glasses full of ice. I don't believe that I have ever seen other tumblers as large as those on the old Pullman cars. We would pour the martini over the ice to the very top of each huge glass. It was a heroic drink. As Flagstad's glass would get half empty, she would jiggle it, look at me pointedly, and say: "Well, what's the matter?—it's plain water." I would make the refill quickly. Her capacity was tremendous. I myself could barely get the one glass down. Then, after a hearty luncheon, I would have to go off to sleep for two or three hours to sober up.

For all this, Flagstad never drank before singing. But immediately following an operatic performance or a concert, the first thing was a good shot of cognac. Many was the time we left

Carnegie Hall while the audience was still applauding and stopped the car halfway down the block while we each took a pull of brandy. She always felt that this helped to avoid a cold. But before singing—never.

Despite her dislike of social functions, Flagstad did enjoy playing the hostess herself. During her San Francisco seasons she always kept a suite high up in the Mark Hopkins Hotel overlooking the bay. One day her second year there she decided to give a small cocktail party for her colleagues in the Wagnerian operas and some of the officers and directors of the Opera Association. Characteristically, she wrote all the invitations herself. The affair was supposed to end at seven thirty, but it went on very much later on account of Lauritz Melchior and his wife, Kleinchen (the great Flagstad-Melchior feud had not yet erupted).

That same Sunday afternoon, Lauritz had a concert to sing in Visalia, California. Flagstad told them that if they got back to San Francisco by seven thirty, they could come and have a drink. On the dot of seven twenty-nine, in walked the Melchiors. All the other guests had left. He really must have rushed through his concert and driven at top speed to get back. Kleinchen and Lauritz would never be the ones to miss any party. And with their gaiety, they were always an asset to any social gathering. They both had infectious laughs and were full of amusing anecdotes. Lauritz also had the pleasant habit of making each prima donna he sang with really believe that she was the greatest he had ever known. Even though in business matters the Melchiors could be hard and unbending, as social companions they were delightful.

Later, in 1939, following my debut as a conductor with the San Francisco Opera, Flagstad gave a large formal cocktail party for all the artists and directors of the company. From her appearance on such occasions one could never have guessed how painfully shy she was. She beamed with radiance, her smile was golden, she was the perfect hostess. I also remember a delightful party after a postwar concert in Zürich at which she honored the great conductor Wilhelm Furtwängler. It was remarkable with what ease she carried all this off in spite of her timidity.

Frances Alda was a great singer. She was also a rather complicated individual, much loved by some and cordially disliked by many. I had the good fortune to be her accompanist for several years, and although I, like everyone else, found her a most difficult person, I must say that the experience during those early years was musically rich and rewarding.

When Flagstad was in California in 1937, I bought her a copy of Alda's book *Men, Women and Tenors*. She had written in extravagant praise of Flagstad. When Flagstad saw this she was as happy as a child. Not only did she know of Alda by reputation; she had been entertained many times by my account of Alda's mercurial, but brutal, criticism of most singers. That season the Metropolitan opened with *Tristan und Isolde*. Flagstad wrote from California thanking Alda for the beautiful things she had written in her book and then said: "As you may have noted, I am to sing on opening night at the Metropolitan. I would be so happy if you will come backstage to see me." Peggy and I went that opening night, and I searched all over the house for Alda. She was nowhere to be seen, and I finally assumed that she must be ill. The next morning I telephoned her to express our disappointment at her absence, and in typical fashion she barked at me over the telephone: "Oh Edwin, you are an idiot! You know I never go to opening nights—I think they are dreadful. Of course I would like very much to meet Madame Flagstad, but it is for you to arrange." Then she went on to ask me how the performance had been.

I said: "Well, Madame Alda, of course opening nights are not exactly ideal—confusion, photographers everywhere, absolutely everything to distract one's attention from the music."

Typically enough, having just told me that she never went to openings, she said: "Yes, I know exactly what you mean. When I was at the opening last year, I was hounded by photographers all through the performance!"

The friendship between Flagstad and Alda was amusing. No two prima donnas could have been less alike in temperament and personality. But Alda, retired from singing then, admired Flagstad greatly, and Flagstad in turn liked and was amused by her older colleague. The old Ritz-Carlton was one of Flagstad's favorite places, and one day I took her, with Alda, to lunch there. The headwaiter knew Flagstad well, but apparently did not recognize Alda. No sooner had we been seated than he asked if we would like *Melba* toast. Little did he know that one of the greatest operatic feuds in history had been that between Dame Nellie Melba and Madame Frances Alda. Alda gave him a stare sufficient to flatten a Caesar and said—or roared— "Melba toast! No! Bring Alda toast!"

Later that afternoon I took the two ladies to a performance of *Otello* at the Metropolitan. Rethberg, Martinelli, and Tibbett were in the cast and it was a memorable performance as well as the occasion of an amusing exchange. I sat between the two prima donnas. Alda leaned across in front of me and said: "I sang this opera with the great Slezak." Flagstad was not one to let this pass. "So did I," she said with emphasis. Despite this kind of amusing rivalry, the two remained fast friends for years.

In *The Chimes of Normandy,*
Norway, 1914

Recording with orchestra,
Norway, late 1920s

As Brünnhilde,
Metropolitan Opera,
spring 1935

Crossing San Francisco Bay,
October 1935

Flagstad was a great admirer of Giovanni Martinelli, the remarkable Metropolitan tenor who was long regarded as the successor to Caruso. His reputation in Italian opera was naturally unassailable, but there was general skepticism regarding his big unfulfilled ambition—to sing Tristan. In fact, Flagstad was practically his only supporter when the matter of his doing the role at the Chicago Opera came up in 1939. She instantly agreed to be his Isolde and said: "He will have only one problem—to sing an entire opera in the German. But I am sure he can do it. Anyone who can do an Otello like his can certainly sing Tristan, regardless of the language. He has my complete cooperation and support." She invited Martinelli to her apartment in the Dorset Hotel, and with me at the piano they went through the entire duet from the second act. Following this he had several working sessions in New York with Herman Weigert. The great part was new to him and came late in his career, but he was an excellent Tristan in Chicago. Flagstad was very happy singing with him and felt that her support had been fully justified. Martinelli turned in a flawless performance—a judgment I feel qualified to submit because I myself was the conductor.

Flagstad was given to doing usually thoughtful simple things. I remember that she had a concert to sing in Washington on February 16, 1937, and that going down on the train from New York I got to talking with her about a singer of other days whom I had accompanied and knew well. This was Edith deLys, a native American who had had little success in her own country, though in the opera houses of Europe during the early days of the twentieth century she had been a great star. "You know her?" asked Flagstad. "I will never forget her as long as I live. Several years ago she came to Oslo as a guest of the opera and was superb."

I went on to say that Madame deLys and her mother were living in New York in rather trying circumstances. When we got to the hotel in Washington, Flagstad asked me if I thought Madame deLys and her mother would like tickets for the following day's matinée at the Metropolitan. "I'll call her and find out," I said.

"Oh no"—Flagstad replied—"I'll do it myself." Madame deLys told me later that she almost fainted when she answered the telephone in New York; she could not believe that it was the great Flagstad herself calling from Washington to invite her to the opera. Of course, she and her mother came, but, paradoxically, Flagstad then refused to see them. Two or three times I tried to persuade her to let me bring them to call on her, but she always said "No." She could go just so far, and then her diffidence ruled.

Flagstad had met Lauritz Melchior in passing once in Brussels before she came to America. As a matter of fact, when she reminded him of this chance meeting, he seemed not even to remember her, and the tenor at her Metropolitan debut was the American, Paul Althouse. She and Melchior sang for the first time together at the Metropolitan on February 6, 1935, in *Tristan und Isolde*. This appearance began their professional friendship. As in a previous generation the pairing of Farrar and Caruso was classic, so in a later time the combination of Flagstad and Melchior became legendary. In the entire history of the Wagner operas there probably has never been such a duo.

It was only natural that with so much work to do together they should become friends, and, of course, they were both Scandinavians as well. Their relationship was complemented by a happy congeniality between Mrs. Melchior and Mr. Johansen. They were both good foils for their glamourous spouses, and they also were both smart business operators.

The cordiality between Flagstad and Melchior in time was rather unfortunately marred by one of those distressing little episodes that seem to plague even the best-disposed professionals. The contretemps had its roots in a minor matter regarding the press.

Unlike many artists, Flagstad never had—or needed—a public relations representative. Publicity came to her unsought, and there was never any problem about newspaper promotion. But during the season of 1936–7 the first negative items appeared in the papers. They were in the form of recurrent questions in gossip columns: "Who is the Prima Donna of the Metropolitan?" I never saw one of them, but their text had to do with Flagstad's position with the company in the light of her spectacular success there, with implied comparisons with other stars. They seem to have come to Flagstad herself from a press clipping service that sent her literally hundreds of items. As a respite from knitting and solitaire, she from time to time spent hours sorting these clippings and discarding the duplicates. She began to mention the continued appearance of this particular article, and presently there was considerable gossip on the subject in the corridors of the Metropolitan. It looked very much like a story planted by some ambitious press representative. Flagstad cared nothing about its origin, but the comment in the trade was beginning to annoy her.

In April, Flagstad, the Melchiors, and I were in Rochester with the Metropolitan for a performance of *Lohengrin,* and one evening we decided after dinner to play bridge in her suite. Over the bridge table, conversation drifted from one subject to another and presently we got into a discussion of the press item. At that time Melchior had as his representative one of the most brilliant of all in the profession, Constance Hope. It happened that Constance was a good friend of mine of long years' standing. One word led to another, and before we could count ten, Flagstad was loudly—and tactlessly—making all sorts of remarks about what she described as "phony" promotion. And she made much of the "prima donna" story from the gossip columns. One of her complaints concerned bills to her for unasked-for photographs with other artists. She said that she preferred to stand alone in her career and, among other things, that she did not even wish to be photographed at a railroad station with any of her colleagues. I could have fallen through the floor. She and Melchior had that very day been photographed together at the Rochester station as they arrived.

Most unfortunately the name of Madame Lotte Lehmann now figured prominently in the heated discussion. It happened that Madame Lehmann also retained Constance Hope as her publicity representative. Madame Lehmann's position as one of the top artists before the public was unquestioned, and Flagstad herself had great admiration for her. But she angrily protested that she would be glad if Madame Lehmann's publicity could be promoted without including, even by inference, the name of Flagstad as a rival for top honors.

Next day Flagstad gave the matter no further thought. For her it had been but a passing conversation not to be taken seriously. But the Melchiors did not exactly agree, and from what was really a casual and innocent beginning, a famous feud grew rapidly. It did only harm to everyone concerned.

When we arrived at the theater for the performance of *Lohengrin*, the Melchiors hardly spoke to us. And when it came time for the curtain calls, Melchior absolutely refused to allow Flagstad to go before the curtain alone, though they had been taking solo curtain calls from the beginning of their association. His behavior was childish beyond description. After the performance, the Melchiors returned to New York and Flagstad and I went west for concerts. We thought the whole thing would be forgotten, but when we arrived in Cincinnati for the May Festival a few weeks later, both Flagstad and I received stinging letters from Constance Hope. The Melchiors had returned to New York with a full report, undoubtedly colored by their own feelings, of that lamentable exchange in Rochester.

Constance took me severely to task for lack of good faith and friendship and sent me a copy of her letter to Madame Flagstad dated April 29, 1937. I am sorry that Flagstad herself did not reply. I did on both my own behalf and Flagstad's and the exact text of the answer was as follows:

> *Hotel Netherland-Plaza*
> *Cincinnati, Ohio*
> *May 2, 1937*

Miss Constance Hope
673 Fifth Avenue
New York City, New York

My dear Constance:
Words would absolutely fail to describe my amazement and surprise upon arriving here this evening and finding your letter waiting.

Upon my return to New York ten days hence, I trust you will do me the honor of getting together to straighten this thoroughly unnecessary misunderstanding, but in the meantime, I feel compelled to write you this reply.

Madame Flagstad and I are both surprised at Kleinchen's and Mr. Melchior's having repeated to you the conversation over a bridge table in Rochester two weeks ago. I cannot help who it is, repeated conversations are never the same.

I personally would never have mentioned such a conversation about anyone to the person whom it concerned. You are far more experienced in this business than I am, and I am sure you hear things every day of your life that you put in your own head and keep there.

And besides, each one has the right to his or her opinion; the whole point in question just now being that if Madame Flagstad has been mistaken she is only too glad to have been corrected. Your impression regarding the pictures in the musical papers is not correct. Just get out your copy of your letter to Madame Flagstad and read the second paragraph. She did not object, and never has or will object, to pictures being published of her with her colleagues, whether they are your clients or not. But the thing she did take exception to was the fact that the Courier sent her a bill and told me that you had authorized them to do so, and that Madame Flagstad would pay half. This information I not only got from the Courier but from your office as well. It was not the matter of the few dollars, but Madame Flagstad did not think it a proper procedure in any way for you to send in pictures and tell the paper she would pay for part without either consulting Miss Mobert[1] or me.

It further happens that the particular picture of Flagstad and Melchior is a very good likeness of him, but not of her. As you know, she cannot control the use of such pictures in the daily papers, but she should at least have a say for what she pays for in the musical papers, and neither in the case of this picture or the one with Mr. Ormandy was she even consulted.

Your impression that she does not want to be photographed with your clients is all wrong. You might be interested to know that last Wednesday morning in Dallas, Texas we made a point

[1] Helen Mobert was for many years in charge of publicity for NBC Artists Service.

of going to the station to meet the train bringing in the Philadelphia Orchestra and to be photographed with Messrs. Ormandy and Iturbi. If this picture has turned out good, it should be very interesting to the papers, and I would very much like to see it reproduced in the Courier.

Now regards the article of "Who is the Prima Donna at the Metropolitan." I myself have not seen the article at all, as Madame Flagstad herself goes through the stacks of clippings she gets from her press clipping bureau, sorts out what she wants, and throws the rest away. But she tells me that this article has come to her from about a hundred different papers this spring, and as it always was exactly the same, she has the impression that it was made publicity.

She has only the highest regard for Madame Lehmann, as you must know, and she thinks such articles as this, and such an exchange of letters as appeared in the Sunday Times this year, is not only stupid, but thoroughly undignified for artists in such positions.

I cannot blame you for feeling hurt with me from the impression you have gotten from Melchior's [*sic*], but in that one angle, you are more wrong than in any other. If you ever want to confirm what I think of you and your work, just ask Madame Flagstad herself some time when you see her, what I have told her. And besides, I told Kleinchen and Mr. Melchior too frankly that I have known you for over ten years, and I have always thought and still think you are the best publicity specialist in your line anywhere in the business.

The only ground on which Madame Flagstad has been disturbed (and it has applied not only to you) is the fact that artists cannot have publicity of their own without always bringing in her name.

As a team at the Opera, the "Flagstad-Melchior" set-up is

unbeatable, and accepted as such. But away from the opera, Madame Flagstad thinks her career has a distinction of its own, just as has Mr. Melchior's and Madame Lehmann's, and she prefers to have it stand alone.

Yours,
Edwin McArthur

Constance immediately wrote me a most cordial reply, and I am glad to say that as far as she and I were concerned, the matter was quickly forgotten. But it was by no means over with the Melchiors. Lauritz was appearing in that same Cincinnati Festival, and he and Flagstad spoke hardly a word offstage. In London, during the succeeding Covent Garden season, the coolness continued, emphasized by Melchior's stupid insistence that there be no solo curtain calls. This may seem completely idiotic to the general reader, but for an opera star a solo curtain call is one of the most important things in life. (It is worth noting that much later Rudolf Bing attempted to abolish this custom at the Metropolitan and was defeated by the invincible resistance of both performers and public.)

After the Covent Garden season the feud continued to grow, and during the next season in San Francisco, Marks Levine made a special trip from New York to discuss it and the future in general with Flagstad. Over a lunch table in the Mark Hopkins Hotel she told him and his associate, Alexander Haas, that the 1937 season was to be her last in San Francisco—the atmosphere was being poisoned by the continued dispute with Melchior. She also asked Max to begin discussion with the Metropolitan for her coming twenty-fifth anniversary as a singer before the public (December 12, 1938). And she made it a condition that the tenor on that occasion was *not* to be Lauritz Melchior.

Max returned to New York with a heavy heart, but did as he was asked. He began conversations at once with the Metropolitan, and among other things told the management there of the solo curtain-call situation. Edward Johnson assured him that Flagstad would have her solo curtain calls in New York. Meanwhile, Melchior himself seemed to go through a change of heart. At a performance in Los Angeles he himself, without warning, literally pushed Flagstad out in front of the curtain alone. And shortly after that when they sang together at the Chicago Opera, they took their solo curtain calls without incident. In the context of this infantile behavior it had better be emphasized that neither Flagstad nor Melchior permitted this personal feud to compromise their professional integrity—for the public their art was as faultless as ever.

Chapter III

1937–1938

THE EPISODES and relationships I have been describing have all been intended to show one aspect or another of Flagstad's contradictory personality—by turns, vain, generous, timid, tyrannical, and obtuse, but also perceptive almost to the point of clairvoyance. Even apart from the intuitive understanding of

her parts in the opera, she constantly revealed almost psychic
talents. Her determination not to like Mr. Morgenstierne was an
unfortunate example. She kept telling me: "I won't like him—
this I am sure of, although I haven't met him yet." Or she would
say to me: "I know the train will be late." There were countless
incidents of this nature. And yet when I would suggest to her
that it would be interesting for her to delve more into the field
of the psychic, she would just laugh at me. "I feel what I feel,"
she would say and let it go at that.

With all this, she was at the same time complete mistress of
her art and profession. What we have seen of her thus far has
been largely concerned with her professional self. At this point
in her life, however, there arose the first of three crises that
reached to the very roots of her being and revealed Flagstad in
a way that her public personality alone could not. This first
crisis involved one of the most delicate and intense of all relationships, that between mother and daughter, and to understand
it one must know something of the child Else and the rather
complex background which formed her.

Else was born on May 17, 1920, to Kirsten Flagstad and
Sigurd Hall, who had married the year before. Although her
parents separated in 1929, Else always maintained an unusually
close relationship with her father. When Flagstad married
Henry Johansen, Else was just ten years old. Johansen's children
by previous marriage were all older than she. Despite her
mother's new-found happiness, Else herself cannot have been
contented. The other children had been brought up in a very
different world from hers, for one thing. And now at a tender
age she had thrust upon her a completely new home life and the
all-pervasive influence of a stepfather for whom she had no
feeling at all.

At the beginning of Flagstad's second marriage, as I have said before, she had little if any thought of continuing a musical career. But as time went on she did accept engagements, and as her professional career grew she necessarily had to be away from home and her daughter. Looking back, it seems fair to say that the usual difficulty of a child in adjusting to a stepparent was greatly complicated for Else by her mother's pursuit of a professional career. This complication, in addition to the deep devotion she had for her father, made Else's teen-age years extraordinarily difficult. I am sure that she must have formed a deep resentment for everything that was "Johansen." And because she was Norwegian herself, with the characteristic independent Norwegian will, the time quickly arrived when she rebelled openly.

Peggy and I first saw Else in the autumn of 1935, when she was fifteen; she had not been in America the previous season, when her mother had made her sensational debut at the Metropolitan. She did come the following year, and it was important to Flagstad that the girl be sent to a good private school somewhere near New York City. After considerable investigation, she chose one in Tarrytown, New York—Miss Weaver's. Tarrytown is not far from New York, and Else was able to see her mother often during the winter months. Also, the school had a box at the Metropolitan and the girls went regularly to the opera. When Christmas vacation came, Else stayed with her mother and Mr. Johansen in New York.

At the time I did not understand why Else so openly resented me and my association with her mother and Mr. Johansen. But I can see now that even at that early age she felt a deep bitterness that her own family life had been so upset. I was only another symbol of that dislocation. Loving her mother, but also cherishing a great affection for her father, Else naturally would have missed the more normal life of a young person. Being the daughter of a woman suddenly world-famous only made it more difficult.

Flagstad herself showed considerable concern about being a good mother in a more usual sense at this period. She went whenever possible to the school to visit Else. I remember one Saturday evening during Else's year there when Flagstad, Peggy, and I went to Tarrytown as her guests for dinner. Flagstad seemed perfectly content to throw off the cloak of fame and for a few hours to be in the company of her own daughter and her schoolgirl friends.

Else remained in America through the 1935-6 season, but when the fall of 1936 came, Flagstad returned to America alone. We had thought Else would return for at least another year at Miss Weaver's, where she had seemed so happy. But when I asked Flagstad why Else had remained in Norway, she brushed the question aside brusquely, and refused for quite a while to discuss it at all. When we returned to New York from the fall tour in December, she announced to me without warning that Else would arrive shortly and asked if I would go to the boat to meet her. "I cannot stand to be without her," was all she said.

Else arrived just before Christmas on the Polish ship *Pilsudski*. Max and I met the boat together. It was a miserably cold day. There was a fine interview; Else denied any ambition to become a singer (she never had any illusions on this subject, publicity stories to the contrary). When the reporters questioned her, she did say that although her mother wanted her to sing, she herself knew that she could never equal her mother's remarkable achievements and didn't want to try. "I'm through with school," she said. "I'm here for a holiday and visit with my mother, and after that I don't know what I'll do."

Else stayed only a very few weeks on that trip, and there was still not the slightest evidence of trouble between mother and daughter. They seemed perfectly happy together, and the fact that there was friction even then was a very well-kept family secret.

Else went from Norway to join her mother and Mr. Johansen in London for that spring season of opera at Covent Garden. I was there with them. During the weeks in London, Flagstad had a few days free of any singing commitments, and Mr. Johansen decided to make the most of them. He hired a car and chauffeur and took us all, including Else, for a lovely five-day trip through the south of England. Meantime, Else and I had become good friends. By this time she had decided that perhaps I wasn't quite so bad after all. Those five days seemed idyllically happy for everyone.

After the season in London, I made my way quickly to Bayreuth for concentrated study and to take advantage of a rare opportunity to attend rehearsals for the coming festival there. Flagstad, Mr. Johansen, and Else returned to Norway.

At the end of July I went to Bremen, to meet Peggy, who was arriving from America, and together we traveled to Oslo to visit the Johansens. When we arrived, there was Flagstad with Leif Stake on the station platform to welcome us. (Stake had been a faithful employee of Mr. Johansen's for years. He became equally devoted through the years to Flagstad, and was with her when she died.) After we had been settled in our hotel rooms, we went to the Johansens' for dinner. I thought Flagstad seemed distraught from the moment we met, but I was not used to such a state in her and could say nothing. I did not learn the reason until Peggy and I got back to the hotel late that night. Then she told me a sad tale. Flagstad had taken Peggy aside after dinner and had confided that without warning, a short time before, Else had packed all her things, had even taken a chandelier off the ceiling, and had moved out bag and baggage to go to live with her father. The next day Flagstad talked to me a little about it, and I realized only then the depth of the bitterness and frustration that had eaten its way into their lives.

As I was to learn in the years to follow, Flagstad was masterful at putting up a good front even in face of great trouble and torture. That week we spent with the Johansens in Norway was the first of many times when she revealed this remarkable characteristic.

From this situation I myself learned a simple but important lesson: there are *always* two sides. All our sympathy had been with Flagstad. We were convinced that Else was guilty of the most terrible ingratitude and was a thoroughly bad daughter to both her mother and Mr. Johansen. But as the years went on I came to realize that nothing is ever so cut-and-dried as that. After a reconciliation with her mother. Else herself made known to me many complications of her life. Although she was not completely blameless, neither was she completely at fault. She had been only a young girl at the time. Beyond that, Flagstad had failed completely to understand that her daughter had a mind and will of her own and also seems to have cared nothing for Else's natural affection for her father. Other breaks were to come, and I was destined to play an important part on both sides. I am glad that so early in the long association I was given some idea of the psychological quantities involved.

Flagstad returned to America as usual for her season in 1937, but her lighthearted gaiety, her enthusiasm for work, and the thrill of her career were lost in bleak professionalism. She certainly continued to sing like a goddess and to live up to the letter of her obligations. But her happiness was crushed. Months on end went by without direct word from her daughter.

For Christmas Eve 1937 she was invited by the National Broadcasting Company to do a network broadcast of "Silent

Night." For many years this had been a ritual of the great Ernestine Schumann-Heink, and Flagstad was the first solo artist asked to continue that tradition. We spent the evening at a dinner party with close friends, and Flagstad seemed in relatively high spirits. At about eleven o'clock we went to the NBC studios in Radio City. After she had sung the carol, the two of us stopped off at her apartment in the Dorset Hotel. We had no sooner gone in than she threw open the French doors onto a balcony, went outside and literally cried out into the night: "Where is my daughter? Where is my daughter?" I was thunderstruck: that was the first of only a very few times in all the years I knew her that I ever saw her lose herself in that way. I did not know what to say or do. We were good friends, to a point at least, but her grip on her private self had always been complete. We both stood for a few moments in utter silence. And then, as quickly as she had broken, she recovered and said simply: "Now, we'll go back to the party."

Flagstad's stubborn courage in the face of this private trial was impressive enough as it was, and this characteristic was to stand her in good stead much later. But her situation at that time began to call for even greater personal control. To maintain her career was not enough. She had to expand it as well. During the 1937 season she decided to accept an engagement from the motion-picture industry. A number of the studio sessions were quite memorable. One that comes most vividly to mind is the occasion of an "official day" at Paramount during the autumn of 1937, a little before the "Silent Night" broadcast.

The previous spring Flagstad had been engaged for an unusual sequence in a film called *The Big Broadcast of 1938*. Every year Paramount produced a *Big Broadcast,* which usually highlighted some of the important events in the entertainment world of the year. There was always some shred of a story line, at least sufficient to tie the production together. (It was in this particular picture that the song "Thanks for the Memory" first appeared. Bob Hope was in the cast, and that song has stuck with him ever since.) This year Flagstad's part, which was filmed in the studios in Long Island City, called for a perform- ance of the "Ho-jo-to-ho" from *Die Walküre*. She wore an opu- lently inappropriate costume and stood on a huge studio rock. The music had been pre-recorded, and she had only to mime the part. I remember when the offer of this engagement came, Flag- stad was dumbfounded at the size of the fee. Even though she was by that time a top box-office attraction in her world, the Hollywood figure of $20,000 seemed to her almost beyond reason.

The spring tour that year was heavily booked, and it was diffi- cult to find time for the engagement. The only day in her tight schedule when she could be available for the filming was her very last day in America—she was to sail for Europe at mid- night. We arrived at the studio at seven in the morning and she worked continuously until after eight that night. After the ses- sion, while she was changing, I sat in an outer office and watched Harlan Thompson, who produced the picture, write her a really touching letter. In it he expressed the admiration of the entire crew for her tremendous energy and patience through the grueling day. There had not been one word of complaint or the slightest exhibition of "artistic" temperament. Those of us who knew Flagstad well took this all for granted. But to Thompson, who had just met her, it was a revelation.

The following autumn we were in Los Angeles and Para- mount gave a large luncheon for her at the studio. She was intensely flattered to be honored by the greats of another world of entertainment. I still have some fine photographs taken that day. One shows her with Adolph Zukor, another shows her being greeted by the late W. C. Fields, and still another charming one shows her with Gracie Allen and George Burns. The fuss all those people made over Flagstad delighted her far more than they knew.

She took childish pleasure in being a film celebrity. One day she was invited by Robert Montgomery to visit the MGM lot. Montgomery was a good friend of Becky Hamilton's, a devoted admirer and faithful friend of Flagstad's and ours for many years. That day the studio was working on one of the Jeanette MacDonald-Nelson Eddy musicals. Flagstad loved their pictures and never missed one, and to her it was heaven to be on location while they filmed one. During the breaks, the two ladies had much to say, and chattered like schoolgirls together. That same day Flagstad had another thrill—meeting Joan Crawford. She had been told that Miss Crawford was one of her fans, and during the long periods needed to get lighting and camera angles adjusted, the two visited like old friends.

One of Flagstad's most poignant Hollywood episodes was her visit to the Twentieth Century-Fox Studios for her first meeting with the Olympic star, Sonja Henie. Flagstad had given a concert the night before in Philharmonic Auditorium in Los Angeles. Miss Henie had been unable to attend because of filming commitments, but her mother had been there and had come backstage. The following day we went bright and early to the Fox studios. In one big building was an enormous rink on which that day they were filming a skating sequence. In her naïve but deeply felt patriotism, Flagstad was like a child visiting a legendary figure out of her dreams. She went to a florist in Los Angeles and bought a huge corsage of orchids for Miss Henie. To Miss Henie, Flagstad was as much a star as herself, and there were tears in her eyes as Flagstad with a few words in Norwegian gave her the corsage.

The great Danish actor, Jean Hersholt, was in the same film. Of all the many interesting experiences of my years with Flagstad, the good fortune of being with those three Scandinavians that day stands out in my memory. After the morning session on the set, Miss Henie, her mother, Flagstad, Mr. Hersholt, and I lunched together. Jean Hersholt was the center of attraction. Of the three famous personalities, he was by far the strongest. He even succeeded in getting Flagstad to talk a little about herself. That usually was not difficult to do. But that day she was in quite another world. To her, the star was Sonja Henie, and I think Flagstad would have gladly forgotten, if only momentarily, that she herself was famous. As a Norwegian, she was content on this occasion to bask in the reflected glory of her countrywoman.

I have had occasion to point out Flagstad's unpremeditated selflessness and generosity. It was a basic feature of the essential simplicity that lay beneath her paradoxical public personality. This characteristic of hers had remained only a thing observed as far as I was concerned. But I was to feel the warmth of her concern and involvement in a direct way, and that in terms of my own career. The episode had its earliest beginnings in Chicago, where Flagstad had sung opera for the first time in 1937. Immediately after that season, the manager, the late Paul Longone, inquired as to her availability for the following season. Flagstad knew well that my greatest ambition was to get a start as a conductor. On her own she seized upon this opportunity to give me a start. Although she had been pleased with the Chicago conductor, Henry Weber, and had no intention to do him any disservice, she had nonetheless come to believe in me and wanted to use her influence to give me a debut. Longone was asked to engage me for some of her performances the following season, and he agreed immediately. I was engaged for two performances of *Lohengrin* and made a fairly successful operatic debut conducting at the Civic Opera House in Chicago on November 21, 1938. But that came about only after a tour that eventually turned out to be a severe trial for almost everyone connected with it.

It is necessary to mention this now. A history of Kirsten Flagstad from 1938 on cannot be complete without placing the proper emphasis on what became something of a "Flagstad crusade"—the promotion of Edwin McArthur's career. It reaped great rewards for me and was the source of enormous pride to her. In many ways it also did a good deal of damage, of which more later. But the seed was planted in 1938. A new and geographically spectacular tour was to give fertile ground for it to grow and flower in.

Marks Levine was the first to believe that Flagstad should go to Australia. He himself had been there twice, first touring with his brother, the pianist Mischa Levitzki, and later with the soprano Dusolina Giannini. He was convinced that Flagstad would take the Australians by storm. The tour was arranged, and NBC made it possible for Max to go with us. We all looked forward to a happy time together. Beyond that, Max's being with us to handle business matters in a strange country promised to be a great advantage.

After the details of the tour had been settled, however, word came from Norway that Mr. Johansen had contracted a serious illness. Flagstad immediately began a series of refusals to leave without him. Such a trip to the other side of the world without her husband was unthinkable. And, typically, she was ready to discard the whole project, regardless of career considerations. This stubborn fidelity was an index of her emotional strength, and it is bitterly ironic to think of the grief it brought her later. But, fortunately for our plans then, Mr. Johansen recovered and was able to join us in San Francisco in time for our sailing.

That the Flagstad Australian tour was a fiasco as far as she was concerned was a source of great sorrow to us all. It really ought to be called a "fiasco-success," for although she was a failure, great steps forward were made in her crusade of sponsoring my career, and I managed to come through quite well. She unfortunately did not. And the worst part of it was that she alone spoiled the enterprise by her lack of interest once we had arrived and by her incomprehensible misbehavior.

The trip began well. There was a loud, happy send-off at the pier in San Francisco. Peggy, who was there to see us off, decided that she wanted to see Flagstad decorated with a traditional Hawaiian *lei*. Unfortunately she would not be with us in Honolulu. Just before we left the hotel for the boat, she put a beautiful *lei* of twenty-four gardenias around Flagstad's neck. A large delegation from the San Francisco Opera, headed by its general manager, Gaetano Merola, was also there to bid us *bon voyage*. We all drank champagne and there was much singing. Our cabins on board were luxurious—nothing was spared on this trip. The Johansens always traveled in style, and they wanted the same for Max and me. The rooms were filled with gifts, one of the most important to Flagstad being two cases of tonic water from Reginald Allen. (Reggie was to be a close friend for many years. We had first met when he was managing the Philadelphia Orchestra, and later he became an important administrative officer at the Metropolitan Opera. His affection and friendship were rare treasures.) The tonic water might well have been available on such a luxury liner, but Reggie wanted to make sure that in the tropics Flagstad would have this special mixer for her favorite gin. Henry Johansen took with him a case of aquavit, the lethal Scandinavian liqueur. Before we sailed he took one bottle to the dining room, called over the wine steward and gave his instructions. "This must be kept ice-cold. When you see we will soon need another bottle, tell me and I will bring it down. Except at breakfast, when my wife and I will not appear, you must bring four small glasses to the table immediately. Fill each glass to the brim with this liqueur and have a large glass of beer on hand to be used as a chaser." That is the way the Scandinavians drink their aquavit, and it is not for the timid.

The voyage across the Pacific was a great lark for Flagstad in spite of her steady concern over Else. She seemed carefree, as she rarely was. We landed in Honolulu with the customary fanfare. We were decorated with *leis,* the band was playing on the pier, and old friends were there to meet us.

The five or six days in Honolulu, during which Flagstad gave two concerts, were a continuous festival. On our first evening in Honolulu, Mr. Castle of the firm of Castle and Cook (one of the large and important industrial empires in the Hawaiian Islands) was giving a large party—a real *luau*—in honor of Mrs. Christian R. Holmes, née Betty Fleischmann, daughter of the famous yeast man, and at that time one of the main supporters and directors of the New York Philharmonic. Flagstad retreated into her reserve at the invitation. She would not go to the party, and she sent Max and me as her emissaries. The affair was carefully prepared; everything was authentically of the islands, and a far cry from the approximations we find in the States. For the first time I felt that I was hearing Hawaiian music as it should be played and eating Hawaiian food as it should be cooked. It was a wonderful evening in every way.

After the feast, Max and I returned to the hotel with Mrs. Holmes, who invited us for a nightcap in the bar. I remember she spent half an hour vigorously defending John Barbirolli, who had just recently succeeded Toscanini as the conductor of the Philharmonic and was very much in the great maestro's shadow as far as the press was concerned. The critics were cutting him to ribbons at every turn and he needed every friend he could find, particularly such a person as Mrs. Holmes. She stuck by him and he handsomely justified her faith and confidence. Not that Flagstad had anything whatsoever to do with the administration of the Philharmonic, but she admired Barbirolli and defended him too in those days. Since those dark days of 1938, Barbirolli, now Sir John, has had a brilliant career and has become one of the foremost conductors in the world.

We sailed from Honolulu on the S.S. *Mariposa* on Decoration Day. The festivities were elaborate. Again Flagstad was literally covered with flowers, and she watched with the familiar child-like absorption as the island boys dove from the decks of the ship, recapturing coins thrown into the water. Two weeks were ahead of us now on board ship before our scheduled arrival in Sydney, and during the trip we made a number of delightful acquaintances. One really unforgettable man, whose friendship lasted far beyond the voyage, was Father James Carroll, a Roman Catholic priest. Father Carroll, who died in 1949, was one of the warmest individuals I have ever met. He was on the faculty of Duquesne University in Pittsburgh, and at the time was being given a trip around the world by a parishioner who evidently had reason for especial gratitude to him. We met the first night out of Honolulu; oddly, it was a gambling occasion.

The Matson liners at that time all had slot machines in the lounges. I had tried to get Flagstad to play the "bandits" all the way from San Francisco to Honolulu. This first night on the *Mariposa* we were in the lounge having coffee and I, having given up on Flagstad, went to the quarter machine and dropped in a coin. I had good luck. At the next machine was Father Carroll, who was in mufti that evening—an open-collared sport shirt and slacks. Just at that moment, he hit the jackpot. He was having the time of his life. Suddenly he turned to Flagstad and not having the faintest idea who she was, said: "Come on, young lady—be a sport—don't be afraid." Flagstad flushed quickly and said: "Why sir, I don't know the first thing about those machines." Taking her by the arm, Father Carroll literally forced her up out of her chair and said: "Come on, now, I'll teach you." She dropped in her first quarter, and for the rest of the trip it was Flagstad whom we had to budget: she was allowed to lose only so much per day.

For the rest of the journey to Australia, Father Carroll became an "official" member of our party. When we stopped at Samoa, Flagstad announced that she would not leave the boat. Father Carroll would have none of that. "You must see the world," he said and took her by the hand again and made her go ashore with him to watch the native dancers and listen to the strange drum beats and the curious sounds of the singing of the inhabitants. That experience she did enjoy, but when we got to Suva in the Fiji Islands a few days later, she was in one of her stubborn moods, and in earnest. She could not be persuaded, even by Father Carroll's charm, and I ground my teeth in frustration. Only five minutes' drive from the pier there is a mountain called Flagstaff Hill, a "must" for visitors. The reader may by this time have gathered that I was something of a camera buff and a photograph of Flagstad on Flagstaff Hill—with its accompanying pun—would have been priceless, especially for publicity purposes. But she would not budge and ordered me not to take my camera out of its case for the rest of the day. Max, for his part, began to foresee more ominous eventualities as her negativism hardened. In any case, the perverse mood stayed with her during our last stop, at Auckland, New Zealand. With great reluctance she allowed herself to be taken to call on the Lord Mayoress, and it was not a pleasant interview, as Flagstad barely observed the most elementary courtesies.

When the boat left Auckland, Max and I decided to discuss this matter seriously with Mr. Johansen. He understood the necessity of good will and good public relations and promised to try to persuade her to be more amenable. But he was not very encouraging. Then we all talked with her. Vainly we tried to make her understand that everywhere people expect much more than just art from artists. A celebrity like Kirsten Flagstad was a legendary figure to her public and had an ironclad obligation to live up to the glamourous image projected by her career. And we did not fail to mention that this was particularly important in Australia because relatively few great artists could go there; in those days air travel to Australia was not regular yet. (Actually, all of the matters of good public relations, etc., had been covered with her to everyone's satisfaction in New York.) The more we talked, the more intractable she became. We did know, of course, that the separation from Else was continually on her mind, and even the happiness of having her husband with her did not make up for the bitterness she carried inside. But nonetheless we were on the eve of an important tour thousands of miles from the rest of the world and she was balking at the simplest prerequisites for success.

The gloom had not dissolved when we landed in Sydney. However, Flagstad was able to force herself to meet the occasion with at least some grace. An impressive delegation had come to the *Mariposa* to greet her. The Norwegian Consul, Niels Storaker, was there with his charming wife. The head of the firm of Taits, under whose management we were appearing, was there in eager anticipation of the star. Reporters of course

were also there, and Flagstad simply had to meet them. It is
an essential duty for any artist, no matter how great her reputation, no matter how black her mood. Surprisingly, she took an
immediate liking to Mr. and Mrs. Storaker and her glacial behavior melted, at least temporarily.

The first concert in Sydney, on June 18, 1938, was a triumph
with both public and press. The Sydney Town Hall is visually
impressive as well as acoustically sound, and her voice rang out
superbly. But immediately after her debut, she made a fatal
error. Lord Wakehurst was then Governor of New South Wales,
and very shortly he and Lady Wakehurst invited Flagstad and
her party to tea at Government House. To our utter despair, she
declined. This is simply not done. Max and Mr. Johansen,
aghast, tried to point out that Lord Wakehurst represented the
King in New South Wales. They emphasized that if a foreign
visitor to Norway declined an invitation to the Palace he would
be insulting the entire nation. But she would not budge. The
day on which she had been invited to Government House, she
had accepted an invitation to the country with Mr. and Mrs.
Storaker, and she would not change it. "I am as important as
Lord and Lady Wakehurst," she declared. It was nothing short
of stupid. When Mr. Storaker learned what she had done, he
was horrified. Her action did not reflect well on his own position
as Norwegian Consul, after all. Also, despite her first success,
promotion of the concerts was essential, and this official visit to
Government House was an important ingredient. But the situation passed as it was.

There were others. The Taits asked Flagstad to spend a few
hours one afternoon in a salon of one of the large department
stores simply to autograph photographs and records. She flatly
refused. It took no time at all for word of these discourtesies to
spread, and our audiences shrank quickly. Max was so embar-

rassed that he adopted the habit of leaving the concert hall before the end of a concert to avoid the unpleasant duty of turning admirers away from her dressing room.

It was soon apparent that we were in the midst of a fiasco. Everyone, including NBC back in New York, stood to lose not only money, but prestige as well. It is very doubtful whether the company would have sent one of its high officials on such a long tour without some reasonable prospect of good return. The Taits, seeing that a good build-up of public response in Sydney was not going to develop, proposed that she extend her tour to New Zealand. She refused. Original plans to give a season in each of the five important cities in Australia were scrapped, and it was decided that she would appear only in Sydney and Melbourne and then get out as quickly as possible. Those days were not pleasant, and it is hard to believe that we ever lived through them. Flagstad was no longer the simple, charming woman she had been. She was in every sense now a most unreasonable, perverse, and exasperating prima donna. She summoned Max one morning, for example, and asked him to investigate sailings back to America, from where she thought of proceeding to Europe, giving up all idea of continuing our beautifully planned journey around the world.

But then something happened which relieved the atmosphere measurably. It changed not only the course of the tour in Australia, but the entire course of my own life. No sooner had the great voice been heard in Sydney than there was a clamor to hear Flagstad with orchestra. ABC, the Australian Broadcasting Commission, organized and controlled the orchestras in the various cities of the country. In Australia, as elsewhere throughout the British Empire, there was a tax on radio sets, and the revenue was used to support first-rank orchestras and to maintain their qualitative level. But for Flagstad to sing with the ABC orchestras in Sydney and Melbourne created a bit of a problem. As a separate enterprise, ABC brought attractions to Australia in direct competition with the Taits. Had Flagstad gone there under ABC management, several orchestral concerts would have been arranged as a matter of course. Now it was necessary for the "competition" to ask for partnership. Flagstad was asked if she would sing concerts with the orchestras and she agreed immediately on the condition that I would be the conductor. I had never conducted publicly in my life, but she said I could do it and that there has to be a first time for everyone.

Max was the one chosen to tell the few necessary "white lies" so often needed to get any career started. Together with Claude Kingston from Taits, he called on the officials of the ABC, and they agreed at once to make their orchestras available for two concerts in each city. But they shied away from having an unknown conductor and would have preferred their own. "Where has he conducted?" they asked. "Oh a lot in America," Max said. "NBC–CBS–WPA, that's *government,* just like you!"

Finally it was agreed on the condition that the resident conductor, Joseph Post, should conduct the first of two concerts in both Sydney and Melbourne. In arranging the programs, we had several conferences with the program committee of the ABC. The atmosphere was staggeringly formal—one would have thought we were settling the fate of the Roman Empire. A little shaken by this unusual severity, I asked that Maestro Post's programs be arranged first. When this was settled, the chairman of the committee turned to me and said: "Now, Mr. McArthur, what would you like to begin with?" Glancing quickly over the programs already decided upon, I said: "We can start with the *Tannhäuser* overture."

The chairman asked: "Isn't that pretty difficult for the orchestra to commence with?"

"Well, Dr. Barry," I said, "when they give the opera, the orchestra starts with the overture."

Everyone laughed, and in Sydney we did begin with the *Tannhäuser* overture. In both of the concerts I conducted in Australia the second half of the program consisted of an hour's excerpt from *Götterdämmerung*, with Flagstad singing the "Immolation Scene" as a finale. In Melbourne, for a little change from Wagner, she sang Beethoven's great scene, *"Ah, perfido,"* and the orchestra commenced with the overture to *Der Freischütz.*

I had my first rehearsal with the orchestra in Sydney on July 10, 1938. Flagstad came to the hall and went over the program with me at a subsequent rehearsal, on July 12. She was forty-three that day. That it occurred on her birthday has always had a great, if not easily described, significance for me. I had alerted the orchestra before her arrival, and as she came in they played "Happy Birthday" and I pinned a corsage on her. Needless to say, I was nervous all through the rehearsal, but Flagstad was a tower of strength and made visible her pride in my work. The afternoon passed without incident. When it was all over I went back to the hotel and was allowed to collapse in exhaustion.

That night Henry Johansen gave a birthday party for his wife at Romano's Restaurant. In retrospect it appears as one of the two or three most important occasions in my whole life, for it determined the course of my career and general focus as a person for years to come. At the table Flagstad took my hand, leaned toward me confidentially, and with her simplicity and directness said: "Edwin, I think you have great talent. My husband and I are determined to do everything possible to help you in a conducting career. I will do what I can to sponsor you professionally, and he will put up whatever money is necessary."

I was speechless. It was an amazing gesture of confidence, all the more not only because Flagstad was at the peak of her career—whereas I as a conductor was barely starting—but also because her endorsement was being supported by an extremely hardheaded and realistic businessman. That evening the course of my career and even of my whole life was determined definitely.

The next night I made my conducting debut in Sydney. I believe I did well, and the concert was a success.

The season in Melbourne which followed was much happier and more successful than the one in Sydney. The difference between the two largest cities in Australia is startling. Though separated by only a few hundred miles, they might well be on different continents. Sydney looks far more American than Melbourne. It has an atmosphere of bustling activity and commercial life, whereas Melbourne has a quiet reserve that one associates with Britain. I liked both cities, and was glad to return to them several times later on during the war years. But despite having made some good friends, Flagstad had been uncomfortable and unhappy in Sydney. Of course, she never really took the opportunity to see what might be there to interest her. And the fact that she had not been a success made it all the more unpleasant. But in Melbourne, it was different. She had been in England a great deal, and she immediately felt at home in that more conservative atmosphere.

And in Melbourne her success was instantaneous—she drew capacity houses and she was again the star. No doubt the relief of knowing that the Australian season was coming to a close was a comfort to her. The whole trip had been planned with eager enthusiasm. That it had been a failure was a bitter pill. And besides this, although no one ever spoke of it, she still carried the sorrow of separation from her daughter. Else had remained completely silent all those months.

For some reason the people of Melbourne did not seem so demanding of Flagstad's time for extra things. It wasn't necessary to say "No" so often. And we had one heart-warming reunion. One evening at a concert Mr. Johansen sat next to Father James Carroll, our buoyant companion from the S.S. *Mariposa*. He was with another priest, who turned out to be his own brother. We learned that the two had not seen each other for seventeen years. Father Carroll had made this voyage especially to see him and their sister, a nun, whom he had not seen for thirty-seven years. The reunion can only be imagined.

At the concert Father Carroll asked if he might bring his sister and brother, together with another nun, to call the next day. Flagstad was overjoyed to see her friend again and to meet his family. They came at noon the next day to the hotel, and Flagstad, realizing that the nuns were unable to attend public concerts, asked if they would like to hear her sing. For an hour she gave of her superb art and the Carrolls could not hold back their tears of joy and appreciation.

Finally, the last concerts in Melbourne were over and we sailed home aboard the S.S. *Niagara* from Sydney on August 4. Max had carefully planned to make connections fifteen days later with the S.S. *Matsonia* from Honolulu to San Francisco. The timing was essential to reach California for three important engagements that Max had arranged by cable. We had a twenty-four hour stop at Auckland, New Zealand, and Max suggested that we use this time for an excursion to the native village of the Maoris called Rotorua. The trip takes some three or four hours by car from Auckland. The Maoris are among the most advanced of aboriginals and are highly respected. They live for the most part in their unembellished natural surroundings, as they have for generations. Modern civilization, though it is just next door, has scarcely touched their lives at all. The locality is crowded with natural wonders, of which one is a large pool of water in which the Maori women do their laundry. Half of the pool is hot, and without any dividing line, the other half is cold.

Flagstad was a very bad tourist. It was rarely that one could interest her in visiting a famous or interesting spot. I know for a fact that although she lived for several seasons directly across the street from the Metropolitan Museum of Art in New York City, she never set foot inside the building. She visited motion-picture studios in Hollywood only when there was some personal attraction. Once I took her inside the great cathedral in Milan, but I am sure that she never visited St. Peter's in Rome, although she was in that great city many times. And, of course, when we had stopped in Auckland before, there had been her snub of the Lord Mayoress—she much preferred to sit in her room playing solitaire.

But something about the way in which Max described the Maori people evidently interested Flagstad. I remembered too, and told her something of the Maori music. Years before I had played several of their songs in concert arrangements for Frances Alda.

We made the trip, and it was an utterly fascinating experience. Except for Princess Rangi, the famous guide for visitors, none of those people on the other side of the world had the faintest idea that they were being visited by a celebrated opera star. And Flagstad didn't behave like a famous opera star that day. She was a plain, simple Norwegian woman with a good deal of wholesome curiosity.

The Maoris greeted her with no fanfare at all, but retained their unaffected simplicity in giving us a warm welcome. She in turn intuitively responded in her own simple Norwegian manner. Princess Rangi asked her if she would like to hear a group of the women sing. Of course she would. "But," said Princess Rangi, "we will sing for you only if you sing for us." Under any other circumstances, Flagstad would have turned and run.

"Of course," she said. For half an hour those few of us had a remarkable musical experience—out of doors in the native Maori village of Rotorua, a group of simple Maori women in their own setting, singing their haunting melodies. We did not understand the words. We did not need to. The music and the expression on their faces was message enough. And then Flagstad sang three or four Norwegian songs. No accompaniment was needed. The rapport was sufficient accompaniment for one of the world's greatest artists singing in that simple way for these simple and honest people. They did not applaud. Perhaps they had never acquired that means of expressing appreciation. But their broad smiles and the animated chatter were proof enough of their pleasure. After each of Flagstad's songs Princess Rangi would say: "They want more!"

She talked about Rotorua many times. Later, using that as an example, I would try to persuade her in our travels to go to see something else. But only a few times would she do so. She always used the excuse that there was no time. For a really inquisitive nature, that is never an excuse. Time can always be found. But a deep respondent chord was sounded that day in Rotorua and it showed those of us there that there were un-revealed depths in Flagstad. Did unconquerable shyness forbid her to relax and enjoy life more? That is a question which I often wonder if I myself can answer.

Just as we sailed from Auckland a violent storm arose, and within a short time we had lost the precious twelve hours needed to insure our connection at Honolulu. We were in a

As Leonore in *Fidelio*,
Metropolitan Opera, 1936

At Vienna, 1936

With Edwin McArthur and Henry Johansen,
Copenhagen, August 1936

At Santa Barbara, California,
November 1936

terrible state, and for days Max spent most of his time sending out frantic radiograms to the United States in an effort to find some other means of travel. It was important to reach California for those engagements, as much for Flagstad's sagging morale as for the considerable financial return involved. Flagstad then conceived the idea that she could perhaps bribe the captain of the *Niagara* to pick up speed (already we were doing the limit). But we were amused and let her go ahead. She invited him to her cabin and offered to sing a benefit recital on board ship. That is often done on ocean liners, and many artists willingly perform, but she had always curtly refused when asked. And here she was making the offer. The recital took place and quite a tidy sum was raised for the benefit of the seamen. Three days out of Honolulu, when we had about given up hope and Max was about to notify America that the engagements would have to be canceled, we were overjoyed to have word that the *Tatsuta Maru* of the Japanese line would be in port in Honolulu en route from Japan. We could continue our trip to San Francisco aboard her and reach our destination in time. Foreign liners were not permitted to carry passengers from one American port to another without payment of fine. This cost Flagstad an additional $800, but we were so relieved that the amount was hardly worth considering.

Flagstad insisted during this journey across the Pacific that the details of her and her husband's sponsorship of my career be further discussed and settled. She refused herself to talk about anything but the music to be done and plans for professional engagements. Mr. Johansen was undertaking the big financial responsibility. He was a thorough businessman and wanted this project organized properly. Max and he talked about the matter many times on board ship, and on occasion I was brought into the discussions. Subsequently a detailed plan was formulated, and Mr. Johansen and Flagstad asked Max if he would put the terms of agreement into a letter that they would sign.

Despite the fact that we had been talking about this subject for days, I can never forget my numb feeling of embarrassment and wonder when Max produced his draft of the proposed letter. It is an extraordinary document that to this day is one of my prized possessions. In it Flagstad and Mr. Johansen affirmed their belief in my future as well as their deep affection for me. The letter explains their hope for my career as a conductor and their earnest desire to sponsor my future. And Mr. Johansen committed himself to $30,000 of financing. I went to my cabin and quite alone in the darkness tried to find answers to the questions of why those wonderful people were doing all of that for me.

It was understandable that Flagstad, because of our close musical collaboration, would want to help me. But her husband? True, we had drawn closer together as time had gone on. He had often referred to Peggy and me as his "adopted American children." His own twin boys in Norway were just my age. I remembered that he had been unhappy that the boys—Henry, Jr., and Frederick—had not been cordial to Peggy and me in Norway in 1937. I never met Frederick, and saw Henry, Jr., only once for a few minutes. Peggy and I had met his eldest daughter, Kate, in Norway, but we were yet to know and love his other daughter, Annie; she was at the time a complete stranger to us. And there was this man, pouring out to me as generously as he would have to one of his own blood. To be sure, he had on so many occasions shown his confidence in me as a person. Even when silly stories began to circulate about a "love affair" between Flagstad and her young American accompanist, he was the first to dismiss the subject as the essence of stupidity. Flagstad and I were of an age close enough to be as sister and brother. On the other hand, Mr. Johansen could well have been father to both Peggy and myself. He was treating us now as though we were actually his dearest children. Can anyone question why I would always have a feeling of responsibility and affection for the man who bestowed on me such unquestioning faith and confidence?

Mr. Johansen's generosity was livened by an accurate sense of humor, and without hurting, he enjoyed embarrassing those he loved. On the very day I made my debut as a conductor in the United States, he directed me to type the letter he and his wife were to sign. "But," I protested, "this is something I cannot do. Please get someone else."

"Edwin," he said sternly, "you are not the conductor yet. For the moment you are the secretary. Now get out your typewriter and do as I say."

Chapter IV

1938–1940

WE LANDED in San Francisco early in the morning on August 25 and flew directly to Hollywood for a Kraft Music Hall Broadcast that evening. This was the first of the three engagements that Max had arranged by cable from Australia. That broadcast was a delight. It was the first of three or four times when Flagstad appeared on the air with Bing Crosby. The character of the Kraft Music Hall was entirely informal and everything was on a first-name basis—something Flagstad would rarely accept.

The next California engagement was in the Hollywood Bowl. Flagstad was visibly happy to be singing again for a sold-out house, particularly after the Australian disaster. It was apparent, however, that Otto Klemperer, who was conducting, didn't particularly like her. She herself was not very enthusiastic about singing with him. There were reasons for frigidity on both sides. Several years before coming to America she had gone to Berlin to audition for him: he had not liked her then and had not engaged her. Also, when this last-minute appearance for her in the Hollywood Bowl had been proposed, it had been suggested that I be the conductor. This Klemperer would not allow. It is only reasonable to believe that he resented what could well be considered impudence on her part in suggesting replacing a great man like him with a young upstart. But Flagstad was stubborn and insisted that in some way I appear at this concert. A compromise was reached. She would sing several Wagnerian excerpts with the orchestra and Dr. Klemperer; I would accompany a group of songs at the piano. The atmosphere at the rehearsal was not cordial. Much to her annoyance, in front of the entire orchestra, he corrected several places in her arias to suit his own particular feeling and taste. Flagstad always accepted the conductor as the final word, and so, as a true artist, she accepted his direction as graciously as possible. But she didn't like him and in his brusque way he showed clearly that he returned her feelings.

Following the concert I flew to San Francisco to prepare for the third and most important California engagement that Max had contracted. The following morning I was to rehearse the San Francisco Symphony in an all-Wagner program for performance with Flagstad that evening. Flagstad and her husband drove early in the morning to Bakersfield, from where they took a train arriving very late afternoon in San Francisco just in time for the evening concert. She had sung a big concert the night before, and the day's travel was not easy. She was still frightened of airplanes and rather than fly she took this much more arduous means of getting there. Despite it, she arrived in San Francisco fresh and ready.

Never before had I seen her so determined. This particular evening was to be a success. Many times I had witnessed her stubborn determination, but never as on that night. The Flagstad-Melchior feud was still at white heat. Much of the unfortunate controversy had flowered in San Francisco, where Melchior had many friends and allies of particular importance and influence in the music world. Some quite openly had already expressed their resentment at her use of position to sponsor me. That night she seemed literally to be saying, "I'll show you who is on top." Seldom in all the years we were together did I see her shed a tear. But when the *"Liebestod"* was finished at the end of the concert, her tears were there. This was the last time Mr. Johansen was in California and the very last time he heard me conduct. I will always be glad that he was there when I got off to a pretty good start in my own country.

Flagstad took pride and pleasure in having members of her family visit her in America during the years of her career here. Before the Australian trip, her mother and sister, Karen Marie, came to New York for an extended visit. Karen Marie came several times more, but the 1938 visit with Fru Flagstad was particularly full of interesting happenings.

Fru Flagstad was a remarkable woman, an embodiment of the qualities we generally consider Norwegian. She was stolid, straightforward, rugged in appearance, and, like most Norwegian women, extremely stubborn. She was also an excellent pianist. Her famous daughter's success had fed her pride and ambition, and unlike the daughter, she had not an ounce of shyness in her. She would have gladly stood in Times Square and shaken hands with everyone. Flagstad's reserve was a constant annoyance to her. Fru Flagstad spoke a maximum of ten words in English. Undoubtedly as a girl in school she had studied English; most Norwegians do. But she had found no need in her life for our language and had forgotten what she knew. We managed to get along quite well in very lame German.

While mother and sister were in New York, Howard Taubman of *The New York Times* invited them all to attend a weekly luncheon of the Dutch Treat Club. This club is made up of professional men of letters in New York City, and an invitation from them is an impressive honor. It was proposed as a response that *all three* ladies perform. Flagstad and her sister as young girls in Norway had often sung Norwegian folk songs in duet. Karen Marie was and is a singer of considerable accomplishment. Taubman had graciously invited me to come with the Flagstads. It was an informal but distinguished affair. No sooner were we seated than I saw, two or three tables away, the late Oley Speaks, one of this country's really first-rank song writers. (Flagstad had never met Oley, but at practically all of her concerts she sang his beautiful song "Morning.") The toastmaster that day was the eminent writer Hendrik Willem Van Loon. During the conversation at the table Mr. Van Loon asked Flagstad if she would like to say a few words. Normally she would have refused, and I was surprised to hear her say that this time she would consent. I quietly went around to her place and whispered: "Oley Speaks is a member of this club and is here today." Nothing further was said.

Before the Flagstad trio, Mr. Van Loon had a few remarks to make, and they were treasures. He spoke eloquently. The world was not yet at war, but there were constant rumblings and an increasing of international crises. In a wonderfully humane way, Mr. Van Loon spoke about the brotherhood of man and the urgent desire of all to be good friends and neighbors. He paid special tribute to the Norwegian guests that day and made us all feel that everyone in that room, Norwegians and Americans, were brothers and sisters in the hand of God. Then he introduced Flagstad. She said simply: "Gentlemen, I am aware that a member of this club, one of whose songs I sing at all my concerts, is here today."

Then she sang Oley's "Morning" and for this, in that setting, received one of the great ovations of her career. The composer was taken completely by surprise. He jumped up from his place, embraced Flagstad, and kissed her on both cheeks.

Then she went on to say that although she was not a speaker, she could not miss the opportunity to express her pride in being in America, her appreciation for the way that the American people had taken her to their hearts, and the family pride she felt in being permitted to present her mother and sister to that distinguished company. Fru Flagstad then went to the piano, and I feel sure that nothing in the annals of the Dutch Treat Club could be compared to the performance all three gave.

Mother and daughters together were also heard by a nation-wide radio audience that spring of 1938. It was under rather dramatic circumstances. Here again the Magic Key program played an important part. The program directors of that hour were as imaginative as ever. Earlier, even before Fru Flagstad and Karen Marie had come to America, they had conceived the idea of having Flagstad sing in New York while her sister and mother performed simultaneously from Norway. It was a challenge to the engineers as well as to the musical ability of the artists. First Flagstad was scheduled to sing with orchestra from the studio in New York. And then from this same studio she would introduce her mother and sister who were standing by ready to perform in a studio in Oslo. To our disappointment, when the big moment came, the communications failed. But the Magic Key directors were not to be thwarted. They scheduled an identical spot the following week. That time everything went off perfectly and the transatlantic performance was a total success. Before long the same directors decided there must be a climax, and when sister and mother were in New York later, on Sunday April 10, 1938, the three Flagstads again appeared on a Magic Key broadcast, this time with Alexander Woollcott.

The year 1938 was filled with unusual and particularly interesting events. Two items in the press especially pleased Flagstad. On February 19, 1938, Mrs. Eleanor Roosevelt attended a matinée performance of *Lohengrin* at the Metropolitan and wrote beautifully of Flagstad's singing in her column "My Day." Then, on Sunday March 20, 1938, the eminent critic of the New York *Herald Tribune,* the late Lawrence Gilman, wrote a remarkable column titled "First Lady of the Opera", devoted entirely to Madame Flagstad. She was perfectly delighted. Now she was able to forget her annoyance of the previous season when all the articles asking "Who is the Prima Donna of the Metropolitan?" had appeared. But the dreary Flagstad-Melchior feud dragged on all the same because of those articles and the famous bridge game in Rochester.

Every year Mr. and Mrs. Esberg came from San Francisco for an extended visit in New York. It will be recalled that they were among Flagstad's warmest friends. On one occasion they made

possible an encounter between Flagstad and the great actor Otis
Skinner. It all began when Mrs. Esberg went alone to a matinée
of *Parsifal*. The performance had reached the scene in which
Kundry—Flagstad was singing the role—washes Parsifal's feet.
Suddenly Mrs. Esberg felt two hands grasping her shoulders
and a familiar voice whispered: "Caroline, what acting—
marvelous!" It was her old friend Otis Skinner, who was scarcely
unfamiliar with acting technique. Flagstad would persuade Mrs.
Esberg to tell this story over and over again. It made her proud,
and it should have.

At about this time difficulties began to arise between Flagstad
and the San Francisco Opera. Mr. Esberg was still a most important member of the company's board of directors. Naturally,
the company wanted Flagstad and needed a firm commitment
from her so that repertoire and other problems could be settled.
Flagstad was being particularly naughty that year. The one person on the board of the San Francisco Opera who was able at
that time to smooth things out between the star and the company was Mr. Esberg.

Luck was with us at this moment, as the Esbergs were in New
York. Soon, together with Flagstad and her husband, we were
invited to dinner at their apartment. We had no idea who else
was to be there. When we arrived, the two other guests turned
out to be the great Otis Skinner and his son-in-law, Alden
Blodgett (the husband of Cornelia Otis Skinner). I quickly took
Flagstad aside and started to whisper to her the identity of Otis
Skinner as one of the world's greatest actors. Loudly she re-
torted: "Don't tell me. I am not so stupid!" Truth to tell, on
many other occasions she had been.

At dinner the great man delighted us all. He seemed to want
to talk about all the roles he had played and presently started on
a long philosophical exposition of the character of Shylock in

The Merchant of Venice. He went into considerable detail, dwelling particularly on the significance of the Jew in society. It was surprising at first that Mr. Skinner should have chosen for this occasion this play and the particular part of the Jew—he was perfectly aware of his hosts' affiliations. But the subject and the way he spoke were all the more admirable when it became apparent that he was deliberately doing this for his close friends.

The entire evening was one of great joy to Flagstad. It is one of the few occasions I remember when she was happy to not be discussing her own career—that evening she was not the center of the stage. And it accidentally did the trick as far as the San Francisco Opera was concerned. As we were leaving, she suddenly said: "Oh, Mr. Esberg, I have been thinking it over, and if you want me back next season, I will come." After weeks of difficult negotiations and discussions it was curious to think that just one evening of social life with a great man holding the center of the stage could melt her determination.

In the entire history of the Metropolitan Opera there has probably never been a party like the one Flagstad gave on the twenty-fifth anniversary of her debut as a singer. The date was December 12, 1938. There was only one sad note to the occasion. The feud with Melchior was still flaming, and not only was he absent from the party, but also he had not sung at the performance. At Flagstad's particular insistence, he was left out. Just before our departure for Australia the previous April, I had gone with her to Edward Johnson's office at the Metropolitan. It was the only pleasant visit I ever had in that office. It will be remembered that I had already experienced two unpleasant days at his desk in 1936, and, unfortunately, more were to come. At the meeting in April 1938, Artur Bodanzky was present and the principal subject discussed was the coming twenty-fifth anniversary performance of Flagstad. It was decided then and there that the opera would be one of her favorites, *Götterdäm-merung*, and the tenor Carl Hartmann. In the cast for that performance Flagstad made another specific request which the Metropolitan graciously granted. She was devoted as a friend and colleague to Madame Dorothée Manski and she wanted Manski on the stage with her that night of celebration. It was one of Flagstad's real sorrows later on that Manski proved to be a bitterly disloyal friend to one who had shown her such affection.

Flagstad decided that following the gala performance she would give a real party in Sherry's Restaurant at the Opera House for the entire staff of the Metropolitan. By "entire" she meant literally *everyone* who worked for the company—stage doormen, ushers, cloakroom attendants, cleaning women, night watchmen, and so on. Everyone was invited. Even the management was surprised at so extensive a list, but she had made up her mind. The only person at the party who was not connected with the opera company in any way was I. Flagstad had charged me with the responsibility of arranging and running the affair. Mr. Ziegler, the Assistant General Manager, was most helpful. But during a conversation in his office when I was settling details of food and drink, he asked in amazement: "Does Madame Flagstad have any idea of what all this is going to cost?"

"Get me the estimate," was all I could say. And when a few days later I quoted a staggering amount to her, she simply instructed me to go ahead as planned.

Sherry's Restaurant was jammed to the walls when Flagstad made her entrance flanked by the general manager and his two assistants of the Metropolitan. The entire assembly rose and sang "Happy Birthday." The banquet was almost Roman in its opulence. Champagne abounded and the men had the finest cigars available. After a little while Flagstad herself began to take trays out to people such as watchmen who, because of their duties, were unable to be at the party in person. Unfortunately, Mr. Johansen was not there. He had been due to land in New York from Europe that morning, but the harbor was totally fogbound and he could not arrive until the following day. But Flagstad was gay and happy that night and momentarily forgot the continued sadness of Else's estrangement.

Flagstad received other tributes on her twenty-fifth anniversary. Probably the most flattering of all came from the Bohemian Club in New York. Each year this club has a special ladies' night dinner to honor some outstanding personality in the musical world. There is no organization quite so distinguished as the Bohemian Club, and to be saluted by them is a coveted experience. Early, in 1937, Flagstad had been asked to sing at a dinner honoring Josef Hofmann, who was that year celebrating his fiftieth jubilee. She wore a special gown of gold cloth for that occasion and prized highly the beautiful letter Mr. Hofmann wrote her afterwards.

Soon after the Hofmann dinner I was approached by an official of the Bohemians, Albert von Doenhoff, who asked if Flagstad would accept an invitation to be the honor guest the following year. It was inconceivable that anyone would refuse such a tribute, but the Bohemians wanted to make sure.

Flagstad of course was very moved, but had one request to make: Might she choose those who would be invited to perform? Naturally, they agreed, and without hesitation she asked that Elisabeth Rethberg, Ezio Pinza, and Mr. and Mrs. Josef Lhévinne appear. The program of music that night in the grand ballroom of the Waldorf-Astoria was unforgettable and the whole affair was dazzling. A long evening of tributes reached a climax when Ernest Hutcheson, president of the Bohemians, proposed a toast to Flagstad. Her response was simple and direct. She said: "I am no speaker, but I would like to sing three songs. All are 'I Love Thee'—the first by Beethoven, the second by Grieg, and the third by Richard Strauss." It was a dramatic touch that I have never forgotten.

It was at about this stage that Flagstad, propelled by adulation like that, passed over into the area of the real prima donna. Although she never really lost her simple and almost peasant-like Norwegian character, it was only natural that with such continuous acclaim and worldwide demand for her she should reach that state. One of the usual habits of a prima donna is the exercise of power, and she realized more and more clearly how much she had and what it could bring her. She gloated over the fact that she could practically dictate the work and cast for her twenty-fifth anniversary. She exulted in keeping Melchior out of the cast that anniversary night.

Another satisfaction to her was that she could dictate terms to so many about my career. Thus I was the beneficiary of an interest that had its selfish as well as its generous side. As this went on, she gradually acquired the queenlike manner that so famously overawed those who were admitted to her presence. She never became genuinely sophisticated, but in being exposed more and more to the upper levels of society, she developed more accurate taste in her clothes and in her mode of living. Up to this time, it had been possible to walk down a street with her without anyone's taking notice. As she came to be recognized, she feigned irritation and complained that the public "will not let me live a private life." The truth of the matter is that she enjoyed every shred of attention that came her way. And as a prima donna, she was acute enough to know that she had to dress and play the part.

The Bohemian Club had honored only one other great feminine personality: Madame Marcella Sembrich. Flagstad was justly proud to follow in the footsteps of that very great prima donna. The business of being a world-famous singer not only awakened in her new responsibilities and a new world to conquer, but also rewarded her with the legitimate privilege of playing the part.

Henry Johansen was in America for most of the celebrations of the twenty-fifth jubilee. His presence added immeasurably to her happiness. He had completely recovered from the previous year's illness and she bloomed in the comfort of a strong man to care for her. But presently his own business in Norway called him home, and their parting seemed more difficult for her than usual. Shortly after his arrival home in Norway however, she announced—with her deceptive calm—that early in the spring of 1939 Else would return to America and to her. Knowng the harshness of their separation and the pain it had caused, I could only be amazed at the matter-of-fact way she told me of their coming reunion. And beyond telling me the date of Else's arrival, she made not the slightest explanation. I found it wise to keep my own counsel.

From the day Else arrived again in America, the tone of Flagstad's daily life changed completely. She no longer complained of the hard work she had to do. She laughed more, and in business matters was much more flexible. Prima donnas can be problems: it seems to be a basic trait of theirs to make trouble, and chronic unhappiness will magnify anyone's difficulties. But with Else on hand again, everything was carefree.

I could only guess at what had precipitated Else's return. Neither Flagstad nor her daughter ever discussed the matter with me in spite of our closeness. Else resembled her mother in very much the same way that Flagstad was like her own mother. Each had the same granitic stubbornness, and the share of personal pride normal to anyone could in these women move quickly into a perhaps unreasonable arrogance. Also, I am fairly sure that Else and her mother never discussed the separation with each other. They had both been through many painful months and too long a time had elapsed without their having communicated about this or any other subject.

On the other hand, a very interested party was Henry Johansen, who had to live with the distraught and broken-hearted mother of Else, whom he considered an errant daughter. I feel almost positive that it was he who determined that peace must be made, and that upon his return to Norway in early 1939, he himself brought it about.

In any case, Flagstad and her daughter picked up the threads of their life in the most affectionate way. Those of us in the family circle fell silently into line as though nothing at all had happened. What went on inside Flagstad's heart and mind during a serious crisis was practically impossible to discover. Her poise was complete, and she had the enviable faculty of putting grief behind her. The separation undoubtedly left scars. But even her close friends were not to hear of them. The important thing was that it was over.

During the winter of 1938–9, Flagstad had chosen to become friendly with a New York family whose warm and affectionate support was eventually to be of inestimable value to her. Katherine Hall and her late husband proved themselves to be of pure gold as friends. Katherine's mother is the only surviving child of the famous Montana Senator William A. Clark. Mrs. Morris is a most remarkable woman—conservative, severely dignified, but intensely interested in everything that goes on. She has owned the same subscription seats at the Metropolitan and to the weekly concerts of the New York Philharmonic for over fifty years. The Halls' children are all wonderful young people.

Every year the Halls go to a ranch called the Diamond J, in

Bozeman, Montana, and in 1939 they proposed that while Flagstad was in Europe, she leave Else with them to go out to the ranch. Else did just that, and a mere chance meeting that summer changed the entire course of her life. When I saw her the following autumn, I could hardly believe that in so short a time a thoroughly Norwegian girl could have become so completely Western-American.

Flagstad's extraordinary energy and vitality were never more apparent than during this happy period following her reunion with Else. Her sheer physical endurance was astounding, and a rather hectic series of spring concerts in Chicago showed to what lengths she could push herself when necessary. She had been engaged to sing at the North Shore Festival at Northwestern University in Evanston, Illinois. Now no longer given, these festivals were important events in American cultural life in those days. Not long before the festival was to open that year, a disastrous fire swept the building where the concerts were given, and for a time it was thought the festival might have to be canceled. But the directors in Evanston were a determined group and carried on. A big section of the athletic field on the campus at Northwestern was set aside and a large tent was put up to cover the bleachers, the chairs on the ground, and the temporary stage which had been constructed. And in that setting the 1939 festival went on as planned.

Flagstad was to sing at the evening concert on Saturday, May 20. Her part of the program came before the intermission. Frederick Stock was the conductor this year, and he had asked her to sing the "Immolation Scene." Following the intermission, Beethoven's Ninth Symphony was scheduled.

Flagstad and I left New York on the *Twentieth Century Limited* on the evening of May 19 and arrived the following morning in Chicago. We were no sooner registered at the hotel than

my telephone rang. It was Henry Vogeli, then manager of the
Chicago Symphony Orchestra and business director of the festival that year. In the gravest tones he told me that there had
been a great catastrophe and begged me to come to Dr. Stock's
office in Ochestra Hall as quickly as possible. I was there
within five minutes. Dr. Stock's face was long as I walked in.
Marian Anderson had been scheduled to sing at the matinée
that afternoon. After Flagstad's departure from New York the
evening before, it had been discovered that Miss Anderson
would have to cancel her appearance because of a sudden illness. It was too late to secure another soloist of such prominence. Max had suggested by telephone to Dr. Stock that when
Flagstad arrived in Chicago I might possibly persuade her to
sing at *both* the matinée and evening concerts that day. The
afternoon concert was to begin at two fifteen, and it was already
almost ten in the morning. And Evanston was an hour's drive
away.

At that moment Flagstad was resting at the hotel with no
thought of anything but the evening's concert. I acted quickly.
"Do you have the materials for things which Madame Flagstad
might sing this afternoon?" I asked. Of course, in the large
library of the Chicago Symphony they would have. All I could
say then was: "Unfortunately, Madame Flagstad hasn't anything to wear at an afternoon concert. She brought only the
one dress for tonight."

Dr. Stock looked at me in amazement. "Is that the only problem?" he asked. "Are you sure she will sing?"

By this time in our lives together I knew her very well and
was sure she would rise to the occasion. She was always the
trouper. I simply said: "I know she will sing, but we have to find
a dress for her to wear."

Mr. Vogeli reached for his telephone and called one of the

officers of the Chicago Orchestral Association, Arthur G. Cable. Mr. Cable agreed to have his wife meet us at a dress shop nearby within half an hour. Meanwhile, I hurriedly called Flagstad at the hotel and said: "You are singing this afternoon as well as tonight and I will pick you up at the entrance of the hotel in five minutes to go shopping for a dress. I'll explain later."

Before she could answer, I hung up.

We met Mrs. Cable within twenty minutes, but it only took a few moments to discover that as good as the shop was, their selection was insufficient for Flagstad.

"Thank you," I said, "we'll have to look elsewhere."

Off we went to Marshall Field's and, rushing into the dress department, we seized the first saleslady we saw. And thus started a sweet friendship with a delightful person, Mrs. Marguerite Dineen. She recognized Flagstad immediately and I explained our problem, and instantaneously that dress department burst into a cyclone of activity. From a selection of over fifty gowns Flagstad chose one that she liked. It was of a lightweight material with spring flowers and had a long, flowing cape of light purple chiffon. The gown needed altering. It was eleven o'clock.

"Can it be ready for me to pick up at twelve thirty?" I asked.

It was agreed, and we left. I took Flagstad back to the hotel and returned to Marshall Field's at the appointed time to pick up the dress.

It must be noted that, in her simple characteristic way, Flagstad never went to Chicago after that without going to see Mrs. Dineen, and the warm reception she always got pleased her immensely.

We left for Evanston at quarter past one. At the afternoon

concert Flagstad sang five big Wagnerian arias, including Brünnhilde's "Battle Cry." Then we drove the hour back to the hotel, and she had a bite of supper alone. After she had changed into her evening gown, we drove back to Evanston for the evening concert. As usual, she was in superb form at both concerts and had her usual triumph.

After it was all over, we drove back into town to catch a night train for Detroit, where she was to do another Ford Sunday Evening Hour broadcast the following evening. Even that was not the end. To make the record complete, she had to be back in New York to sing a group of arias with orchestra at a gala concert the next evening for the benefit of the Musicians' Emergency Fund. Any one of that string of concerts would have been sufficient for almost anyone. But Flagstad did them all in splendor and finished the final one in a blaze of glory.

Now, while I am writing about Mrs. Dineen, I must jump ahead a few years.

Came the war, and after that the Metropolitan Opera, thanks to Rudolf Bing, invited Flagstad to return to its stage. One day shortly before that memorable night in January 1951 Flagstad received a letter from Mrs. Dineen. She wrote that she hoped that Flagstad would remember her. Meanwhile, she had moved to Los Angeles and was then employed in Bullock's store. Among her customers was a wealthy woman with whom she had often talked of Flagstad. This lady believed that Flagstad would never return to the Metropolitan Opera, and Mrs. Dineen was equally sure that she would. The generous lady had promised Mrs. Dineen that if Flagstad ever did return to the Metropolitan she would give her the gift of a trip to New York to hear her. And so Mrs. Dineen assured Flagstad that when she stepped out on that stage to re-enter Metropolitan Opera life, she would be in the audience.

Now we go back to 1939. Disappointing trouble in business negotiations occupied much time and thought. I have always regretted that I and my career were the pivot around which so many of these unpleasant technicalities revolved. I confess I would rather it had never started, and at one crucial point a little later, I asked that we forget it. But Flagstad was immovable. She believed in what she believed in and would not be deflected. My debut with the Chicago Opera Company had been a success, and without any trouble whatsoever Longone had re-engaged me for the 1939 season to conduct all the Wagnerian repertoire. He died before that season took place, but his successor, Henry Weber, honored as a gentleman all of Longone's commitments. Four Wagner operas were scheduled within a period of nine days. On but twenty-four hours notice within that short period, an additional performance of *Tristan und Isolde* was added. Performer that she was, Flagstad finished that fifth heavy performance in better form than she had been in at the beginning. In addition to the particular interest surrounding Giovanni Martinelli's historical Tristan, the fine young American soprano, Rose Bampton, sang her first Sieglinde in *Die Walküre* during that season.

Meanwhile, Flagstad had already announced in 1937 that she would not return to the San Francisco Opera. But she was a woman and reserved the woman's privilege of changing her mind. "If," she said, "the San Francisco Opera Company will engage Edwin McArthur to conduct some performances, I will return. If not, that's the end of the matter."

The general manager, Gaetano Merola, agreed at once. He wanted Flagstad badly enough to make any sacrifice. But important members of the board, most notably Robert Watt Miller, resisted vigorously. Mr. Miller was an important director, and his close friendship with Lauritz Melchior added an obvious complication. Unfortunately, the Flagstad-Melchior feud was still very much alive. When general discussions began, Flagstad would have liked very much to keep Melchior out altogether. But that was a condition which the San Francisco Opera Company would not accept.

At that point the negotiations stopped dead, and here—as with Else—Mr. Johansen turned out to be the peacemaker. He was annoyed at the obvious childishness of the feud, with its burden of unnecessary inconvenience. Besides, he quite frankly missed the company of Mr. and Mrs. Melchior. So he simply asserted the dictatorial privilege of a Norwegian husband and insisted on an end to the nonsense. Flagstad capitulated and quite suddenly we were all friends again.

Erich Leinsdorf had conducted successfully in 1938 for the San Francisco Company following his auspicious Metropolitan Opera debut the previous season. There were those who chose to interpret Flagstad's sponsorship of me as an attempt to displace Leinsdorf. Nothing could have been farther from the truth. She simply felt that an American of the same generation as a foreigner should have at least an equal opportunity in his own country. There had been shockingly few American conductors, particularly in the operatic world, before her campaign for me.

Despite the difficulties that some in San Francisco chose to create, Flagstad never wavered in her determination, and eventually I was engaged for the 1939 San Francisco season. At one point in the discussions, the San Francisco Opera expressed concern over my ability to prepare *Tristan und Isolde,* the opera officially assigned to me. They would allow only sixteen hours of orchestra rehearsal. When she heard this, Flagstad said: "If Edwin goes over the alloted time, I will pay the difference myself." For the record, I used only fifteen hours.

Else came down from Montana for the 1939 opera season in San Francisco. Together we went to the opening performance that season. The work was Massenet's *Manon,* and Bidú Sayão and Tito Schipa had the leading roles. The following morning we crossed the bay to meet Flagstad's train. That night the three of us went to a movie and afterward to a drugstore, where, believe it or not, the prima donna sat on a stool at the counter and had an ice cream soda. Right in mid-soda, she suddenly said: "Edwin, Peggy must come out here for your first performance. Call her tomorrow and invite her for me."

I made my debut in San Francisco on October 20 conducting *Tristan,* and my Peggy was in the audience. The performance went well—I felt easy and confident the whole evening, and Flagstad and Melchior were stunning. Two other dear and old friends, both Americans, were in the cast: Kathryn Meisle sang Brangäne and Julius Huehn was the Kurvenal. Their being on the stage that night gave me added confidence and a really warm feeling. The notices next day were enthusiastic, and for the moment I was walking on air.

But difficulties still lay ahead. I had also been engaged to conduct one performance of *Die Walküre* which technically belonged to Leinsdorf. He used up all the orchestra rehearsal time for it himself. Knowing that this was to be my first, had he been a good colleague, he would have given me a little time with the orchestra. But this he did not choose to do. And so when I went into the pit in San Francisco on October 24, 1939, to conduct my first *Walküre,* I had not had even thirty seconds work with the orchestra on that very complex score. As an added responsibility that night, the cast included Marjorie Lawrence, who was doing the first Sieglinde of her career. The performance went off without incident, however, and the occasion was a success.

My only regret was that Mr. Johansen was not in San Francisco for that season. He would have been as proud as Flagstad of my debut there in opera. But he had sailed for Norway the previous spring and he never returned to America.

RCA Victor soon learned of the reconciliation between Flagstad and Melchior and also that they were to be singing together in California. They lost no time in arranging for new recordings of the two artists. In order to tell the story completely, we must return to 1935, when Flagstad had first recorded for Victor. The outcome of that session was completely satisfactory, and another recording session was arranged for April 1936. As all had gone so very well at the first recording, it was surprising as well as distressing that, for inexplicable reasons, practically everything went wrong at the second one. It turned out to be a complete catastrophe. Flagstad was very unhappy, aghast at the recorded result, and refused to allow the issue of anything. She was so furious that she swore never to make records in America again.

As I have said, she and I recorded in Copenhagen in 1936 and again the following year in London. These were albums of songs. But naturally both Victor and His Master's Voice were eager to have more from her with orchestra, and were particularly anxious to record in the United States. She spent so much of her time here that it would make a significant difference in production expense, and it was much more practical generally.

Max, as her manager, had the responsibility of making peace. He arranged a meeting in his office between Mr. Johansen and Charles O'Connell, who was still in charge of classical recordings for Victor. I was there as well. Flagstad's most serious complaint about the unhappy previous session had been that everything was so rushed that a satisfactory performance became impossible. O'Connell promised that this would be corrected and that Eugene Ormandy would be asked to conduct. Mr. Johansen undertook to do all he could to change Flagstad's position. He succeeded, mainly because of the probability of Ormandy's services at the proposed recording session. Flagstad admired Ormandy immensely.

O'Connell fulfilled most of his promises. A session was arranged for October 17, 1937, in the Academy of Music in Philadelphia. The orchestra was drawn from the Philadelphia Orchestra, and Ormandy was on the podium. A formidable list was scheduled: *"Ah, perfido"* of Beethoven; *"Abscheulicher, wo eilst du hin"* from *Fidelio;* *"Ozean, du Ungeheuer"* from *Oberon;* *"Du bist der Lenz"* from *Die Walküre;* the "Balcony Scene" from *Lohengrin.* This was quite enough for a single three-hour session. But then O'Connell reneged on his guarantee against rushing. He was determined to get a recording of Brünnhilde's "Immolation Scene" from *Götterdämmerung.* This is probably the most exhausting dramatic excerpt in the repertoire, but O'Connell insisted on crowding it into the occasion. It did not go well, and Flagstad was displeased even that day over the result. When she heard the playbacks, she okayed everything but this "Immolation Scene." Victor was unhappy: they had gone to great expense and naturally were dismayed at seeing their investment thrown out the window. Flagstad could not be moved, and once more said she would not record in America.

But now to return to 1939. Not only had the Flagstad-Melchior feud evaporated, but also I was on the scene as a new quantity in further negotiations. Here was the opportunity for Victor to record the two great singers together and, as O'Connell quickly discovered, it was not very difficult to get Flagstad to agree to record again if I was in the picture. But she also had other conditions, particularly in the matters of artists and repertoire.

Naturally the big love duet from *Tristan* would be an important item; then there had to be a new recording of the *"Liebestod"* and of the first-act duet from *Götterdämmerung.*

But Victor also wanted the "Immolation Scene." Here Flagstad made her most important condition: she would re-record this scene only if Ormandy was to be the conductor, *or* if he was willing to release her from what she considered an ethical obligation. She had never intended the slightest criticism of his conducting at the previous ill-fated session in Philadelphia. We made this clear beyond any question to O'Connell, who presently reported to me that Ormandy expressed no objection at all to another conductor's recording the scene with Flagstad. In *The Other Side of the Record,* a book he published some time later, O'Connell rather pointedly implied that he had been coerced. "Eventually I was required to record the 'Immolation Scene' with Mr. McArthur conducting," he wrote. That is totally false.

But, meanwhile, Ormandy was indeed very unhappy, as we were to discover much later. I have never been sure just how O'Connell presented the matter, and unless both Flagstad's intentions and my own had been made clear to him, his feeling was indeed understandable. Actually, Flagstad never appeared again with Ormandy and she always remained disturbed at what seemed to her a gross misunderstanding. Many years later, in 1952, when she and Ormandy were both appearing at the Sibelius Festival in Helsinki, she wrote him in an attempt to correct this old unpleasantness. Unfortunately, Ormandy did not seem to forgo his pique. On June 27, 1952, he wrote her a curt reply, claiming to have no recollection at all of the matter and went on to say that circumstances beyond his control had made it impossible for them to work together.

In any case, on November 11 and 12, 1939, in the RCA Victor Studios in Hollywood, with the San Francisco Opera Orchestra, Flagstad and Melchior recorded under my direction the love duet from Act II of *Tristan* and the opening duet from Act I of *Götterdämmerung*. Flagstad also made solo cuttings of the *"Liebestod"* and the "Immolation Scene." They were by no means the best records made during the careers of either singer. Later recordings that Flagstad made with the incomparable Furtwängler far surpass those old issues. But they did serve an urgent need of the record market at the time and had an enormous sale. It is worth noting that at those sessions, O'Connell did not "rush" matters.

After making those records Flagstad had three orchestra concerts, with me conducting, to give in California before leaving for the opera season in Chicago. Two were in San Francisco and the third was in Los Angeles. They proved to be mistakes. Despite her great popularity, the houses were far from sold out and the local impresarios lost money. She was always deeply hurt at less than a full house. How could it be? Truth to tell, after so many appearances with the opera, Californians had had quite enough of Flagstad for a little while. Strange as it may have seemed to her, she was not the only artist before the public. In small matters of this kind she was curiously childish. For example, she chose to forget that it took her several years to build up a concert public in England. I remember the first recital she sang in Albert Hall in London. It was on June 27, 1937. The late impresario Harold Holt had presented her and had guaranteed her a large fee. Despite her success at Covent Garden, the sale for the Albert Hall concert was so poor that only a few days before the date Mr. Holt called on Mr. Johansen at the

Savoy Hotel and suggested that the concert be canceled. Mr. Johansen would have none of it. She sang that concert—I played for her—for a miserable handful of people. And a handful of people in the enormous cavern of Albert Hall is pretty frightening. Of course in later years she won her public even there. But like all artists, she came quickly to believe that one need only hang a name outside to persuade the public to come rushing. It is never to be counted on.

We left San Francisco the evening of November 19 eagerly looking forward to the opera season in Chicago and to seeing dear old friends there.

Thanksgiving day that year fell on November 23, one day after we reached Chicago. I reminded Flagstad of how much she had enjoyed her first Thanksgiving in America and tried to persuade her to go out for dinner. But she preferred to stay quietly in the hotel. My mother had come from Denver, and she, Max, and I joined some other friends for the appropriate feast. When we got back to the hotel, I found half a dozen frantic messages in my box asking me to go to Flagstad's apartment no matter how late I returned. Peggy had telephoned from New York earlier in the day the tragic news of the death of Artur Bodanzky. We knew that he had been ill, but did not realize it was so serious. It had never occurred to Flagstad that she would not always have the guidance and leadership of that great man. He had practically brought her up in her big Wagnerian parts—she had sung all three of the Brünnhildes and Kundry with him for the first time. He had shown his affection and admiration for her always. The Wagnerian repertoire had taken on a completely new life at the Metropolitan since her coming, and Bodanzky himself had risen to his greatest heights as a conductor. It was a magnificent collaboration. Personally, he was someone with whom she always felt relaxed, and he was one of the very few for whom she expressed real affection. She not only admired his genius; she loved him as a daughter would a father. And he seemed to look upon her as one of his children. I believe that his death brought her one of the deepest emotions of loss which she had yet experienced.

This sad event of course inevitably raised the question of Bodanzky's successor at the Metropolitan.

This is the most important point now to make absolutely clear. From the moment in Sydney, Australia, in 1938 when Flagstad and Mr. Johansen proposed sponsoring a career for me, we had all agreed that the Metropolitan was not to be considered as a possible place for me. Bodanzky had brought in the talented young Erich Leinsdorf the year before as his associate and to conduct several Wagnerian operas. Leinsdorf had made his successful debut with *Die Walküre* at the Metropolitan on January 21, 1938. There was no room for another conductor and certainly no place for me. Flagstad requested of other opera companies and many managers that I be engaged as a conductor. But never up until that Thanksgiving night in Chicago had she given any thought at all to the Metropolitan. She had never even mentioned it.

But now it seemed evident that the situation was quite different. For one thing, the rift between Flagstad and Melchior had healed completely. Melchior had been most enthusiastic over my conducting in California that very season, and Flagstad felt she had in him a partner in her sponsorship of my career. And it was true. I will always be grateful to Lauritz Melchior that he joined her wholeheartedly in helping me along.

That night in Chicago she said to Max: "Surely life has to go on—it could not be out of order to ask the Metropolitan to give Edwin at least a chance."

Max was also Melchior's manager and knew that Melchior

was in Toronto that very night. Flagstad herself telephoned Lauritz from Chicago, and he immediately offered to add his influence to what seemed really a very simple request: to give an American conductor an opportunity at the Metropolitan.

After the telephone call, Flagstad, Max, and I drafted a telegram to Edward Johnson. She sent it the following day, and I still have a copy of it. It clearly expresses Flagstad's own grief at the loss of Mr. Bodanzky, and in the most courteous way asks— on behalf of Lauritz Melchior and herself—that I be given an opportunity at the Metropolitan.

It is folly for anyone to say that Flagstad, I, or anyone else believed for a moment that I could have filled Mr. Bodanzky's place. And for that matter, I could not have filled Leinsdorf's shoes at that time either: by then he had had far more experience than I. But it never occurred to Flagstad that the Metropolitan would put on the shoulders of the young Leinsdorf responsibility for the entire Wagnerian repertoire at that time when the schedule called for at least three Wagner performances a week. All she wanted was a hearing even of only one performance, after which it would have been up to me to sink or swim. Three days later an evasive reply came from Johnson. He put it to her that it had not been possible to make plans with the executive committee, a transparent attempt to escape.

Shortly thereafter the Melchiors returned to New York and met with Johnson and assistant general manager Ziegler. Max wrote me a full report of the conversation and Kleinchen Melchior told Flagstad about it herself. The Melchiors had felt that Flagstad's request would be granted in some way, although they were aware of resistance on the part of the Management, particularly from Edward Johnson. If I had been a flop in San Francisco and Chicago, the resistance could have been easily understood. But that had not been the case, and now in 1939 it seemed that the difficulties of 1936 with the Metropolitan were coming home to roost.

Flagstad finished the season with the Chicago Opera and then returned to New York for a Carnegie Hall recital on December 5. Her first Metropolitan performance was a matinée of *Parsifal* two days later. Johnson avoided meeting her at rehearsals, but both he and Ziegler visited her briefly in her dressing room that afternoon. Not one word was spoken about her request. Several subsequent performances went by, and on Flagstad's advice I stayed away from the opera house to avoid embarrassing Johnson. He still avoided the subject.

Meanwhile, the choice of Mr. Bodanzky's successor became the conversational occupation of everyone. Flagstad and Melchior made no secret of their dismay that Leinsdorf had been given everything; and the impression of course could not be avoided that their displeasure arose from a desire to force me in. It quickly became so distasteful all around that on December 22, 1939, I asked Mr. Johnson for an appointment to discuss the matter myself. He received me in his office during a performance that evening of *Der fliegende Holländer*. Flagstad was singing Senta on the stage while we were going through a singularly unpleasant conversation. I told him that what had been intended as a generous gesture to an American by Flagstad had become a scandalous cause and had best be dropped. He was unforgivably rude. He claimed that Flagstad had placed him in a position of ill repute and declared that the whole matter would be seen through to some sort of a showdown.

But Johnson and his colleagues at the Metropolitan made one fatal error in their estimation of Flagstad's character. They overlooked her Norwegian stubbornness. If Johnson had simply said: "Madame Flagstad, much as I would like to grant your request, I do not find it possible to do so," she would have accepted his decision and the matter would have been closed. He failed to see that and evaded the issue instead. Nothing could have reinforced Flagstad's determination more.

Then the Metropolitan made a silly mistake. Flagstad's contract for that season, which expired on March 17, 1940, contained no provision for her singing on tour. There was a provision which gave the Metropolitan the right to one extra week, beginning March 18, 1940, provided that they exercised this option in writing by January 15. Although there was no possible contractual commitment beyond that last week, there had been informal discussions regarding some performances in Boston and Cleveland, even in spite of the frigid atmosphere.

For some inexplicable reason, the company let the important date of January 15 pass by without exercising the option in writing for the week of March 18. Flagstad immediately let it be known that she would finish that season on March 17. This obviously placed the Metropolitan in a terrible position. They had committed themselves to Boston and Cleveland for performances with Flagstad, and that week of March 18 they had scheduled two performances of *Parsifal* and one of *Tristan und Isolde* in New York.

On January 31, 1940, Mr. Johnson telephoned me at our home in New York and asked if I would come down to the opera house to see him that evening in his office. This time he was charm itself. He went to considerable lengths to congratulate me on the progress of my career, particularly because he realized what it meant to Flagstad. Then he said that after considerable thought he had decided to offer me an appearance at the Metropolitan. It would be a post-season performance of *Tristan und Isolde,* with Martinelli in the title role. He really must have thought me very stupid. Flagstad and I had both thought

Martinelli's Tristan in Chicago very fine. But we were not at all convinced that he could put it over for the New York critics and public, accustomed to the perfections of Lauritz Melchior. And, of course, any flaw in such a performance could have been blamed too easily on the young conductor's inadequacy.

I went straight from Johnson's office to Flagstad's apartment and gave her a full report of my talk with him. It was too obvious that Johnson was trying to use this means of passing over his careless blunder in failing to sign her for the additional time needed in New York and on tour. I have seldom seen her so angry as she was that night. Nor had I often been so unhappy —how I wished the whole affair had never begun! It was no longer Edwin McArthur's case. It was a battle royal between Kirsten Flagstad and the Metropolitan Opera.

On February 1, 1940, I wrote Mr. Johnson as follows:

Dear Mr. Johnson:

Since our meeting last evening I have given careful thought and consideration to the matter you tentatively laid before me at that time, and have carefully reviewed in my own mind the circumstances which have led up to my possible engagement as a conductor at the Metropolitan Opera House.

You will recall that on the evening of December 22nd last, you received me kindly in your office for an interview. At that time the subject of my engagement as a conductor had become a matter of such "public gossip" and in so many ways had seemed to resolve itself into an almost international situation, that I felt it advisable to seek your advice in the matter. And at the same time, for my own part, I asked you to forget that the subject had ever been raised. You will also recall that you gave

As Senta in *Der fliegende Holländer,* Metropolitan Opera, 1937

As Isolde, San Francisco Opera, 1937

With Edwin McArthur outside Albert Hall, London, June 1937

most freely of your advice to the effect that you thoroughly disagreed with the manner in which Madame Flagstad was fostering my career as a conductor, and that in your opinion it would be a good long while before I would have proved myself worthy of an engagement at the Metropolitan Opera House. Although I could not exactly understand upon what you then based your opinion, inasmuch as to my knowledge you have never heard me conduct a performance of Grand Opera, I nevertheless had come to you for your opinion and was therefore willing to accept it.

In view of your positive attitude at that time, I am considerably at a loss to understand why you feel that you can offer me an appearance in your opera house now. And acting upon your original advice, I have decided that it will be best for me not to accept your offer at this time.

You know what is already back of me—successful appearances in San Francisco, Los Angeles, and Chicago. And you also know what is ahead of me in the immediate future, prominently so my engagement with the Philadelphia Orchestra. Those who have arranged my engagements have had confidence in my ability to perform satisfactorily my duties. Thus far I have not let anyone down. Those who are guiding my career are seriously concerned with its course and progress, and I am not willing to make a false step which would betray their confidence in me, if such a step may be avoided.

A good opportunity and engagement at the Metropolitan would of course be a most advantageous event in my life as a conductor. But I do not believe it would be advisable to make any appearance at all unless I were assured that I had the wholehearted belief and support of the direction of the Opera Company.

And so I believe it far the wiser to take your advice and

wait until I more fully deserve the golden opportunity which
may some day await me in 39th street.

> *Very sincerely yours,*
> *Edwin McArthur*

After that, all hell broke loose. What was the Metropolitan to
do? On February 5 Flagstad wrote Johnson that, fulfilling a
promise she had given him to communicate her intentions regarding touring with the Metropolitan, the decision was in the
negative. She also drew to his attention that the Metropolitan
had not exercised the option for the extra week by the pre-
scribed date, but added that if he would let her know at once,
she would be willing to hold the time available.

He replied immediately mentioning "certain notations" that
Mr. Villa of the Metropolitan had made in Flagstad's contract as
the result of earlier discussions.

She wrote back that she could take no responsibility for any
notations in their copy of her contract which did not agree with
her recollections of their conversations on the subject and asked
him to take her letter of February 5 as final.

At this point Flagstad's devoted friend, Mrs. Rebecca Stick-
ney Hamilton—whom we know as "Becky"—came prominently
into the picture. By chance she was a guest at dinner together
with David Sarnoff, chairman of the board of RCA and at that
time one of the most active board members of the Metropolitan
Opera Association. Becky outlined Flagstad's dispute with the
Metropolitan to Mr. Sarnoff, to his very considerable concern.
He appreciated the importance of Flagstad to the Metropolitan
far more than did the management itself down on 39th Street,
and he asked at once if he might call on her. They met within a
day or so and she told him her whole story.

Shortly after this first visit, Mr. Sarnoff invited Flagstad and

Else to lunch with him on February 11 at his home in New York. Only the three were there. Around four o'clock Flagstad telephoned me herself and asked if I would come at once to Mr. Sarnoff's house. When I got there, in his very direct way he told me that Flagstad had described the situation to him and said frankly he felt her wishes should be considered. He went on to say that if I wished to conduct a performance with the Metropolitan in Boston, he would undertake to arrange it. In exchange for this, Flagstad would give the Metropolitan the extra time. In her own interests as well as the Metropolitan's, she should not disappoint the public. I assured Mr. Sarnoff that I felt from past experience that I could do justice to the Metropolitan, to Flagstad, and to myself.

A smashing battle was to follow, but David Sarnoff is a strong man. Because of his support, I was engaged by the Metropolitan and conducted a performance of *Tristan und Isolde* in Boston on April 1, 1940. It is correct to say that Flagstad agreed to sing the performances that spring in Boston and in Cleveland because Mr. Sarnoff had arranged that engagement for me. But it is false to claim that she refused to sing for the Metropolitan at all unless I was to be the conductor. That very spring and in subsequent seasons, she sang many performances for the Metropolitan when I was *not* in the pit.

Many people said she had their neck in the noose, which was not so. She fulfilled every one of her contractual obligations. From her point of view, the Metropolitan was indebted to her for having literally saved its life in 1935. She felt that one favor which she had chosen to ask in return could have been graciously granted. And she had a simple conviction on the subject. In a later conversation she told Mr. Johnson: "Mr. McArthur is the only one who has anything to lose. If he is a failure, he will have it as a blot on his career the rest of his life. If he is a success, not only will it be to his credit, but it will be to yours as well. You will have brought before the public a native American conductor for the first time in the history of the Metropolitan." To her it was as clear as that, and she carried the attitude through life, and to many issues more important than whether or not I would conduct for a few hours in an orchestra pit.

The performance in Boston, I must really say, was a great success. The press was good. Mr. Johnson did not pay Flagstad the courtesy of being in Boston when her protegé made his debut. But Mr. Sarnoff was there and made a fine speech from the stage during the second intermission. He spoke in glowing terms of the three Scandinavians on the stage—Flagstad, Kerstin Thorborg, and Melchior—and warmly praised the young American in the pit.

Back in New York, on the evening of Monday, April 8, 1940, I put Flagstad on the train for Cleveland at Grand Central Station together with other members of the Metropolitan. Within twelve hours we had the tragic news of Germany's invasion of Norway and a period of trial and torture began which was destined to blight our lives for more than a decade.

PART TWO

PART TWO

Chapter V

1940–1941

EVEN BEFORE Flagstad's train reached Cleveland on the morning of April 9, 1940, the world knew that Germany had invaded Denmark and Norway. Lauritz Melchior knocked on her compartment door and broke the news to her. Many members of the Metropolitan told me later of her stoic behavior that week—she was not one to weep in public. But she told me many times later of her inner suffering and, naturally, of her concern for her family at home.

When we read the news in New York, I thought at once of flying to Cleveland. But on quick second thought I decided that to do so would be pointless and melodramatic. We spoke by telephone as soon as she was at her hotel and each day thereafter until her return to New York the following Sunday.

That day in Cleveland saw the beginning of an emotional torment—and even a physical one—that never left her as long as she lived. She was never again able to relieve herself completely of tension. And even Peggy and I were unable to break through the stoic reserve to give her some simple human comfort. She remained a difficult person to get close to until the end.

Millions of human beings saw their lives torn apart during the horrors of the war. There was no reason that Flagstad should have been an exception, and, to be honest, she was far more fortunate than many. But I have always felt that it is particularly difficult for a public figure to carry on against that sort of adversity, and most especially a performing artist whose responsibility is to bring pleasure to a musical public.

The following Sunday, April 14, she returned to New York and that same morning received her first direct word from Norway. It was a cable from her husband and said simply: "STAY WHERE YOU ARE. WE ARE ALL RIGHT." I was with her in her apartment when the cable arrived.

This message was her only clue so far as to the fate of her family in Norway, whom she had intended to join that summer. Everything then made it appear very much as if she would be stranded in America for the duration of the war, however long it might be. And after absorbing all of the implications of the situation, she asked Max to see what he could do to book her for a complete United States concert schedule that summer. In spite of last-minute complications, that was easily accomplished. Everyone wanted her, needless to say, and Max soon had a full summer's tour constructed for her. I remember that she made it a condition that I conduct everywhere.

Before these events, she had promised to sing a benefit concert on April 16 at the Academy of Music for the Norwegian Hospital in Brooklyn. She had chosen the date herself, and for it had made a program that included two groups of German *Lieder* and two Wagnerian excerpts. (The previous March she had given an all-Norwegian concert in New York's Town Hall which she had intended as sort of a farewell to her public. Like all prima donnas, Flagstad was forever talking about a "final season," and with war already raging, she seemed this time really to mean it.) The concert in Brooklyn for the hospital was to raise money, and she knew as well as anyone that Schubert, Brahms, and Wagner were better box office—especially for her —than Norwegian songs, and, as a matter of fact, better than any of the music of Scandinavia.

A few days before the concert, she began to get letters of protest against the program she was going to sing. "How can you sing in the language of the enemy?" she was asked.

For several days she showed me the letters—always, curiously enough, without making any comment.

The night of the concert finally came and I went to her hotel to pick her up. Before we left for Brooklyn she said to me: "Are you going to play from memory tonight as usual?"

"Of course," I replied.

"Well," she said, "those awful letters I have been getting were not necessary. I made up my mind before receiving one of them that at this particular concert I will sing nothing in German."

On the stage she made a few simple remarks explaining that she felt that under the circumstances it would be better to change the program. And as we went along she announced what she would sing. Sitting there at the piano I did not know myself what was to come next until she had introduced it.

A happy feature of the concert was the presence of the Norwegian Minister and Mrs. Morgenstierne. At the end of the concert the audience called out for them. Mr. Morgenstierne rose in his box and made an impressive tribute to Flagstad as both an artist and a great Norwegian. This public tribute made Mr. Morgenstierne's bitter enmity so short a time later all the more difficult to comprehend and face. Afterwards we all went to the Norwegian Club for supper, and again there were toasts and tributes from all. That was the last time Flagstad and Mr. Morgenstierne met.

Strangely, we had hardly discussed the war situation at all. The newspapers were full of it, and I am sure Flagstad read every word of the reports. But she said nothing and seemed to be seeking some kind of outlet for emotional relief.

Just at that time she was asked to sing at a special dinner of the American Newspaper Publishers Association at the Waldorf-Astoria in New York, an invitation that gave her particular pleasure. A presidential election was to take place in 1940, and already in April there was great interest in the possible candidacy of Wendell Willkie (his actual nomination as the Republican candidate came only a few weeks later). The association had invited the future candidate to be the principal speaker on April 25, and Mrs. Helen Rogers Reid, Vice-President of the New York *Herald Tribune,* invited Flagstad to sing. She sang several American and Norwegian songs as well as one Wagnerian excerpt and won the usual spectacular ovation. I played for her that night as usual, and I cannot remember her ever looking more radiant or singing more beautifully. She felt it a distinct honor to be there.

Meanwhile, I had urged her to get her mind off the disturbing events of the time, to take some kind of vacation. Immediately following the Willkie dinner she left with Else for a good Western trip. She had no engagements until June 20, and during those free weeks, she and Else were able to spend several days at the Grand Canyon, go on to southern California, and celebrate Else's twentieth birthday with Reggie Allen in Santa Barbara. I went out to Hollywood to play for her June 20th engagement with Bing Crosby. Else went again to the Diamond J Ranch in Bozeman, Montana, and at the end of June, Flagstad returned to New York.

During the vacation interval, Flagstad had written me several times expressing her anxiety over conditions abroad. Else had herself received a cable from Norway assuring her that everyone was well and that the family's business was apparently safe. Flagstad wrote me somewhat inscrutably that they had not considered it necessary even to try to answer the cable.

All this time she was being assailed by letters of protest regarding her announced program for July at the Lewisohn Stadium in New York. It was to be an all-Wagner evening, and she would not take my advice to ignore the letters. She answered them all. Only later on did she learn that silence is often the better part of wisdom in situations of the sort. Writers of crank letters seem never to be satisfied with a fair and honest reply.

When I joined her in California and brought up the matter of the European situation, I could arouse neither interest nor response. I realized that though she must certainly be preoccupied with the subject, she did not wish to discuss it. For the moment we maintained an understood agreement to ignore troubles.

Meanwhile, the whole country was engrossed in the presidential campaign. It was a particularly important one, not only on account of the war, but also because it was the first time any president had sought a third term. Flagstad's behavior during that period made it clearer than ever before to me that, though she was living in the midst of all this activity, she had not the slightest understanding of or interest in politics.

Her first consideration was of herself. She resented her difficulties and the change forced in her own life. Remembering the anxious letters she had written me earlier, I suddenly realized that I had misinterpreted her meaning. Her concern was only for herself—she feared that her singing days might be numbered on account of the war. This was of course completely illogical, and I quickly pointed out to her that even on short notice Max had been able to arrange a full schedule of singing engagements for that very summer.

She did worry a great deal about Norway. It was folly for anyone ever to have accused her of being unpatriotic. She loved her country with a simple affection that sprang from her peasant roots. Her principal concern for the liberation of Norway was, however, that her own life and the lives of her husband and family should be safe and secure. This was simple evidence of an uncomplicated mind wherever politics, either national or international, were concerned. Norway just should not have been occupied by the Germans. There was no reason for Norway to have become involved. Flagstad was completely unmoved by the implications of any political philosophy—democracy, monarchism, fascism, communism, or whatever.

During this period George Engles had begun negotiations with the Metropolitan for the 1940-1 season. No formal talks had taken place during the spring of 1940, and the atmosphere remained anything but cordial, largely on account of Flagstad's crusade in my behalf. It would have been so much easier for the Metropolitan if I had been a flop at the performance in Boston. But I did not oblige them, and after my success there, we were naïve enough to believe the Metropolitan would come forward with an offer of a re-engagement. They did not.

Ziegler lunched with Max and Mr. Engles and, without mentioning my name, asked if Flagstad could be available to them for sixteen performances the coming season. This was surprising in itself because she had always sung close to thirty performances each year. Max made a special trip to California, where she was visiting Mrs. Esberg, to discuss the Metropolitan contract and other plans for the season, and although Flagstad did not sign the contract until much later, she agreed to the sixteen performances. And, temporarily at least, my name dropped completely out of discussion as far as the Metropolitan was concerned.

At the end of June, Flagstad and Peggy went off to Lake Champlain and had a fine ten days together there. Flagstad enjoyed it so much that later on she went back alone for a week in July. It was one of the few times she traveled unescorted in prewar days, and almost like a child she bragged about having gotten on so famously—she had even remembered to tip the Pullman porter.

The first of her big summer concerts with orchestra took place on July 8 in New York. Lewisohn Stadium was packed to capacity, and it was a joy to see how happy she was to be singing again. The program remained as originally planned—all Wagner—and she had another great triumph before a wildly enthusiastic audience. The following Friday was her forty-fifth birthday. Mr. and Mrs. David Sarnoff gave her a beautiful dinner party at their home in New York to which only her special friends were invited. What a moment for her when the cake was brought in! Mrs. Sarnoff had gotten photographs of both Mr. Johansen and Else, and they were encrusted in icing on the top. As she put the knife in, a music box in the cake began to play "Happy Birthday."

Early the next morning I was awakened by a frantic telephone call from her asking me to come at once to her hotel. As I raced across the city my only thought was that something terrible must have happened in Norway. When I got to her apartment, she handed me a telegram from Else which read: "MAMA, PLEASE, I WANT TO MARRY ARTHUR AND YOU MUST SAY 'YES.' " I could not make out at once just how she felt about it. I suppose any mother is concerned about a daughter's choice of a husband, and I had an immediate suspicion that Flagstad did not like the idea of losing Else even to a husband.

Arthur Dusenberry was a typically fine young Western American boy whom Else had met the previous summer on her first visit to the Diamond J Ranch. They had been attracted to each other almost immediately. Although Flagstad had said many times that she hoped Else would find a Norwegian lad for a husband, I know that she was as happy as any mother would be that her daughter had found the boy she loved and wanted to marry. But I also think that here there was an added personal satisfaction for her of another kind as well. It was to her, and not to Else's father, that Else had turned for permission at that moment.

In the light of this news we restudied the heavily booked summer schedule and itinerary. To make a side trip to Bozeman, Montana, was something of a project. We finally determined that we could leave Chicago by train right after a concert on August 8 and reach Montana by Saturday morning the 10th. Flagstad asked me if I would give her daughter in marriage, an honor I have never forgotten. And so Else married Arthur Dusenberry at a noon wedding in Bozeman on August 10. We had a sumptuous wedding luncheon, including two cases of champagne we had taken from Chicago, after which Flagstad and I continued the journey to California for the rest of the concert schedule.

The following March, Else and Arthur joined us in Ogden, Utah, and then went on to Tucson and Phoenix, Arizona, where Flagstad was singing concerts. Mother and daughter said goodbye after the concert in Phoenix and did not see each other again until after the war. When Flagstad left for Europe in April, I suggested that Else should come to New York to spend a few days with her. Flagstad definitely refused. I think she herself wanted to avoid that extra emotional strain, and mother and daughter had a brief farewell by a mere telephone call.

And so the summer was a busy one. Most of the concerts were successful, but there were a few failures too. She sang to a mere handful in San Antonio. This was a shock to her, but only went to prove again that an artist's popularity is not always universal. Those people down in Texas just did not know who Kirsten Flagstad was. Also, we made a mistake by insisting that I myself conduct at Ravinia Park in Chicago. John Barbirolli had already been engaged as the conductor for the dates of Flagstad's appearances. He was persuaded to relinquish the baton for one of the concerts, but it would have been better if he had conducted both of them. Although it was a thrill for me to be conducting the Chicago Symphony Orchestra, and I did have a success, Mr. Barbirolli rightly resented the intrusion and future personal relations were impaired, a fact that I have since regretted. In any case, the net result of the tour was that Flagstad was occupied and relatively contented. I did what I could to keep her mind off Norway and what might be happening there.

Without warning in the middle of the summer a cable came from her husband asking why she did not come home and saying that he was waiting for her. She was of course shocked to receive it. We had all assumed from his message in April that she was to stay in America, and there was no explanation of the contradiction between the two telegrams. Nor was there ever one, for that matter.

It was war and there was no way of knowing what might be behind his having sent such a message. Was he being forced by the Germans to demand the return of his famous wife? We discussed, just she and I, all the many possibilities we could think of, and presently composed a reply to her husband which explained that she had accepted professional engagements that obliged her to remain in America for the present. She hoped that whatever his situation was, he would understand that she was only trying to follow his original instructions.

Then word came that Mr. Johansen's daughter Annie had succeeded in getting out of Norway, had traveled across Siberia, and was coming by ship from Japan to San Francisco. We were completely baffled by this.

I have never to this day understood how Annie had managed this. She is a dear friend of ours, and also a very clever girl. If there is ever a way, she will find it. And in 1940 she did. There is no denying either that at that time, although Flagstad definitely did not know it, Mr. Johansen was a member of the political party then in power. I suspect that it was through his influence that Annie was able to make the trip.

Meanwhile, the tour went on. And despite this strain Flagstad met all her engagements without incident. The last summer concert was in the Hollywood Bowl on August 29. After this she went for two weeks to the Klamath River country with Mrs. Esberg and Milton Esberg, Jr. I remained in San Francisco, and one of her most contented letters of all the years was from up there in that peaceful country. She did not make a single reference to the troubled times. One would have thought the world and her life to be in complete and peaceful normalcy. She was just happy to be there quietly with one of her dearest friends. How really extraordinary that a person could put her problems aside so completely!

On September 18, Flagstad wrote that Else had found a new 1940 car she wanted to buy and asked me to send Else a check for it. She was also helping a young Norwegian friend with money to go home and asked me please to take care of the matter.

A little later she wrote me that she would be back in San Francisco for my birthday, September 24. That was a great day for me. The American Society of Composers Authors and Publishers (ASCAP), under the aegis of its co-founder and president, Gene Buck, gave two concerts on Treasure Island in San Francisco Bay. It was the second year of the Fair there. I conducted at both concerts and Flagstad was thrilled to see and hear all the famous composers in both the classical and popular fields of American music. Such greats as Jerome Kern, Sigmund Romberg, Carrie Jacobs Bond, Irving Berlin, W. C. Handy, Howard Hanson, and Deems Taylor were present. It was really a historical occasion.

On September 26, Flagstad sang again on Bing Crosby's show. As I look back I think she got more pure pleasure from those broadcasts with Crosby than any other performances in her career. She loved his charm and informality. And he liked her well enough to ask her back many times.

Meanwhile, George Engles had been telephoning me from New York that the Metropolitan Opera was anxious to have the signed contract back. Flagstad was not in any hurry to comply. She was still cross with Johnson and his colleagues, and the whole season was to be pretty well mixed up in any case.

When it became evident that Flagstad was to be stranded in the United States at least for a while, it was too late to arrange appearances with the San Francisco Opera. Max suggested and booked a special tour of small towns in Minnesota and Wisconsin; there are many Scandinavians in that region, and she had never been able to sing for them before. Some of those concerts were very pleasant. Some were nightmares. The houses, even though small, were not always full. A house less than full always made her unhappy. Then too, surprisingly enough, many of the Scandinavians seemed to have little taste for music. None of the towns in this short autumn tour could begin to pay her regular fee. That did not concern her, but when looking forward to singing for fellow Scandinavians, she had particularly arranged a special program with a predominance of Scandinavian songs. Imagine her surprise when from everywhere came complaints that there were too many Scandinavian songs and they wanted to hear her sing Wagner. The only possible reaction was a shrug. She had just been severely criticized for singing German programs—Wagner in particular—in New York and Washington. And here people of her own descent in the Midwest were dissatisfied that she was not singing those very programs for them.

Meanwhile, I was scheduled to leave Los Angeles for New York on the morning of September 27 and was determined to take back Flagstad's Metropolitan contract with her signature. That morning she was in one of her more stubborn moods, and it was with the greatest difficulty that I persuaded her to sign it. She was still angry over the Metropolitan's having failed to invite me to conduct. I was as disappointed as she was, perhaps more so, but of course nothing could be done then.

After three weeks in New York, I was scheduled to meet her again in the Midwest for the Scandinavian tour. She was to follow this with the gala opening of the Chicago opera season, on November 4 in *Tristan und Isolde* with Melchior. I was in the pit that night.

Now Flagstad was alone in southern California awaiting the arrival of Annie. On September 27, Alexander Haas, California representative of NBC Artists Service, wired her that the S.S. *President Coolidge* had arrived in San Francisco *without* Annie aboard. Flagstad wrote me from Hollywood that she would go to San Francisco to await the arrival of other boats. She was sure that Annie would turn up soon. A very few days later she did, and it was good that her stepmother was there. Her papers were not in order, and she would not have been allowed to land even with her visitor's visa had not Flagstad guaranteed that Annie would either leave the United States within six months or apply for quota admission. Annie eventually did the latter.

Annie also brought another puzzling message from Henry Johansen: that he wanted his wife at home and could not understand why she had not come before. It was all extremely confusing, and even Annie did not understand the decisions that Flagstad had made until there had been a face-to-face meeting and some discussion of the whole matter. Over all of this hung the cloud of wartime censorship and there was never any certainty about the actual meaning of a written message.

Flagstad then started her autumn concert schedule and Annie went to Bozeman to visit Else, later joining us for the opening of the Chicago opera season. How well I remember the night of November 5 on the train from Chicago to New York. Annie, Peggy, and I went to the diner, and I soon realized that even then Flagstad had not made clear to Annie the real problems she had faced in making her decisions. Annie's coming had brought her the satisfaction of direct messages from home, but it had also renewed her anxiety and tension. How she kept her mind on her singing those days is hard to understand.

This is not the story of Henry Johansen. It is the story of his wife. But I have my convictions regarding his activity during the occupation of Norway by the Germans. It is only right and fair that I set down here an account of many conversations I had with Mr. Johansen and my own feelings on the entire subject.

We talked about the whole problem of political ideologies and international problems generally on many occasions. From him I heard a point of view that I believe was shared by many businessmen in the small countries of Europe. He depended on trade with the outside world for his very existence. He reacted as did the rest of the civilized world to the insane brutalities of Nazism, but he feared the spread of Communism and spoke of his growing concern over that threat. And while he was revolted by everything connected with Hitler, he apparently recognized in German power at least a temporary bulwark against the much-feared takeover from the Left. No doubt he accepted it as an expedient to the pursuit of his business and life as he had always understood them.

He was one of many prominent men caught at home in April 1940 when the Germans invaded Norway. His behavior, had he been out of the country at that time, might very well have been different.

Nevertheless, that he apparently chose to make his peace with the enemy, even if to only a slight degree and for a short time, can have only our hurt and angry condemnation. But for all that, as a human being, I can never repudiate my own affection for and loyalty to his memory—that of the friend who, long before this ghastly time, showered upon my wife and myself unbelievable generosity and care.

I have always believed that his insistence that Flagstad leave America to join him in occupied Norway was an act of selfishness and a great human error. It is impossible now to know what might have happened to him or to her family had she not gone back. There was a strong feeling that because of her prominence, her own loved ones might be in more danger than if they were relatively unknown Norwegians. One cannot say a flat "Yes" or "No." There has never been any evidence that Mr. Johansen was put under pressure to insist upon the return of his wife to Norway. Many another woman would have refused to give up the safety of America. But not Kirsten Flagstad. More than career, more than daughter—yes, and almost literally more than life itself, she loved and respected her husband. He asked her to return to his side and to her that was then the only thing to do.

Thus, in the middle of very heavily booked professional activity came this consuming and hysterical state of unrest. Flagstad paid me the high honor of her confidence and discussed everything with me in great detail. Music making during these months was of secondary consideration. I held tenaciously to one point of view. I reminded her constantly that she could not possibly understand what motivated her husband in urging her to come home, this despite his most recent message, brought by his daughter. I also pointed out that Henry Johansen could not possibly know the circumstances of her life in the United States and that the length and even the outcome of the war were still doubtful. But in all good faith, she had committed herself to professional engagements, and my opinion was that it would be a tragic error to break contracts and burn bridges that could never be reconstructed. This reasoning quieted her for the moment, and she continued.

During the summer of 1940, Max Levine suffered a severe heart attack and was out of his office for many months. Flagstad always had depended on him, and she missed his counsel badly, as of course I did too. But life had to go on, and not only did George Engles take the reins in New York more actively than ever before, but also we had the great good fortune to enlist the unusual talents of Elsie Illingworth of NBC Artists Service. She handled some extremely difficult negotiations with Norwegians in arranging benefits and was able to smooth over a situation that for a time threatened a complete rupture with the Metropolitan.

A crucial episode occurred on October 15 and 16 in Fargo,

North Dakota. Flagstad had signed her Metropolitan contract
the month before and had settled in her mind that she would
sing sixteen performances with them that season.

On October 15, Mr. Engles telegraphed me in Fargo asking
me to relay to Flagstad a request by the Metropolitan for two
extra performances. I hesitated even to bring the matter up. The
important thing for Flagstad was to finish the engagement already signed and to find some means of getting home to
Norway as quickly as possible. On the other hand, in addition to
the income the extra performances would bring, two other fea-
tures would, I knew, attract her. The extra dates requested were
to be for additional performances of one of her favorite operas
—*Fidelio*—and she was to be singing it with Bruno Walter
conducting.

I discussed the matter with her over lunch and found that
although the subject had not even been mentioned for three or
four months, she was more determined than ever that she be
given her old quid pro quo for any additional services to the
Metropolitan: that I be re-engaged to conduct.

Alas, there I was in the middle again. It would be foolish
and insincere of me to say that I no longer wanted to conduct at
the Metropolitan, but I did hate to see the whole battle flare up
again. At the same discussion, before we even approached
agreement for more performances at the Metropolitan on any
conditions whatever, she suddenly turned on me and said:
"Edwin, don't argue with me any more. I simply cannot go
on."

Max was at that time in St. Petersburg, Florida, convalescing.
She picked up the telephone herself and got him on the line.

"Please, Max," she pleaded, "help me. I want to cancel my
contracts and go back to Europe."

What could Max do? He said that upon his return to New
York several weeks later he would see what could be done. This

was no solution at all, and there we were in Fargo with a concert to do that very night—and we were only a few days away from the gala opening of the opera season in Chicago.

She dismissed me angrily. I have never felt so desolate and helpless, and as I walked down the hall to my own room I had no idea what was to happen.

An hour later she telephoned me and said: "Please, dear Edwin, come back."

When I was back in her apartment again, she was quiet and composed and said to me: "Now Edwin, tell me once more. What do you honestly think I should do?"

All I could say was to repeat what I must have told her a hundred times: "Madame Flagstad, finish your season, then go home. But leave the slate clean."

As though it were today, I can see her as she rose, walked across the room to me, took hold of both my hands, and said: "Edwin, you are a real friend, and I will do exactly as you say."

Very calmly she then told me to telegraph Mr. Engles that she would remain to finish the commitments for which she had been signed. But she emphatically instructed me to advise him that under no circumstances would she add performances to her Metropolitan contract without courteous consideration from them.

That day I wired George Engles as follows:

YOU GAVE ME A TOUGH JOB STOP I HAVE SUCCEEDED IN FULFILLING IT STOP FLAGSTAD WILL REMAIN HERE AND HAS CABLED SWEDEN[1] TO THAT EFFECT. GREETINGS. EDWIN

---

[1] By this time, Mr. Johansen, apparently not being sure that cables from occupied Norway would reach America, had established a contact in neutral Sweden with whom we communicated.

A few days later in Quincy, Illinois, where we had gone for a concert, I received a very cordial note from Mr. Ziegler, dated October 21, 1940. He thanked me for the Metropolitan for having persuaded Flagstad to remain. I replied to him on October 26 as follows:

Dear Mr. Ziegler:
Thank you for your kind note sent to Quincy.

Madame Flagstad's near decision to go home a few days ago came as a result of having received many urgent messages during the past weeks from Mr. Johansen. I have never seen her more disturbed or upset over any situation, and I am very glad indeed that I was able to be with her and give her what advice I could for her best interests.

With kind regards,
Sincerely yours,
Edwin D. McArthur

Before returning to New York and the final disposition of matters with the Metropolitan, Flagstad interpolated another recording session into her concert tour. It proved to be a particularly happy occasion. She had always been eager to record her favorite cycle of songs: Grieg's *Haugtussa*. I believe that our very best recording session of all took place in September 1940, again in Victor's Hollywood Studios. We made the first of her three recordings of the lovely Grieg cycle. Another great singer and a very close friend of both Flagstad and myself, Dusolina Giannini, was living in California at that time and agreed to attend the recording session and to monitor the session from the control room.

Dusolina had had a formidable career in her native land, but she was one of those Americans who rose to greater heights in the musical capitals of Europe than in her own country. Flagstad had heard her sing Carmen several years before in Berlin and often had told me that Dusolina's portrayal of that role was one of the greatest she had ever heard.

The recording of the *Haugtussa* cycle that day turned out extremely well, and its success was owing in no small part to Dusolina's careful direction. Many times she would hold up her hand to stop and would flatly declare that it would have to be done over again. For me it was a memorable experience to see two great singers working together so well.

In the autumn there was another session with orchestra and with Melchior. This time I again was the conductor. Victor had been satisfied with the records made in California and much of the press had been full of praise. We spent two days in Philadelphia and the orchestra again was drawn from the Philadelphia Orchestra. For Melchior I conducted several large tenor excerpts, and with Flagstad and him together we made the big duet from Act II of *Parsifal* and the "Bridal Duet" from Act III of *Lohengrin*. Flagstad often said that she thought these the best recordings she had ever made. The orchestra was superb, and the wonderful acoustics of the Academy of Music in Philadelphia enhance the quality of any recording. These were the last recording sessions Flagstad had until after the war.

The main thing to occupy our minds during these days, of course, was the search for a means of getting Flagstad to Norway when her engagements were over. But at this tense and delicate time, there was still another explosion at the Metropolitan. It seemed she was never to be free of that situation.

For the 1940–1 season, the Metropolitan had engaged another famous Wagnerian soprano, Germaine Lubin. Suddenly word came from Madame Lubin that she was unable to leave occupied France. The other leading Wagnerian soprano of the Metropolitan, Marjorie Lawrence, already had a completely full schedule. And in addition to her Wagnerian performances, the Metropolitan was producing for the first time in its history Gluck's *Alceste* with Miss Lawence in the leading role. It thus became absolutely imperative for the Metropolitan to have more performances from Flagstad. She had just recently turned down such a request from Fargo, North Dakota, but had left the door open for negotiations. The relationship between her and the management, however, by that time did not permit direct conversations.

At this point, Elsie Illingworth became the all-important intermediary. She made it clear to Edward Johnson on what basis additional performances could be negotiated. Continuing to hold his ground, Johnson adamantly refused to engage me. Mr. Sarnoff rightfully stayed out of the picture this time. He had settled things the previous season and he seemed to feel that my success had justified his intervention, but that from there on it should be nothing more than a normal negotiation. Miss Illingworth had a particularly stormy session with Johnson on Friday, January 3, 1941. She reported the unpleasantness to Flagstad, who asked me to stay away from the opera house the following afternoon (she was singing a matinée of *Tannhäuser*). That was one of the very few of her performances at the Metropolitan which I missed.

Frankly, neither Flagstad nor I gave much thought or concern to the matter those January days. We were busy as it was, and the whole affair had a really bad taste for us by then. But the Metropolitan was in trouble, and her apparent indifference to it made their irritation even more acute. She sang her performances, dined quietly with us and a few other close friends, and talked incessantly of the necessity of arranging her trip to Norway.

Finally the Metropolitan capitulated. They had to. Only a

week before the crucial date—January 20, 1941, when they absolutely had to have her for a performance of *Siegfried*—a contract was arranged for me. It called for three performances in New York and one each in Boston and Cleveland. Flagstad was happy. So was I. And it is to Mr. Johnson's credit that he arranged an auspicious debut for me in the opera house in New York. He chose a Monday evening, the most important night of the week. The occasion, February 17, 1941, was also the fifteenth anniversary of Lauritz Melchior's debut at the Metropolitan. On that night, too, Flagstad sang her one hundredth performance of Isolde. Messrs. Johnson, Ziegler, Earle Lewis, Melchior and I sent Flagstad one hundred roses with a charming verse that Mr. Ziegler wrote:

> *The hundredth Isolde of Flagstad "die Holde"*
> *Rates one hundred roses*
> *Plus quelques autres choses*
> *And all our love.*

The final line was in Norwegian. Mr. Johnson came to that performance; he even had come to the orchestra rehearsal and introduced me to the orchestra. On that occasion, he took defeat like a gentleman. All three managers, in white ties and tails, were photographed backstage with Flagstad, Melchior, and myself, and the event turned out to be really glittering. The press the next day was excellent and I feel justified in quoting here a few lines from the distinguished music critic of *The New York Times*, the late Olin Downes:

From the New York Times—Tuesday, February 18, 1941

Edwin McArthur appeared last night for the first time as a conductor in the Metropolitan Opera House when Wagner's "Tristan and Isolde" was sung with Kirsten Flagstad and

Lauritz Melchior in the title parts. The novel feature of the occasion was Mr. McArthur's reading of the score.

He read it with much passion, conviction and feeling for the color and excitement in Wagner's music. There is no question of his talent for conducting and for opera. His first act had thin spots which can be specified. The second act, at least up to Marke's entrance, went extremely well, and so did the third. As a whole this was a full-blooded and moving performance in which, despite evident and more or less inevitable immaturities, Mr. McArthur showed his temperament and, one would say, a genuine capacity for interpretation on big lines.

What the orchestra might have done if more accustomed to the young conductor and he to them is a matter of conjecture. But it is to be said that most of the time Mr. McArthur knew what he wanted and with conspicuous ability got it.

And so those days in early 1941 were full of excitement, and at the time it was always good for Flagstad to be well occupied. Just a short time before my debut she was asked by the New York Philharmonic to donate her services for one of the pension fund concerts. I conducted the Philharmonic that evening of January 22, 1941, in Carnegie Hall. Even apart from the musical significance of the concert, it proved by accident to be of importance in both Flagstad's and my own personal life. A few days after the concert, Mrs. Walter Damrosch telephoned and invited Peggy and me to luncheon. We had never met the Damroschs and keenly appreciated the honor of the invitation. Another guest that day at luncheon was the eminent Nadia Boulanger. At the table Dr. Damrosch talked of the Philharmonic concert. He related that as he and Mrs. Damrosch were riding to Carnegie Hall that evening he had said to her: "Of course, my dear, I look forward to hearing Kirsten Flagstad as I always do, but I am unhappy about this evening. She has imposed a young conductor on the Philharmonic and upon the public. I do not approve of this." Then he went on to say that when we were half way through the "Leonore" Overture No. 3 of Beethoven, which opened the program, he nudged his wife and said aloud: "My dear, I was wrong. The boy has real talent."

Dr. Damrosch made a point of coming to a later performance of *Tristan* which I conducted at the opera, and Flagstad was very proud of his association in her "crusade." But his really great gesture for her came in later years of terrible trouble when he publicly repudiated her detractors and offered to play for her in public. She never forgot that support for her in her worst days.

Just three days before my first Metropolitan *Tristan*, Bruno Walter made his much belated debut at the Metropolitan. For years the New York public had been privileged to hear this great conductor in orchestral concerts, and it was eager for an impression of him in the opera house. The work was to be *Fidelio*, and I was present in Flagstad's apartment one Sunday evening before the performance when Dr. Walter showed her the consideration of going there to rehearse it (it would have been much more usual for her to go to him). She had sung *Fidelio* many times before. During the rehearsal session she deferred to Dr. Walter's authority and experience, just as she did with all conductors. She did not always agree with the conductors with whom she sang, and Dr. Walter was no exception. But to her he was the master, and she did just as he wanted. Naturally, Dr. Walter's debut was a tremendous success and it is doubtful if in the entire history of the Metropolitan there has been such a production of *Fidelio*.

Another important evening for Flagstad was Sunday, February 16, 1941. The late George Sloan was at that time chairman of the board of the Metropolitan Opera Association. On this occasion he and Mrs. Sloan gave a dinner in Flagstad's honor at their home in New York. Frank Chapman, Gladys Swarthout's husband, was Flagstad's dinner partner. During the conversation Flagstad told Mr. Sloan of her determination to go home to Norway and of her great difficulties in arranging the trip. We had been completely unsuccessful up to that time in getting her a seat on the plane to Portugal, the first stage of the only possible transatlantic route. Time and again we had explained to her that she need not go through Europe and that she could avoid crossing occupied France and Germany itself. Neither Japan nor Russia was yet at war, and she could have made a trip by boat across the Pacific and then by trans-Siberian railway to Sweden and eventually to Norway. This would have taken several weeks and the journey would have doubtless been hard. In any case, every time it was mentioned, she firmly vetoed the idea. "I want to go home the shortest way, and it must be arranged," she said. To get to Norway and to her husband the shortest and quickest way was her only thought.

Mr. Sloan was sympathetic and immediately offered his help. A few days later he took an official of Pan American Airways to call on Flagstad in her apartment at the Waldorf-Astoria. Almost immediately the much-sought reservation on the Clipper across the Atlantic was secured.

Mr. Sloan also arranged for Flagstad to spend an hour at tea with the late ex-President Herbert Hoover, who lived in the same hotel as herself. Mr. Hoover tried in vain to dissuade her from going to Europe.

No one wanted Flagstad to leave America. I myself, probably more than anyone else, completely disapproved. Yet nothing I could say could bring home to her the danger and the probable eventual consequences of this reckless project. Her determination was unshakable, and there came a time when everyone began to realize that it would only cause her further sorrow to be crossed. Too often she had made it clear to me that I was the one person she could count upon. Whenever even a slight question was raised, she quickly said: "My husband has asked me to come home. I will go—and Edwin will arrange everything for me."

Chapter VI

1941–1945

I T H A S repeatedly been charged that Flagstad returned to Norway in 1941 through aid she had received from the German Embassy in Washington and that she traveled on a German passport. The fact is that, as far as I know, she never met anyone at all connected with the German Embassy in the United States. The charge that she traveled on a German passport is incredible. She was a *Norwegian* with a legally valid *Norwegian* passport, and she never had one of any other nationality in her life.

Mr. Stephen Spiegel was then and is still one of the outstanding professional immigration consultants in America. He is a real specialist. He had handled Flagstad's affairs for many years.

It was he who took her to Niagara Falls in early 1941 to arrange her entry into the United States on a quota visa. He handled the immigration and naturalization of Else and was a thoroughly reliable consultant in all of Flagstad's affairs in this complicated field.

At this point Mr. Spiegel's office was given Flagstad's Norwegian passport and instructed to secure the necessary visas for her trip.

On March 1, 1941, Flagstad tried to reach her husband by telephone in Norway. (The previous November on Thanksgiving day she had been able to talk with him. Without first asking Flagstad's permission, Annie had secretly arranged that Thanksgiving day call.) Flagstad had been completely shaken for days over his pleading insistence that she come home. There had also been one call in January of 1941 from Chicago. From New York on March 1, she could not get through. It was often charged later that because of his alleged influence with the Germans, Mr. Johansen had talked by transatlantic telephone with his wife every week. Actually she and her husband spoke only twice by telephone during those years of separation.

We left New York on March 4, 1941, for a month's tour of concerts on the Pacific Coast. I instructed Mr. Spiegel to keep us constantly informed as matters progressed.

By the time we returned to New York early in April, he was able to tell me that Mary Martin of his staff had gone to Washington for the express purpose of securing the transit visas for the countries through which Flagstad would have to pass: Bermuda, Portugal, Spain, Occupied France, and Germany.

Miss Martin returned from Washington with the report that there was some delay in securing the visas, particularly that for Portugal. I was told that the Portugese Embassy in Washington could have stamped the passport with the necessary transit visa

Final scene of *Fidelio*, San Francisco Opera, 1937 (René Maison as Florestan, Julius Huehn as Fernando)

At Paramount Studios, Hollywood, November 1937

In Brünnhilde costume for *The Big Broadcast of 1938*, Hollywood, 1937

on its own responsibility, but was unwilling at that time to do so without firm authority from Lisbon. Spiegel told me further that the Norwegian legation in Washington could have requested this transit visa as a diplomatic courtesy for Flagstad and that the Portugese Embassy undoubtedly would have acceded to such a request. Naturally the Norwegian legation in Washington was the official representative of free Norway, with no connection whatever with the Quisling regime. The Norwegian government at the time was established in London, and I was told that the legation in Washington acted directly on instructions from there.

Miss Martin went to the Norwegian legation with the proposal, and was told—so it was reported to me—that the Norwegian legation had no objection to Flagstad's returning to Norway provided that she did not cross enemy territory. Had she gone via the Pacific and across Siberia, the understanding was that the Norwegian legation might have assisted her. But having chosen the route across Europe, she closed the door to any help from official Norway. It had never occurred to Flagstad that she, as a Norwegian, would be denied assistance by her own government.

I insisted that Miss Martin go to Flagstad's apartment and tell her this story in person. This Miss Martin did the day before Flagstad flew to Europe in 1941. I was determined that there should be no misunderstanding as long as she herself had chosen this course.

It was a foregone conclusion that the German authorities had to be dealt with in her behalf for the necessary visas through the occupied territories, as well as through Germany itself. The National Broadcasting Company, particularly through its vice-presidents John F. Royal and George Engles, took an active part in making all the arrangements. But Flagstad herself had abso-

lutely no contact with any German, and no one in the German
Embassy or connected with the German government was ever
used by her personally.

All this time it had been my suggestion and hope that Mr.
Johansen would meet her in Sweden, and that perhaps they
would decide that she should not enter Norway. As I look back
now, I wonder at my stupidity at that time on this point. It was
amazing that we could have been so naïve as to think that the
German occupation authorities would have allowed Henry
Johansen to leave Norway to meet his wife in a neutral country
and to return home without her.

It was clearly apparent then that official Norway frowned
upon her plan to return. No one can deny the justice of their
position. But even then I often thought how much better it
would have been if the personal relations between Flagstad and
the Norwegian Minister had been friendly. Officially his position
might not have changed, but at least the atmosphere would not
have been so clouded and the bitterness and enmity to be faced
in the years after the war would have been lightened.

Flagstad's Norwegian friends in America remained loyal and
affectionate then, but she was sadly betrayed by many of them
later. One of her supporters in those days was Consul General
Lars Christensen. He and his wife were old friends of hers. In
my presence at a party at the Waldorf-Astoria in 1941, Mr.
Christensen expressed approval of Flagstad's plan to go home,
observing that it was important that some strong people be
there during the occupation to help prepare for better days to
come after the war. Everyone seemed to co-operate—except the
officialdom of Norway in Washington.

At the beginning of the 1940-1 season Flagstad told NBC
Artists Service that she would like very much to sing some concerts for Norwegian relief and asked that they be arranged

wherever possible to coincide with other bookings. Elsie Illingworth took charge of the arrangements. It was tentatively planned to do three concerts—one in New York, one in Chicago, a third in San Francisco. Miss Illingworth communicated with Mr. Andrew ("An") Rygg, who was in an official position to arrange such Norwegian benefit concerts in America. A concert in San Francisco proved impossible, but dates for Chicago and New York were arranged.

At a completely sold-out concert at the Civic Opera House in Chicago on January 17, 1941, over $6,000 was raised. Actual arrangements for this Chicago concert were supervised by Rev. Mr. Ingvolstad, Secretary of the Norwegian Relief Agency in America. Following the concert, a dinner was given in a private dining room in the Opera House building. The escaped Mayor of Narvik was among the guests, as was Mr. Rygg. Rev. Mr. Ingvolstad explained to everyone concerned that the money being raised for Norwegian relief in America could not reach Norway until after the war. He went on to say that thousands of dollars already had been raised for help to Norway and that this money would be available immediately upon the cessation of hostilities. When Flagstad later gave an account of this in Norway, she was called a liar.

The concert in New York had been set for March 3, but it never took place. Mr. Rygg saw fit to insist upon insulting and embarrassing conditions, and we were not to learn the reason until years later. He insisted that the price of the tickets be reduced so that poor Norwegians in New York could attend the concert. Flagstad annually sang several times each season in New York and at the highest prices, and it would have been damaging to her standing to have sung at a reduced admission scale. And the point of the concert was to raise money, as far as she was concerned. She refused to cut the admission charge.

Then Mr. Rygg countered with the suggestion that if he could persuade HRH Princess Martha to attend, the high prices could be retained. There was never any question of Flagstad's respect for Crown Princess Martha, but after all, she herself was an attraction sufficient to fill the house. Then Mr. Rygg demanded that the program she proposed to sing be submitted to him for approval. We could not understand such an impudent request.

Flagstad furiously canceled all plans for the New York benefit concert. The Metropolitan was delighted. Immediately they seized upon the free date and sold out another performance of *Fidelio*.

But some things, even in those frantic days, made Flagstad happy. On December 19, 1940, Allen Wardwell, a prominent board member of the Metropolitan, wrote requesting her participation on a committee to raise funds in memory of Artur Bodanzky. Mr. Wardwell sent a list of names of those it was thought might be contributors to the fund and asked Flagstad to indicate those to whom she might appeal. This was a project very dear to her heart, and she devoted an impressive amount of her own time writing personal letters to possible donors. Every single individual she wrote to responded with a contribution. I remember the letter she had from the late Mayor La Guardia. He wrote that he was honored to be a part of the memorial to Mr. Bodanzky, but even more honored to have her letter and to send his contribution to her. (La Guardia had previously been quoted in the newspapers as saying he would be happy to go down in history as the Mayor of New York during the time of Kirsten Flagstad.) The money was raised, and a beautiful bronze bust of Bodanzky by Malvina Hoffman was unveiled in the Metropolitan Opera House on February 5, 1942. By then Flagstad was in Norway. The account on February 6, 1942, in

The New York Times mentioned everyone possible connected with the memorial *except* Kirsten Flagstad: even then there were those who thought it would be unpopular to be connected with her name. It was saddening. She had been one of Mr. Bodanzky's great prides and she herself had raised more for the memorial than anyone else.

Her final prewar performance in the Metropolitan Opera House took place on Saturday afternoon, April 12, 1941. The opera was *Tristan,* and I conducted. After many curtain calls, Melchior got permission from Edward Johnson to make a few remarks to the still-applauding public. He announced from the stage that a week later Flagstad would be leaving for home and that all wished her Godspeed and a safe return.

There was a roar from the public: "Flagstad! Flagstad!" She raised her hand and said simply: "I am very happy to be going home, but I shall be even happier to return to you."

Two days later she sang another musicale for Mr. Speyer, and that evening we went together to Cleveland for a performance of *Tristan* with the Metropolitan on April 15. The only time I distinctly realized from her expression and her conversation that she was apprehensive over the coming trip was on the train an hour before we arrived in Cleveland. I never have told this before to anyone, even Peggy. But that morning Flagstad blurted out to me that she was "scared." I quickly asked her if she wanted to give up the project. She changed in an instant and vehemently said: "Oh no, no!" I returned to New York by air after my performance leaving her there for a final *Walküre* on Thursday.

More important to her those days in Cleveland than singing was her final luncheon with Edward Ziegler, the assistant general manager of the opera. They had always been devoted to each other and for several years they had observed the odd tradition of lunching together in, of all places, the lunchroom in the Cleveland railroad station. (She once told me that the corn-beef hash in that restaurant was the best she had ever eaten.) She never saw Mr. Ziegler again. When she came back to America after the war he was ill and had retired from the Metropolitan.

On April 18, Max and his wife called on Flagstad at her hotel in New York for a farewell visit. He asked her at that time what she would do if the Nazis asked her to sing.

"Max," she said, "I am not going to sing for them. You know a singer can always be ill."

He then got her permission to arrange the following season tentatively, with the definite understanding that she would let him know by July 15 if she could come back.

Of first importance, it was also settled that day that she would communicate with everyone in America through me.

When Flagstad left, there was no signed contract with either NBC Artists Service or the Metropolitan Opera Association. There had been only last-minute conversations and a verbal understanding of a highly tenuous nature.

Meanwhile, I had devoted myself to making every possible arrangement and to taking care of such details as the storage of her clothing, jewelry, and other personal effects. I also had arranged with her bank to send a special representative to her hotel to arrange the purchase of some four thousand dollars in traveler's checks. She was to take with her only three hundred dollars in cash and the barest essentials of clothing and personal needs. I remember making a long list of the many things to be taken care of and I tried to think of every possible detail.

She and Annie together spent most of that last night packing. Next morning I called for her in a limousine, unfortunately without Peggy, who was ill in bed. With Annie we drove to the airport, where a group of affectionate loyal friends had gathered to wish her farewell.

No one wept but me—it was all too much for me. I had pinned a corsage on her, and she at least looked brave and smiling.

And so at ten o'clock that morning of April 19, 1941, the *Dixie Clipper* lifted off the water and we all stood there in helpless silence as the great star who was our beloved friend soared off into the perilous unknown.

We had done everything humanly possible to arrange things for Flagstad as far as Berlin. From there on, she would be on her own and would have to try to reach her husband in Norway. Not one of our well-organized plans succeeded. We had sent a special cable to Lisbon asking that she be met and that a reservation be made for her at the Palace Hotel in Estoril, a suburb. It was ignored. All along the route of travel she cabled me until her arrival in Berlin, from where she was forbidden to communicate with anyone, even her husband.

After a short stop in Bermuda en route to Europe, she landed in Lisbon on a Sunday, just another stray passenger and not the important personage she was accustomed to being.

On April 22 she wrote me a letter from Madrid full of details of the trip that far. (This letter reached New York three weeks later to the day.) She had had great difficulty in redeeming any of her traveler's checks (eventually she had been able to cash $300 of them) and felt indeed fortunate to have some American dollars in cash with her. The ticket that we thought was all in order for travel beyond Lisbon had not been honored, and she had had to purchase another. She had never given a thought to details of this kind, and I shuddered to read of her having to do it all then. But she rose to it, apparently only out of the strength of her determination to reach Norway, home, and family.

Finally, after three difficult days in Berlin and the final discovery that she would somehow be able to go direct to Norway —instead of Sweden as we had hoped—she arrived in Oslo on Sunday, April 27, 1941. We first read the news in the papers on April 28. Then a cable came from her to me dated April 29. All we could do then was wait for further word and hope that she would be able to return.

Then began a series of complications which could well have been avoided if everyone had followed our original plans.

On May 15, Henry Johansen wrote me that he and Flagstad were safe and happy together again and that they had decided that she would remain at home until the end of the war. This letter reached me on June 23 with another long, detailed letter from Flagstad herself. Her letter also was dated May 15.

But unfortunately before I received the letters, Mr. Johansen apparently gave an interview to the press in Norway on June 17 in which he let it be known that his wife would not be returning to America. It was immediately published in American newspapers, unfortunately before I or NBC Artists Service had had any direct word from Flagstad or Mr. Johansen.

Max had arranged a tour for the following season and both the Metropolitan and the San Francisco Opera Company had scheduled many performances for her the following autumn.

Disregarding our agreement that I be the single official "contact" with Flagstad, George Engles cabled her on June 18 asking for direct word from her. None ever came. Both she and her husband evidently felt that his letter to me completely covered the question of her possible return.

When the letters of May 15 did arrive, I immediately notified

NBC Artists Service and wrote the Metropolitan as well. That was on June 23.

On June 24, Engles again cabled Flagstad asking for a direct message. She could have sent one, but she did not. And by that time she herself had given a press conference in Norway and her statements were already being misinterpreted.

Now she was purposely staying out of communication. It was not a new routine. For years her husband had carried on correspondence for her—why should his doing so not be in order this time?

On July 1, 1941, Max wrote to Flagstad, again appealing for some word from her. Among other things he indicated that the reason a tour had been booked for her was as a "protection." She told me after the war that she never understood this point of view. What was Max protecting her from?

Finally, on July 9, Mr. Johansen did write directly to George Engles, but only to repeat to him what had already been written to me seven weeks earlier. As far as the Johansens were concerned, the matter was settled.

The San Francisco Opera had to change its already well-made plans, and Max had the difficult task of notifying all his clients that Flagstad would not be back. The Metropolitan continued for a short time publicly to disbelieve the word from Norway, but finally it too had to alter its plans.

All this damaging confusion could have been avoided if (1) no discussion of possible return had taken place until Flagstad's arrival in Norway, (2) Mr. Johansen had not given his interview to the press on June 17, and (3) NBC Artists Service had abided by our agreement that when word came to me and I passed it to them it would be accepted as valid.

The public, because of the continued publicity, was given the impression that Flagstad had left America with definite commitments to return and that now she was going back on her word, which was completely untrue. As I have said before, she had no signed contract whatsoever when she left New York on April 19. But the damage was done and it caused trouble for a long while.

Disturbing speculative headlines began to appear in the press: "KIRSTEN FLAGSTAD DISAPPEARS IN NORWAY" —"FLAGSTAD SILENCE STIRS U.S. ALARM"—"EFFORTS TO FIND FLAGSTAD FAIL"—"OPERA STAR MISSING IN OSLO." And then of course items in the gossip columns began: "Kirsten Flagstad, former Metropolitan Opera favorite, whose husband and stepchildren are in Nazi-occupied Norway, has been ordered to do a concert tour of Germany 'or else' "—"and a grapevine rumor has it that Kirsten Flagstad and her husband have escaped from Norway."

No one knew what to believe. I never thought that Flagstad had actually "disappeared": there simply is no normal international communication in wartime. I knew further that the Johansens were matter-of-fact people. They had simply done what they thought was right and that settled it.

The gossip-column items did not worry me, and it was thoroughly proved in later years that they were baseless. The misfortune was that so many people believed every word they read.

When on Pearl Harbor day we ourselves were attacked, it seemed clear to me that only a miracle could bring us in contact with Flagstad again until the conflict was over. But I did keep trying to find some means of getting through to her.

Presently, it occurred to me that perhaps the great Swedish contralto Kerstin Thorborg and her husband, Dr. Gustav Bergman, might be in touch with their own relatives in neutral Sweden, and that through them I could get some word to Flagstad. I went to call on them one Sunday afternoon, and they immediately offered to help. They were indeed corresponding regularly with people in Sweden, and although mail to neutral countries was being heavily censored, we felt sure I could compose a letter vague enough in its language to pass.

On January 26, 1942, I wrote a long letter to Madame Thorborg's brother, C. W. P. Thorborg in Hedemore, Sweden. It took a lot of thought to write a very personal letter to a man I had never met. Much of the letter concerned his own sister's life and activity in America. But I succeeded quite admirably in getting important news for Flagstad into the body of the letter. Months later Flagstad received this unusual communication. It had taken a long time to reach her, but I could not help feeling really proud and satisfied that my little scheme had worked.

She had received all my letters in 1941 up until Pearl Harbor, and those she wrote me from Norway eventually reached America. Her last was dated August 23. But after December 7, I gave up all thought of writing except via routine Red Cross communications. The letter through Mr. Thorborg was the only exception.

Suddenly on May 9, 1942, came a shock. Flagstad cabled from Zürich, Switzerland, asking me to write her there airmail in care of the Stadttheater. I felt very excited. I remembered that on her previous visits to Zürich she had lived at the Dolder Grand Hotel. At once I placed an overseas call and, amazingly, got through to her around midnight. We were specifically advised by the overseas telephone operator that because of wartime restrictions, our conversation would be monitored and that we must avoid any possible reference to anything but the most casual topics that would have no bearing whatever on the war or could be of any possible use to the enemy. This was a regular restriction on all overseas telephone calls during the war years.

Our conversation was therefore restrained and stilted. But I was overjoyed to hear her voice again, and it was a great relief to learn that she and her family were as comfortable as could be expected under the occupation. She was in Zürich to sing at the opera. There had been considerable difficulty in getting permission to leave Norway, and she told me that after four or five weeks she would have to go back. This last bit of news was a blow, although I suppose I should not have been surprised. When her cable had arrived earlier that day, I had immediately conceived the faint hope that she had "escaped" from Norway and was going to try to return to us in America.

On May 10, 1942, Flagstad wrote me a long letter from Zürich. She too had been overjoyed at hearing my voice. Her sister was with her that trip in Zürich and she was very specific in saying that she had not sung *at all* since her last performance with the Metropolitan in Cleveland on April 17, 1941. She had had offers, but had refused them all.

I telephoned her once more in Zürich on the afternoon of June 17, 1942, and of course had meantime written her a long, detailed letter as full as possible of every kind of news I felt sure she wanted to have.

She wrote me again on June 25, 1942, just ten minutes before leaving Zürich for Norway. Both of her letters reached me in New York in July. There was really nothing of world-shaking importance in either of them—just affectionate and warm personal letters for a loved one who longed to hear from her and her request always that I look after Else. In her second letter she sent press clippings of her performances at the opera in Zürich and then gave me the name of a Dr. Henry Bodmer in Zürich through whom I was to write her in the future. I did this, of course, but it turned out that none of my letters via him reached her until the war was over.

Chapter VI　　　　　　1941–1945

After her second Zürich letter, there was another period of
blackout, which lasted until November 7 when she cabled again,
this time from Stockholm. This was followed by a letter, also
from Stockholm and dated November 12, telling me she was
there partly to sing a concert, but mainly to communicate again
with Else and me. I cabled her in Stockholm, but did not write;
she was to be there only a few days. Her letter was very tender
and she expressed her longing for America and for us, but also
said, "I am longing for home and my dear Henry."

She had been optimistic enough the previous Christmas to
mail seventy beautiful souvenir books of Norway to friends in
America, but they had all been returned. It was amusingly naïve
of Flagstad to think that in wartime, with its stringent restrictions on all mail, souvenir books could ever reach their destination.

In her letter from Stockholm she gave me a long list of friends
to whom she asked me particularly to send her greetings. I did,
and Edward Johnson, Edward Ziegler, David Sarnoff, and many
others wrote me very pleasant acknowledgments and expressed
their happiness at having heard from Flagstad. On this same
visit to Stockholm she also wrote to Else and Mrs. Esberg.

Meanwhile, the gossip and unpleasant rumors about Flagstad
continued, and rightly or wrongly I decided then on a policy
about them. I did not feel I would accomplish anything by
trying to refute false stories. How could I, on the basis of our
rather fragmentary communications? And I did not believe the
antagonists and gossip-mongers would take my word in any
case. It was my feeling that in time everything would settle as it
should. Only a handful of close friends and business associates
knew that we had been in touch, and, moreover, her letters were
entirely personal. Her own friends of course believed her. But I
doubted then as I doubt now that any of her increasing number

of enemies would have taken her word for anything in any case.

Our next word came from Malmö, Sweden, on March 30, 1943—first a cable and then another long, detailed letter. Always her letters would begin with the explanation that she was there to sing, but mainly to use the opportunity to write to Else and me. And always the firm statement that she had not sung at all at home or in Germany.

Then in June of 1943 came a cable from Zürich, this time signed by Annie Bodmer (obviously a relative of the Dr. Bodmer referred to earlier). It read: "PLEASE SEND NEWS OF ALL."

I myself was at that time in the Southwest Pacific in the war. Peggy answered by cable: "ALL WELL—LETTER FOLLOWS—EDWIN AWAY WITH SERVICE." Peggy's letter never reached Flagstad until the war was over.

On July 4, 1943, Flagstad had apparently become impatient at not having had Peggy's letter and had Miss Bodmer cable again: "YOUR CABLE RECEIVED STOP LETTERS BEING VERY SLOW SEND NIGHT LETTER WITH MORE INFORMATION ABOUT ELSE—HAS SHE A BABY."

To this Peggy replied: "ELSE WITH ARTHUR WHO IS IN SERVICE ON COAST. ELSE HAS NO BABY—NONE EXPECTED." Shortly after that Arthur went overseas in the service.

Once again the Zürich Opera tried to get her for a season. But despite vigorous efforts even of the management of the Stadttheater, the authorities would not give her permission to leave Norway. Mr. Johansen had meanwhile resigned from the National Samling Party, which was in power during the occupation, and they had no other means of getting further special consideration.

It is clear, then, that Flagstad led a quiet and inactive life in

Norway during those war years, with the specific exceptions I have just described—when she went to Switzerland and Sweden to sing.

There were false and libelous accounts of her singing for the occupation authorities in Norway. One story even had it that at a concert she was supposed to have given, all the tickets were bought by Norwegians, none of whom came. She was supposed to have appeared to a completely empty house. According to Flagstad, this story was a complete fabrication. She told me herself after the war that no such appearance had ever been suggested. Her word was enough for me.

It was folly to accuse her of being unpatriotic. Many did feel a keen disappointment that she had chosen to remain inactive. Some felt she could have done far more for Norway had she stayed in America to use her talents to raise money for Norwegian relief. Which would have been right is difficult for anyone to judge. She chose what *she* believed was the right behavior during those war years, and she remained loyal to her own convictions. She believed her place to be with her husband and in her homeland, and her significance as a public figure was a matter of secondary importance to her.

The irony of her life is that this courage of her convictions stood its major test not during the war, but after it, when she fought and won the most brutal battle any artist, any innocent person, might face.

PART THREE

PART THREE

Chapter VII

1945–1946

ON SUNDAY, May 13, 1945, only a few days after the end of battle in Europe, Flagstad and her husband were strolling in the garden of their home in Kristiansand. Suddenly officers of the law appeared and arrested Henry Johansen. He was not permitted even to go into the house for his coat. He kissed his wife and was taken away. She herself described the scene to me many times: "It was all so quick, I did not really know what was happening!"

She never saw him again. Our first word of this was a dispatch from Oslo in the newspapers on May 26. (Actually, Mr. Johansen had been arrested by the *occupation* authorities a few months earlier. He was later accused of having "arranged" this first arrest in an attempt to clear his name later with Norwegians. Whether or not this was true I do not know.) In any case, being certain that any communication to Flagstad would be intercepted, I decided to await word from her before writing myself.

Our first letter from Norway was a short one from Leif Stake of the Johansen personal staff addressed to me in care of NBC

Artists Service. Although sent by air, the letter did not reach New York until July 5, and had been through censorship. There was not one word of news whatever. Nothing had been suppressed, but it was an extremely curious communication. All that was wanted was the address of Mr. Johansen's daughter, Annie. Since I already had read of Mr. Johansen's arrest, Stake's failure to mention either him or his wife made me all the more determined to await first word from her.

Finally, in the last days of August, came her first postwar letter, dated July 22, 1945. She told of having received various Red Cross letters and of much loving correspondence from Katherine and Jack Hall, who had sent many packages. She spoke of her hope to come to us as soon as possible. And she pleaded with Peggy and myself not to believe her to be a "bad person." Naturally, she included the news of her husband's arrest, but seemed to believe that in short order things would be cleared up.

From the very beginning we were faced with the most difficult of all possible conditions. As long before as 1932, Mr. Johansen had been involved in a large legal case in Norway and eventually had won it. The opposing attorney was a Ingolf Sundför, and from 1932 on, Mr. Johansen and he were the bitterest of personal enemies. When we learned that this very Sundför had been appointed prosecutor of Mr. Johansen in the postwar case, we could hardly believe our ears. From this point on, I must use the word "we," for almost immediately I became a vital part of every problem.

I have never understood why the indictment of Henry Johansen as a collaborator should have been simultaneously leveled at his wife. I felt then and still believe that she was the victim of a pointless and unmerciful harassment. It was understandable that in the endeavor to justify the charges against her husband the government would undertake a thorough investigation of his financial affairs and the structure of his business. To a certain degree this would have to include an investigation of Flagstad's financial affairs as well. But the insulting way in which totally irrelevant matters were dug up and publicly aired in court hearings was incomprehensible. It is fair to say that she was victimized on account of being Mrs. Henry Johansen. But it is also fair to believe that in addition to the personal enmity of Prosecutor Sundför, Mr. Johansen's case became the more prominent by virtue of his being the husband of a famous woman. Each suffered at the other's expense.

I wrote my first letter to her in this period from St. Louis, where I was fulfilling my annual engagement as musical director of the St. Louis Municipal Opera, on August 28, 1945.

"Where to begin?" I wrote. "Madame Alda even said in an interview that you were such a close friend of hers and would not have gone to Europe unless you were sure that you could return to fulfill your obligations to the Metropolitan! Leinsdorf got into the press too, but mainly to the effect that the Metropolitan could get along very well without you. Of course the Opera tried to give the impression that you had a contract with them, which was not true. —There were discussions in the press as to why you had gone, by what means, and all of that, but not one single reporter had the nerve to ask me, and I alone was the only person in America who knew all the details." Then of course I spoke of Else, and also of Annie's recent marriage, assuring her that I had taken care of all the bills for that. On March 21, 1942, Annie had married Svend Haug, a fellow Norwegian and old friend of her father. It turned out to be a most happy union for all concerned.

"You will be grieved to know," I continued, "that Oscar Thompson who was one of your loyal defenders died some six

weeks ago." Oscar Thompson had been one of America's most
distinguished music critics for many years. It was he who had
heard Flagstad in earlier years in Oslo before she came to America in the beginning. At the time he died, he was the chief music
critic of the *New York Sun*. On May 19, 1945, he had written a
very provocative article in his column which he headed "Flagstad's Projected Return." At that time the whole subject was still
speculative, for no one had heard a word from Flagstad or
anyone else in Norway. But Mr. Thompson obviously assumed,
as did many others, that the day would come when her return
to the musical scene would be a natural expectation. His first
article stirred up a violent storm. The following Saturday, May
26, 1945, he continued the discussion and quoted from some of
the letters he had received. The most vocal of objectors was
Marcia Davenport, who violently objected to any suggestion
that Flagstad be permitted to return to our musical life. (Mrs.
Davenport was the daughter of the famous singer of days gone
by, Alma Gluck, and the wife of Russell Davenport of *Fortune*
magazine.) Mrs. Davenport had in earlier years written several
articles and reviews on Flagstad, many of which were favorable.
I never felt her to be particularly friendly to Flagstad, and was
not surprised at her burst of protest at this time. The following
week, Mr. Thompson wrote still a third column and printed
some of the rebuttals to Mrs. Davenport and other detractors.
Then the series stopped, and for a time Flagstad's name was out
of the papers. But it was a very short time indeed.

Meanwhile, Flagstad had herself given out statements of her
desire to return to America. In *The New York Times* of May
14, she announced plans to return to America as soon as possible
"to see my daughter, if not to sing." In other dispatches she
declared her bitterness over the charge—one of the most scur-

rilous—that she had sung in Berlin, and went so far as to say that she would never sing again in her native Norway.

Then on June 15, 1945, *The New York Times* carried a rather lengthy article by Irving Spiegel. He quoted Edward Johnson as saying: "The first question to consider is her re-entry into the United States, and that is a matter which rests entirely with Washington. Until she is in the country and her position is clarified I can see no reason why the Metropolitan should even consider the question of her re-engagement."

The article then went into a lengthy account of a special statement from the Norwegian Embassy in Washington which substantiated recent reports from Norway of Flagstad's unpopularity at home.

I was still in St. Louis when this article appeared. Max Levine wrote me on June 16, sending me a copy, and understandably expressing concern over the effect of all this. He wrote of the possibility of engaging a public-relations representative, but went on to ask what, without direct information at hand, such a representative could do?

In the same letter Max said that Henry Johansen's brother Alfred, who lived in New York, had called at his office and reported that he had cabled Mr. Johansen and received a reply that everything was all right and that a letter with details was then on the way. I never saw such a letter and it is strange that Alfred Johansen received such a cable when Mr. Johansen was already in prison. The contradiction was never explained.

One of the most remarkable articles about Flagstad at the time appeared in *The Musician,* a musical journal of questionable importance, in June 1945. A whole page and a half was devoted to an amazing recital of falsehoods. Except that we were very much involved in more important things, an immediate suit for libel should have been instituted. After a whole string of shocking accusations and lies, the article ended with this paragraph:

Flagstad will never again sing in Norway, of that one can rest assured. No amount of whitewash will ever cover up the mark of "traitor" with which the Norwegian people have branded her. Is any decent American willing to share that brand before the world for the privilege of hearing her sing? Not even if she sang with the tongue of an angel!

But there were a few voices in our favor, too. On July 16, 1945, the magazine *Newsweek* printed the following letter:

The Flagstad Argument:
Apropos the Flagstad argument (*Newsweek,* June 25) the lady is a great artist and I for one (a veteran of five campaigns in the European theater) should like to hear her sing again. Her political background and sympathies (her husband is an accused collaborationist) have no bearing on the quality of her voice or our enjoyment of it.
By all means, let us welcome the singer, Kirsten Flagstad, to our concert halls.

Jewett Campbell QM 1/c
Ft. Pierce, Florida

And the following in the *New York Post* of July 19, 1945, by the eminent Dr. Daniel A. Poling, one of the most revered clergymen of our time:

The case of Kirsten Flagstad, leading Wagnerian soprano of the Metropolitan Opera from 1935 to 1941 is not as simple for most Americans as it seems to be for C. J. Hambro, president of the Norwegian Parliament. Mr. Hambro at a Town Hall meeting in

164

New York said that as far as the Norwegians are concerned
Kirsten Flagstad is "dead."

Flagstad's husband, Henry Johansen, wealthy lumber merchant, has been arrested, charged with being a member of
Vidkun Quisling's National Samling party, and accused of
profiteering during the occupation by selling lumber to the
Germans.

Flagstad herself is not charged with being either an active or
"passive" Nazi. It is not known that she gave a single concert in
Norway, but she did give an interview to the official Quisling
paper soon after her return from the United States, via Portugal
and Berlin. Recently she was quoted as saying "I am glad for
Norway's freedom; I am a true Norwegian, but our freedom has
not been made too happy for me."

With the legal implications of the Flagstad controversy this
column is not primarily concerned. But if Kirsten Flagstad returned to Norway to be with her husband, then something remains to be said. She may or may not have known that he was
under suspicion as a Nazi, but Kirsten Flagstad took vows in
marriage, vows that gave her no alternative (if she seriously
regarded them) but to go to her husband. If she herself remained outside the Quisling movement, she also gave a rare
demonstration of loyalty to the "royal in herself." In a time
when marriage vows are so often forgotten and so widely
broken, Kirsten Flagstad may have something to say that the
world needs now to hear.

The gossip columnists had not yet started their ugly campaign
in earnest. But they were gathering steam. One item from Elsa
Maxwell was amusing. It appeared on November 8, 1945. The
following paragraph from this article is evidence of its complete
lack of truth or authenticity:

She sang almost exclusively in light operas until my friend Lauritz Melchior discovered and introduced her to Metropolitan audiences as Sieglinde in "Die Walküre."

But by then Flagstad and I were deep in correspondence about far more important subjects than whether or not she would resume her singing career in America. Her husband was in prison, charged with a serious crime. Already the pattern of the prosecution was evident. The apparent aim was to confiscate not only all of Mr. Johansen's wealth and property, but his wife's as well. The wording of Norwegian law, so she wrote me, protected the confiscation of a spouse's property. But now a bitter campaign began in the attempt to show that she had never earned anything herself and that which was in her name really belonged to Henry Johansen and was therefore liable to confiscation.

She began to ask for help and her letters became almost frantic. She told me of her excellent lawyers, Trygve Bendixen of Oslo and A. L. Gullestad of Kristiansand. Bendixen was Mr. Johansen's lawyer, but worked in close co-operation with Gullestad, who officially handled Flagstad's affairs. They gave her long lists of information demanded by the prosecution, and I began to receive letters from her asking business questions and discussing matters of finance and so on in a way quite unlike anything I had experienced from her before. She had never needed to give such things even a passing thought. But now here was a real emergency, and the rare quality of organization which she had always brought to her art she applied rigorously to the matters at hand.

Later her attorneys wrote directly to me, but in the beginning she did everything herself. Every conceivable kind of information was demanded. The government insisted that she produce accounting of her income in all the countries in the world where she had ever sung and copies of her tax returns from the year 1935 on, as well as a statement of her assets in America at the time of the inquiry.

It was no small task to get all this information together. NBC Artists Service had by this time gone out of existence. It had been succeeded by a new firm, National Concert and Artists Corporation (NCAC), and fortunately Max was one of its leading officers. Despite the fact that for various personal reasons Max and I were not on friendly terms at the time, I did not hesitate to ask his help, and he did everything possible to provide the necessary records. Joseph Henry Ide, Flagstad's accountant for many years, was also of great assistance. I carefully assembled everything that was asked for and forwarded it to Norway.

But there were more demands. The prosecution refused to take Flagstad's word for all this, or even the word of her agents. Sundför wrote to the Metropolitan Opera Company for a detailed statement of her earnings through her entire career there. The Metropolitan replied that it was against policy to reveal fees paid to artists without written authority from the artist herself. I myself remembered the number of performances she had sung each season and at what fee. I provided this information, but still it was not accepted as valid. In desperation, Flagstad finally did ask the Metropolitan for the information, through me as her American representative.

On August 27, 1946, the comptroller of the Metropolitan Opera, F. P. Keppel, Jr., sent to Gullestad an official summary of fees paid to Flagstad from the season 1934-5 through the season 1940-1. The figure agreed to the penny with the one she had testified to months earlier.

During all this, items of other interest came in her letters. She

inquired in a letter dated August 12, 1945, as to the status of her
return clipper ticket on Pan American which had been purchased in 1941. I wrote her on September 14, 1945, that I had
long since secured a refund. Also, she was concerned about the
status of her quota visa. Already I was in constant touch again
with Stephen Spiegel, who continued to handle all Flagstad's
immigration affairs. I advised her that when the time came, he
would take care of things.

In her letter of August 12, 1945, she reported the first inquiry
from Frederick Horwitz about resuming her singing. Horwitz
had been a partner of Flagstad's earlier personal representative,
Eric Semon. Semon had died during the war years, and Horwitz, after having spent many months in a concentration camp,
was resuming his business in Paris. She wrote asking me what
she should do and made it clear that she did not want to make
any decisions herself.

It was hard to advise her, but already it was evident that the
Johansen case would drag on and on and that, although there
were hopes of his being released from prison, no one could be
really optimistic. Flagstad and her husband were permitted only
the scantiest correspondence on open cards, and she wrote me
that he strongly urged her to start singing again and get out of
the country.

Then a blow fell in America. In the best of faith, Flagstad
wrote a long letter to Mrs. Marie Whitbeck Clark in Rochester,
New York, giving a long and rather personal exposition of her
predicament. Why she wrote the letter I never understood. The
only reason possible is that she was by this time almost hysterical and simply needed to pour out her feelings. Mrs. Clark was
the most casual acquaintance—and that only by virtue of being
the mother of a son, John, who as a small child had been one of
Flagstad's fans.

Mrs. Clark, in good faith, I am sure, immediately sent the letter to the newspapers, and it found its way into *Variety* and *Nordisk Tidende*, the American-Norwegian newspaper, among others.

Immediately wild public discussion pro and con broke out again. Mrs. Clark sent me a copy of the letter and almost demanded that I publicly defend Flagstad. I happened to be in San Francisco at the time, and I telephoned Mrs. Clark, telling her to mind her own business and angrily reprimanding her for having made public a purely private letter. At the same time I wrote Flagstad what had happened. She wrote back on October 15, 1945, expressing her utter dismay and her conviction that everything was against her. She had sunk to what she thought was really the bottom then, and told me that surely things could only get better. How little she knew at that writing of what terrors still lay ahead.

The day before, October 14, she had written me a more cheerful letter—seven pages long. She was so happy to have heard from Herman Weigert (assistant conductor and her coach at the Metropolitan); Helen Mobert (director of publicity for NBC Artists Service, whom she dearly loved); Cleone Pottenger (who later became for a short time her secretary); Carleton Smith (music editor for *Esquire* magazine and an ardent fan); Beatrice and Julius Huehn (he was one of her favorite colleagues at the Metropolitan, and his daughter had been named Kirsten, after Flagstad); and many others.

She spoke of disappointment that she had not heard from Lauritz Melchior when he was in Denmark, but said that she really had not expected to. A friend had heard him sing the last act of *Siegfried* in Hamburg and had told her it had been "grand."

Also, she had been to the movies and seen *Here Comes Mr.*

Jordan, with Robert Montgomery, and it had reawakened all her nostalgia for America.

She constantly asked who was still loyal to her and who was not, and was particularly relieved and happy to know that Reggie Allen was for her.

Niels Storaker and his wife, whom we had known so well in Australia in 1938 when he was the Norwegian consul in Sydney, had been in Oslo, but had not communicated with her.

Consul General Lars Christensen had also been there and her family felt sure that he would communicate with her. But her intuition told her he would not—and she was right. She did not know then that Mr. and Mrs. Christensen, though they were old friends, had refused to see Annie in New York all through the war years.

And then came the request that we send her clothes. "As far as I know the *Stavangerfjord* sails from New York November 1 for Norway," she wrote. She asked also that Peggy please wear her pearls "to keep them alive." Also, she insisted that Peggy accept her platinum fox as a gift and hoped that I had not let anyone get into her briefcase.

Then came a request of the highest personal importance to me—for the very first time, she asked that I call her "Kirsten." It had never occured to either Peggy or me that we would ever use her first name, however close we might be. But in this letter she was determined, and so from then until she died she was "Kirsten" to us.

Then came requests for figures for an accounting of her earnings in London. Again I remembered her fee at Covent Garden, and I wrote to Harold Holt there asking him for a statement of Flagstad's earnings through his management. At the time I was en route to New York from San Francisco, and I wrote her from

Denver on October 8, 1945, that more detailed information would be coming soon.

Meanwhile, in San Francisco I had seen Kleinchen and Lauritz Melchior. They had been to Europe that first summer after the war—1945—and he had even been to Berlin! They made a point to tell me, however, that they had not even tried to contact Flagstad when they were in Denmark. I was really shocked: it was apparent they were turning their backs on an old friend with whom association just then might tend to make them unpopular. I had to hold my temper not to tell them off. I purposely did not write Flagstad this disappointing piece of news. She already was hurt enough.

She wrote me on October 24, 1945, of her satisfaction that the Metropolitan had refused information to Sündfor. She had had a letter from Gerard Semon, son of Eric Semon, who had inquired about managing her. She asked me to answer Semon. It was easy to put him off. She told me that she thought it wise, and now probably financially necessary, to resume her singing. She was happy to be working through Frederick Horwitz—was pleased that I too was satisfied with him—but asked me again to advise her on every detail. She said she had been invited to sing again in Zürich the following summer, and was particularly gratified to have the offer.

On November 2, 1945, I wrote my first letter to her in which I addressed her as "Kirsten." I remember how strange I felt as I began. Peggy and I had been to the storage warehouse and unpacked many trunks and then repacked three of them with things that we were sure would be useful to her. I advised her that they would be arriving soon, and sent them on the *Stavangerfjord* on November 1.

On November 12, 1945, a request came from Kirsten for detailed information from the Hanover Bank regarding her account. Later both the Hanover Bank and the National City Bank conducted an extremely helpful correspondence with her attorneys and me and provided a detailed statement of deposits and withdrawals throughout the lives of her various accounts. Mr. Sundför never wrote to the National City Bank as far as I know, but he did write the Hanover Bank and met the same wall of resistance which he had encountered at the Metropolitan. The bank absolutely refused to give him information without his giving proof of his unquestioned legal right. As it was, the prosecution was being provided with every bit of information asked for, and Sundför's writing directly to the bank seemed just another endeavor to be troublesome.

Then came a demand from the prosecution for all of her hotel bills while in residence in New York City, of all things. She kept writing how sad she was to be such a bother! I hesitated at nothing. The Astor Hotel, Dorset Hotel, and Waldorf-Astoria provided the information and it was dispatched at once.

The next development was a series of letters from an interested stranger and friend. On August 24, 1945, Miss Edith Faigman had written a long letter in defense of Flagstad and asked that I act publicly in the matter. Miss Faigman also corresponded with Flagstad herself and, what is more important, with the director of the University Library in Oslo. She was a most thorough investigator. She received a most cordial and enlightening letter from the Library which, if it had been made public, would have cleared up a great many questions, and in favor of Flagstad. But we had adopted the policy of not getting into a public controversy. On November 28, 1945, Miss Faigman wrote to Flagstad literally offering to defend her publicly. On December 19, 1945, Flagstad responded, thanking Miss Faigman for her interest and trouble, but asking her to refrain from any public use of her correspondence. It is to Miss Faigman's credit that she acceded to Flagstad's request, a welcome contrast to the undisciplined behavior of Marie Whitbeck Clark.

During all this time we, and I myself in particular, were being severely criticized for our public silence. On that point I was deliberately stubborn. I was convinced that our enemies were merely baiting us and that an attempt to reply even to deliberate lies would only fan the flame. I am glad to say that I did not stand alone. And, most fortunately, Kirsten too kept still. It was not easy to face the scurrilous accusations in silence. But I still think we were right and that the later years proved it.

One of Kirsten's most important letters was that of November 22, 1945. It began innocuously enough: would we please understand that Peggy was to have the platinum fox? Also, please would I send her some American magazines? And she spoke of more singing engagements, three orchestra concerts in Amsterdam, on November 28 and 29 and December 1. She asked affectionately after Elisabeth Rethberg and thanked Peggy for some silk stockings we had sent. Then—would I believe her serious? —she missed the smell of cigar smoke. Would it be all right for her to light up a cigar and take a few puffs herself? But then came the blow: in the normal way, she had applied for her passport so that she could fulfill her singing engagements, and it had been refused. The prosecutor would not hear of her leaving Norway. She was needed for further questioning! Everything possible already had been asked and answered over and over again. Neither she nor her attorneys could have possibly anticipated this. She could not get out. Her husband was behind bars legally accused of crime. She was not accused of anything, but she was a virtual prisoner nonetheless. And then even worse still, she sadly continued that she had trouble with her arm— great pain, especially when she wrote. This had been with her ever since she had left America in 1941, and she blamed it on her nervous knitting on the Clipper to Portugal. Quickly it flashed across my mind—the beginning of something physically dangerous!

The letters back and forth from America to Norway were a continuous stream, usually three or four of them a week. No sooner would I send asked-for documents and explanations than another request would come.

On December 2, 1945, a happy letter from her at last. The trunks had arrived, and how delighted she was with the clothes and the many personal things we had been thoughtful enough to include and her joy to have music from America again.

Meanwhile, the concerts she had arranged had to be canceled because of the passport situation. On December 16, 1945, she wrote that she had informed Horwitz that all thought of a projected tour of South America and Mexico was to be abandoned. There was still no discussion at all of her singing in America.

One of two letters from her dated January 4, 1946, was almost heartbreaking. I had previously written her that with the resumption of her career it might be better to have another collaborator, and I have to admit that I put in no explanation of this advice. She had not understood at all and thought it meant that I was deserting her! She had wept bitterly.

I quickly explained that my intention had been to indicate that she must not feel the necessity of carrying me along—the day of "Flagstad's crusade for Edwin McArthur" was over. I assured her that of course I would make music with her whenever it was possible—how unnecessary her plea for me not to desert her!

A letter dated February 3, 1946, relates how she had described in Norway the routine of her business in America. How helpless I was when I read her letter. I had gone into the greatest detail in providing every scrap of information demanded and had sent the most explicit instructions to her as to how to explain everything. I admit that it was difficult for her purely because she had never known any of the details. But now she had completely failed to follow simple instructions, and it seemed that her attorneys were at sea too. I was learning too how differently things are done in other countries.

Then she wrote on February 5: "The other day I was thinking of Mabel Search again and again. Did something happen to her or were her thoughts here with me? I feel such things strongly usually." Miss Search, a well-known literary consultant and writer, was a wonderful friend and later a brilliant advisor to us when Kirsten returned to America.

On February 22, 1946, I telephoned to Norway, and she was overjoyed to hear my voice. She practically cried over the phone: "Oh Edwin, Edwin!"

All during the autumn of 1945 and the early weeks of 1946 the name of Flagstad had been almost completely out of the American press. Then on March 20, 1946, *The New York Times* printed the following:

FLAGSTAD HELD WELCOME

Mrs. Belmont says artist's music transcends politics

The return to this country of the Norwegian Wagnerian soprano, Mme. Kirsten Flagstad, is a matter for the State Department to decide, but the Metropolitan Opera would "welcome back her glorious voice," it was declared yesterday by Mrs. August Belmont, founder and president of the Metropolitan Opera Guild, Inc. She spoke in the Women's National Republican Club, 3 West Fifty-first Street.

"We have always felt," Mrs. Belmont said, "that an artist's

175

music is his nation and transcends politics." Her audience of several hundred women warmly applauded the speaker's remarks. Mme. Flagstad, who returned to her native country shortly after the outbreak of war, has been charged with collaborating with the Germans.

Mrs. Belmont is without a peer among those who have guided the destinies of opera in America. She always championed Kirsten's cause and never failed to show her affection, not only for the artist, but for the woman as well. I sent Kirsten a clipping of the story, and it goes without saying that it gave her some badly needed encouragement.

Now came a very interesting exchange. On April 7, 1946, I wrote Kirsten as follows:

Please write me if the story I heard like this is true. I understand that Martinelli telephoned you a few weeks ago, introduced on the telephone his friend, Mr. Hild who manages the Cincinnati Summer Opera and they asked you to come to sing Tristan this summer with Martinelli there. Your only reply was continually "Get in touch with Levine—get in touch with Levine." You do not mention this in your letter to me and I wonder if the story is true.

On April 17, 1946, Kirsten wrote me the details. Martinelli had cabled first to her in care of the Royal Opera House in Oslo, briefly advancing the proposition and asking for a more private address. He also asked Kirsten to treat the matter confidentially. Kirsten replied to Martinelli that she was in no position to discuss such a proposition and suggested that he contact either Marks Levine or perhaps myself. Subsequently she received a longer cable and later a telephone call from Martinelli. But owing to his request that she treat it confidentially, she had not mentioned it to me.

It did strike me as strange that she constantly took me into her confidence on matters of the greatest importance—matters almost of life and death—but deliberately failed to tell me this. I seemed to have forgotten the curious Flagstad habit.

Her letter of April 17 with the details reached me April 24, and I wrote her as follows:

Since writing you last, Martinelli telephoned me and I saw him and the manager of the Cincinnati Opera at my apartment in New York. This manager is Oscar Hild, and he is a very important national officer in the Musicians Union and as such is an influential person in the entire musical set-up here in America. They told me their story frankly and I was frank and honest with them about the reasons you were still in Norway. As I wrote you before, I do not think Cincinnati summer opera would be the place for you to make your first appearance in America, but I was diplomatic with them, knowing that in the future it might be advantageous to have this connection. We therefore made a deadline of May 15th at which time Mr. Hild will have to make definite plans for the summer. If by that time you do not have your passport, we will forget the whole thing.

Nothing came of this for several reasons, the main one being that the passport did not come through. Kirsten would have loved to sing with Martinelli, but I believed, as I wrote her, that this would not have been exactly the correct re-entry into American musical life.

In that letter of April 17, there was an item of considerably greater importance—Henry Johansen was seriously ill. He had been moved to a hospital in Oslo, still under guard as a prisoner.

Even in jail he had been bedridden for a long time. Now in the hospital he was able to have his own doctor.

I had to go to San Francisco again for conducting engagements, and wrote Kirsten from there on May 1, 1946, that I had arranged that Cleone Pottenger should handle her secretarial work whenever she might be able to come to America and that I had also given Cleone the title of "personal representative." We were beginning to hope that perhaps by autumn Kirsten would be able to come back. Our most serious problem naturally was the denial of Kirsten's passport, but I never doubted for a moment that it would eventually be given her. Once she had it in hand, she could quickly resume a singing career and of course we would be making plans for her to sing again in the United States. I also wrote her that I had made formal arrangements with Milton Esberg, Jr., to handle her public relations when she returned. She wrote me later of her delight in and approval of all these arrangements.

I have said that for some time during this period there had developed a regrettable strain in the relation between Max and me. No doubt there were faults on both sides. Much had happened in both of our lives since Kirsten's departure from America in 1941. I had spent two years in war service in the Pacific and had not found it easy to pick up the threads of a career. For my part, I perceived a strange coolness and lack of interest on Max's part, and it hurt me.

Actually, he was having serious private problems and these seemed to affect his relations not only with ourselves, but also with many of his close friends.

And a great change had taken place in his business. With O. O. Bottorff, who for years had been in charge of a branch of NBC Artists Service as managing head of Civic Concerts, he had formed a new firm, National Concert and Artists Corporation (NCAC). This new firm continued to handle my own career as a conductor. But life had not developed for me as we had anticipated, and perhaps, being oversensitive, I thought that I felt a diminishing interest on their part.

Max made no secret of the fact that he resented my having been in continuous communication with Kirsten without taking him into complete confidence. At that time I did not feel that his confidence was a safe one. If my judgment was wrong, then I was the one to suffer eventually. The main thing of real concern to me was what effect this rupture might have on Kirsten's career when she returned to America. Max chose to misunderstand completely the intent of our engagement of Cleone Pottenger. On this particular subject he wrote Kirsten a rather insulting letter in which he went to considerable length to belittle Cleone's ability. He described her as having been no more than an adequate employee in his firm in previous years.

It was important that Kirsten know of this strain between Max and me, and she wrote me several times questioning my recommendation of her going with Max as manager when I myself no longer had the former warm personal relationship with him. I tried to keep the two problems separate. In her case, I wanted only what would be best for her. At that time it seemed only right that Max and his new firm should be her American managers, and I felt that Max eventually would accept new conditions that we considered to be practical and advantageous.

Chapter VIII

1946

O N M A Y 17, 1946—Norway Day—Kirsten wrote me a letter that began with one piece of news which brought her great joy—Else had written her to prepare her to become a grandmother! But she continued with the heartbreaking word that her husband was fatally ill—the doctors had given him but two months to live. She wrote simply and frankly. During this final illness, her lawyers had been pressing Sundför and the highest police to allow her to visit Mr. Johansen. After a long wrangle she was told she would be given permission to see him with a policeman present. Bendixen asked Mr. Johansen if he wanted to see Kirsten under those conditions and he had replied that he and Kirsten knew where each was in the affections of the other and that it would be too hard a meeting. Kirsten agreed, but she wrote me on this date that even if her passport were granted, she would not think of leaving Norway with her husband in his final illness.

From St. Louis on May 19, 1946, I wrote: "The Metropolitan Opera has been here on tour. I saw Jennie [the faithful wardrobe mistress] and she cried about you and said to send you her very best love. Also, on the street about twelve of the old or-

chestra men from the Metropolitan stopped and spoke to me
and said to send you word that they are longing for you back
and that the Metropolitan has not been the same since you left.
Thought you would like to hear these nice things."

Shortly after that I telephoned her again, and on May 29,
1946, she wrote that her spirits had been greatly raised at hearing my voice and that there was no change in her husband's
condition.

On June 24, 1946, I received the cable:

MY HUSBAND PASSED AWAY SUNDAY EVENING—LOVE KIRSTEN

When this word came, I immediately telephoned Milton
Esberg, Jr., in San Francisco in an attempt to have the press
release of Mr. Johansen's death originate in their public-
relations office. Milton and his partner tried, but were not successful. Two days later the wire services from Oslo carried the
notice in the American newspapers, and on June 29 *The New
York Times* printed an article dated from Oslo on June 28 to the
effect that Mr. Johansen's estate had been confiscated and that
the Norwegian authorities would not permit Madame Flagstad
to leave the country. This of course was nothing new—they had
been holding her there for months.

Mr. Johansen's funeral took place in Oslo on June 27, 1946. I
was fortunate to reach Kirsten by overseas telephone from St.
Louis just before she left the Grand Hotel for the service. She
often told me that call had meant more to her than anything
else right at that time.

The hardest letter I ever had to write was to Kirsten after this.
Words can completely fail to express one's feelings at such a
time. But now we were involved in a new controversy. Bitter
criticism had come into the investigation over concert programs
she had sung in Washington, D. C., in 1940-1, and in my letter

to her of June 28, I tried to explain. The silly charge was that she had sung a predominance of songs in German, as well as Wagnerian excerpts, and that she had paid particular court to German officials in Washington. We now realized the basis for Mr. Rygg's insistence on examining the proposed program for the benefit concert in New York. This whole subject caused us no end of trouble. The entire issue was silly, and it is incredible that it was to be a sore point of discussion for many months.

On July 6, 1946, Kirsten wrote me the details of Mr. Johansen's death as she knew them. She of course had not been there, but the faithful Leif Stake had been, as he was destined to be with Kirsten when she herself died in 1962. She described to me the dignity of the funeral and told me of the large wreath of red roses from her. Another wreath from Else was beside his bier. She wrote me: "The minister was my former teacher in religion and he spoke on the word 'God is Love.'—I was very quiet and dignified—Henry would have had it so."

She had been very touched to have a telephone call from Sol Hurok on June 24, the very day that her husband died. Mr. Hurok was in Paris, and called to ask when she was coming back. She had known him but slightly in earlier days in America, and thought it extremely kind of him to have called her. Also, Elsie Illingworth telephoned her later that same week from England.

I next heard from her August 9 when she asked for additional and more detailed hotel bills. She also begged me to write to her more often: she needed my letters. And she spoke of the visit of a certain Captain Thorkild Rieber; we were not then aware of what crucial importance this man's support would eventually be. He and his daughter Ruth were the kind of friends that one usually only hears or reads about. They will figure most prominently in the later pages of this story.

On August 26, Kirsten wrote that though she had carefully quoted in her letters to me the exact demands of Sundför, nothing we did seemed to satisfy him.

She said, too, that Becky Hamilton (the same Becky who had been instrumental in bringing David Sarnoff into our lives in 1940) had been to visit her in Norway, using her own business as an excuse to get there from Paris. She had persuaded Kirsten that it was foolish to think of not singing any more. Then Kirsten complained that she had not received some promised material from either Peggy or Katherine Hall and was much in need of black for mourning.

But to me her most important message, also dated August 26, was her cable to St. Louis saying, "YOU ARE MORE THAN WEL-COME." I had been pleading with her for weeks to allow me to go to her, and I understood. She warned me that she had very low moments, as I would soon see, but said that she was not giving up. "Please hurry," she added almost pathetically. I had to go at the earliest possible moment.

Our season at the Municipal Opera in St. Louis closed September 1, and Peggy and I left for New York the following day. With the greatest difficulty I had secured a place on an American Overseas Airlines flight to Oslo for the following Saturday, September 7. I spent that week in New York busily gathering together items to take to her—Andrea Cowdin (she and her husband Cheever had been her good friends in prewar days and were to prove invaluable in the days ahead) sent me a dozen pairs of silk stockings, which were impossible to get in Norway and were not easy to find in those days even in America. I also took many American magazines and several pounds of chocolate candy. At ten o'clock that Saturday morning the plane took off from La Guardia Airport and I could not help thinking then of that Saturday morning five and a half years earlier when I had seen Kirsten off from the same airport—and into the unknown. It hardly seemed possible that in only a few hours we would be together again.

Our plane landed the following day shortly after noon. It was a long bus ride into Oslo from the airport and my impatience to see Kirsten once again made it seem even longer. When we arrived at the city terminal directly across the square from the Grand Hotel, there, with the faithful Leif Stake, was Kirsten waiting for me. She was a sad figure. I was not surprised, knowing only too well what she had gone through. But seeing her dressed in mourning and showing faint traces of tears was a shock. She was not given to weeping. Even in New York when she had left us over five years before to go home, she had kept up appearances stoically all through that morning of farewells. At this moment of reunion, however, she made no attempt to hide her grief. But she composed herself after a few moments and we walked hand in hand across the square to the hotel to have our first *skaal* together after the long separation. She watched impatiently as I unpacked my bags to give her the things I had brought over. Her delight at receiving even those simple things was touching. Finally I said: "Now, down to business. When do I meet with your lawyers?"

Startled, she cried out: "For heaven's sake, what for?"

"My dear Kirsten," I said, "you must understand that of course I have come to Norway to see you, but even more important than that, I have come to try to straighten out your affairs. Something is terribly wrong here."

Before that day, as she had written me many times, Kirsten had gone out to theaters and so on, but she had not dined in public. That September 8 was the first time she had entered a public restaurant since the end of the war some sixteen months earlier. As soon as we had had our *skaal* in her apartment, we

went down to the dining room of the Grand Hotel and had dinner publicly with Stake and her sister. The following evening she
and I dined alone in the same public dining room. On this
occasion the room was completely packed with people, and this
is rather important. Dozens came to our table to greet her and
to tell her how very happy they were to see her again. I could
hardly eat a mouthful between introductions to her fellow Norwegians. It was therefore difficult to understand either the content or motive of an article appearing in the *New York Journal-
American* on September 22, 1946, by one Ned Nordness under
the dateline of September 21, 1946, from Kristiansand, Norway,
which read as follows:

> *Kirsten Flagstad sits in a restaurant ignored by other
> diners as completely as if she were not there.*

My account of this incident and the newspaper article were
admitted as evidence in the court hearing in Kristiansand a few
weeks later.

On Monday, September 9, I had my first meeting with
Bendixen (I would be meeting Gullestad later in Kristiansand).
Bendixen went into great detail and spoke of the apparent difficulty there had been in clarifying the mass of questions. In my
opinion, much of that which was questionable was so only because Sundför had chosen to use every means to be difficult.
There were disputable items of finance. But of even greater
difficulty was the tremendous animosity that surrounded her
and seemed to be feverishly fanned by vengeful enemies. In
times of hysteria, reckless accusations are perhaps inevitable,
but some of the stories being circulated about Kirsten were
simply not to be believed. Earlier we had heard in America that
Crown Princess Martha was unfriendly to Kirsten because Her
Royal Highness had been jealous of Kirsten's having been called

the "first Ambassadress of Norway." Crown Princess Martha may have not had the warmest feeling for Kirsten, but we never knew of it. And it was folly and insulting to Kirsten even to indicate any attitude but respect and admiration for Norwegian royalty on her part.

Bendixen told me that in his opinion I, and I alone, could answer and explain the charges against Kirsten's behavior in America. To my dismay, I quickly discovered that in the court hearings prior to my arrival in Norway, Kirsten understandably had given incorrect answers and explanations to many questions. I rightfully use the word "understandably." I say this because there was no reason why she should have remembered minute business details of which actually she had little comprehension and which had largely been handled by others, myself in particular, many years earlier.

On September 12 Kirsten and I drove together from Oslo to Kristiansand. Then began a strenuous period of ten days of conferences with Gullestad. Soon after my arrival in Norway we had requested a court hearing for my evidence. Although I had originally intended to remain but a few weeks, when the court hearing was arranged for October 10, a month hence, I changed my plans and spent all the necessary time preparing for what proved to be a hearing of the greatest importance. Much of the voluminous material I had sent from America had been either misunderstood or distorted. From Norway, during my stay there, Kirsten and I both wrote to various agencies in America either for new information if any could be discovered or for more official corroboration of that which had been sent earlier. We all resolved that there would be absolutely no slipup of any kind this time. In conference with both attorneys I soon saw that not only Kirsten herself, but even the lawyers, had not thoroughly understood important documents. We had provided copies of her tax returns for all the preceding years, but none of the Norwegians could understand them.

Meanwhile both Bendixen and Gullestad went over with me the many phases of controversy about which I would likely be questioned in court, and convinced me that the hearing might take several days. No one wanted to give so much time. It was therefore suggested that I write certain explanatory letters to Gullestad as well as several statements on controversial subjects with the hope that these letters and statements would be accepted as bona fide evidence. The letters (there were three of them, dated September 13, 1946, September 20, 1946, and September 28, 1946) covered particularly the disputes regarding money matters and tax returns. The statements covered a wide range of subjects: "Type of programs sung in America"— "Arrangement of concerts for Norwegian Relief in America"— "Dinner honoring Wendell Willkie"—"Of Telephone Calls" —"American Social Life and Parties"—"Arrangement of Trip to Norway in 1941"—"Of Publications." (See Appendix A, pages 311 ff.)

But those ten days in Kristiansand were not quite all business. To my great joy, Kirsten felt like singing, and we spent hours together making music. She had promised her mother that upon our return to Oslo she would sing through with me at the piano all her big Wagnerian parts. And of course after five and a half years of separation, it seemed that we would never catch up on all the news, and so we chattered for hours. She insisted from the beginning that I tell her everything without omitting the unpleasant. She already knew of Mr. Morgenstierne's enmity of course, but she was unhappy to learn that a man whom she had counted as a real friend, the portrait painter Brynjulf Strandenaes, had turned bitterly against her. Strandenaes has to his credit a fine portrait that he painted of

Kirsten in the early years. It now hangs, having been given in her memory by her grandson, in the Metropolitan Opera House. Kirsten had been generous to Strandenaes and she wept that he had turned against her. There were others too in the Norwegian colony in New York who had been happy to bask in reflected glory when she was triumphant, but who had run for cover when the clouds appeared. But then how happy she was to know of the affection of Margaret Johansen, her sister-in-law, of her good friend Miss Astri Knutson, of Dr. Arne Ingels of San Francisco, of Rolf Andersen, and of others too numerous to mention here. I was struck by how important her good name among Norwegians in America was to her.

September 24 was a day on which we put aside all thought or talk of trouble. It was my birthday, and Kirsten and her faithful housekeeper, Beret, planned a special celebration for me. The day was made even happier for her when early that morning she received a cable telling her that she had become a grandmother. Sigurd was born on September 22. It meant much to her that I was there when she received the news. We opened a bottle of champagne and, standing either side of her portrait (the one that now hangs in the Metropolitan Opera House), we drank a *skaal* to the new baby. Just the two of us had a wonderful birthday dinner, and I will always remember the cake—it was covered with little American flags to celebrate that anniversary for me.

And then we had to return to Oslo for more business. Among those I had met when first arriving in Norway on this trip was a young Norwegian composer, Arne Doerumsgaard, whose music Kirsten occasionally had performed. It was he who earlier had ascertained the seriousness of Mr. Johansen's illness and had told Kirsten that her husband could not recover. Now he came forward with a very good suggestion. He proposed that we approach an attorney named Anneus Schjoedt with Kirsten's case. Mr. Schjoedt was the leading lawyer in Norway at that time, as he may still be, and by general consent had not the slightest taint of having been a collaborator. Of course, neither had Bendixen nor Gullestad for that matter. Mr. Schjoedt had the highest standing as a Norwegian, was most prominent after the war as a leading government prosecutor of Norwegian traitors, and had himself prosecuted the case against Vidkun Quisling. There was no doubt in my mind that if so distinguished a patriot could become active for Kirsten, the case would immediately take on a different complexion. This was intended as no reflection whatever on the integrity or ability of Messrs. Bendixen and Gullestad. But they did seem to be banging their heads against a stone wall. The most discouraging aspect of everything at this moment was Kirsten's inability to get a passport.

Bendixen agreed that Mr. Schjoedt's entrance into Kirsten's case would be an important step in the right direction, as did Gullestad, who came to Oslo from Kristiansand for discussion of the matter. Both Bendixen and Gullestad realized more and more the importance of my knowledge and were eager that conferences with Mr. Schjoedt be arranged while I was in Norway. A meeting was set up for the two attorneys, Kirsten, and me in Mr. Schjoedt's office. Mr. Schjoedt was formal, but extremely cordial, and for about an hour the whole case was discussed in detail. I understood the subject matter so well that although I could not participate in a Norwegian conversation, I was able to follow the trend of discussion closely. Presently Mr. Schjoedt turned to me and with great kindness, and in perfect English, spent half an hour discussing the case with me and speaking of places in the United States where I understood he had been in earlier years. There had never been any question of

Mr. Schjoedt's entering the case against Henry Johansen. We sought his help only in behalf of Kirsten, and he was shocked to learn of the difficulties over her passport. His last words as we left his office were that he would enter immediately into this phase of her case.

Kirsten was encouraged after this meeting—she had reached a state in which she was skeptical of practically everyone and everything, and not without reason. She had been sure that so prominent and busy a man would not be willing to take on another responsibility, although she was willing to grasp at any chance. She knew very well what the prestige of Mr. Schjoedt's representing any interest in her behalf would mean. That he agreed to do so was a good sign for us all, and did much to relieve the almost total despair she was feeling.

Although most of our time was occupied in preparation for the court hearing, which was scheduled for October 10 in Kristiansand, we did manage some pleasant diversions those days in Oslo. Kirsten fulfilled her promise to her mother, and we spent several evenings going through all her Wagnerian parts. She laughed heartily, which was so good for her, at hearing me sing the other parts in my terrible voice. And it amazed and heartened us that her great voice was still itself. After the long silences and troubles she had endured, this was truly miraculous. After that, I could not refrain from bringing up tentative plans for the resumption of her career once her passport was in hand. And then she asked almost fearfully if I would again make music with her! It had never occurred to me that I would not. But I did make a firm condition that never again would she make it obligatory that I appear as her conductor.

That she nonetheless decided to make these requests a few times in the years to come was entirely her own decision. That all these requests in her later professional years were denied, both she and I accepted gracefully. When she later did some quite extensive recording, both she and I would have been happy if I could have appeared at least once as her conductor. But that was not to be. At one orchestral concert in April 1950, which we presented ourselves in New York, I was the conductor, and then when she came out of her retirement for the two glorious concerts in Carnegie Hall in 1955, I was again on the podium. But except for those three occasions, our postwar musical collaboration was confined to my being once again her piano accompanist.

On my arrival in Norway, Kirsten had spoken briefly of the visit from Captain Thorkild Rieber which I have already mentioned. Presently she gave me the full details. She had met him only casually during her earlier years in America. He was at that time chairman of the board of The Texas Company and was recognized then and now as one of the greatest authorities of the world on the oil business. He and Mr. Johansen had been only casually acquainted.

As an introduction to the man and his daughter Ruth, who were destined to be the most important and generous people in Kirsten's life for years to come, I quote here, with Captain Rieber's permission, from his letter to me dated September 3, 1963:

On Thursday, June 27, 1946 I left New York with associates via Pan American Airways on an important business trip to London, arriving on the afternoon of the 28th. This was my first postwar visit to Europe.

With business affairs in England behind me, I decided to pay a short visit to the Scandinavian countries, particularly Norway. Inter-European communications, especially air, were still very much subnormal but I succeeded in chartering a de Havilland

Dove and took off on July 12th for Paris, France, where I arranged for proper credentials, visas, etc. for my British pilots and myself and eventually left Paris for Copenhagen, Gothenburg and Oslo, where I arrived on the 18th day of July.

My father (who had been my only personal tie to the Old Country) had died in his home in Ulvik, Hardanger, in January 1940, shortly before the German invasion in April of that year. On arrival in Oslo and settled in the Grand Hotel, I reached out for my former close business associate, Haaken Mathiesen, Managing Director of The Texas Company in Norway, and through him got a fair line on the condition of the country and the state of affairs of my many friends and acquaintances in Norway. I had met Madame Flagstad on a few occasions in New York when she was a Prima Donna at the Metropolitan Opera. When Norway was occupied, I knew that she was anxious to return to her country to be with her family but was subjected to many annoyances, scurrilous attacks by unscrupulous columnists and propagandists and indignities on the part of petty officials attached to the Norwegian Embassy and Consulate, who were doing everything they could to prevent her departure. But she finally succeeded in making her departure and eventually was able to join her family at their home in Kristiansand. From various sources I had learned that during the Occupation, Madame Flagstad had a rough time at home because of allegations against her husband, Henry Johansen, who was arrested in the garden of their home a few days following Norway's liberation and spent a year in prison before he died prior to being brought to trial. Kirsten Flagstad was not only a great artist but a very great person as well and had been more of a credit to her country in America and elsewhere than any single individual that I can think of. As a Norwegian by birth, I felt very badly and indignant about the way she had been treated not only here but in her own country as well.

Because of this, while in Oslo I decided to reach out for her and asked the Grand Hotel telephone operator if it was possible to communicate with Kristiansand and, if so, that I should like to reach Madame Flagstad. Imagine my surprise when the operator told me that not only was Madame Flagstad in Oslo but in the Grand Hotel in a room on the same floor where I had my accommodations. Within an hour Madame Flagstad and I were in personal conference during which I learned from her of her desire to leave the country as soon as possible.

She informed me that she expected her former accompanyist, Edwin McArthur, to arrive in Oslo at some later date and we concluded that McArthur should contact me as soon as he returned to New York after his contemplated Norwegian visit.

Captain Rieber's visit to Kirsten had done more to lift her morale than anything else, and of course it was decided that immediately upon my return to New York I should meet with him.

The hearing in court took place on October 10, 1946. Just at the beginning there arose a situation so exasperating that it became almost funny. Sundför had provided an interpreter. The routine to be followed called for every question to be put in Norwegian and translated into English. Then my reply in English was to be translated into Norwegian. The process was laborious in itself, but in addition, the interpreter was anything but efficient and very soon everyone expressed annoyance at his ineptitude. The thing began to look endless. The official court stenographer, a really charming lady, spoke up and said: "Please, I can take this dictation in English. It is not necessary to go through all of this translation."

What a relief that was! Bendixen and Gullestad conducted a

thorough direct examination, but to my disappointment Sundför cross-examined me only very briefly. I was aching for a fight with him, and therefore complained later to Gullestad about it. He told me that my information and my answers had been so clear and so damaging to the prosecution's case that had he himself been in Sundför's position, he would have refrained from questioning me himself. One startling and curious aspect of the entire hearing was that music was never mentioned. This affair had to do only with such matters as business, finance, and personal behavior.

Kirsten sat beside me at the table with the memorable composure that she had been able to maintain, even during this worst unpleasantness up to then. With the consent of the opposing attorney, the three letters and the rather lengthy statements I had written were admitted officially into the evidence and court record. It was a difficult day. Except for those who have chosen the law as a profession, I doubt if anyone enjoys being a witness. But the importance of this day and what I would say on the stand were monumental. We had Mr. Schjoedt's assurance that he would step into the matter of Kirsten's passport, but it was important that the prosecution be satisfied with the clarity and veracity of my testimony immediately.

When we returned to Kirsten's house that evening, not only did she show tremendous relief and appreciation, but also both of her attorneys went to great length to express their great satisfaction. Subsequently a copy of the court hearing was sent me in New York for such corrections as I might wish to make, and with it there was a letter from Gullestad again expressing profound appreciation of what had been accomplished on that day and during my whole stay in Norway. Although it does not sound particularly modest, there is no question that if I had been unable to go to Norway at that time and testify officially as

I did, Kirsten's affairs would have continued in complete chaos for a very much longer time.

I had long been satisfied that Sundför was a bitter personal enemy of Henry Johansen and that his appointment as the prosecutor in his case was a deliberate act of revenge. But to support my convictions, I wrote much later to Bendixen asking him as an attorney to put the subject straight to me. He replied that when Sundför had been appointed as a trustee for the sequestrated Johansen properties, he himself had protested immediately and pointed out that Sundför and Mr. Johansen had long been enemies as the result of the earlier case. He said further that Sundför's conduct in the earlier case had been so reprehensible that it had been brought before the Association of Norwegian Lawyers as well as the Ministry of Justice. Both parties had complained strongly against Sundför's behavior, and as a result he had resigned his membership in the Association of Norwegian Lawyers.

But despite this old antagonism and Bendixen's protest, Sundför continued in Kirsten's case. One cannot possibly avoid the conviction that Sundför's appointment was predicated on revenge and undoubtedly was effected as a result of bitter intrigue and chicanery. It was evident that as a prosecutor, because of his enmity for Henry Johansen, he could not proceed objectively. Had Mr. Johansen not died before being actually brought to trial, even his case might not have been so bad. We will never know that. But I was glad to have this clarification from Bendixen and to satisfy myself that Sundför had wrought vengeance not only on Henry Johansen, but on Kirsten as well and had subjected her to an unbelievably bitter persecution. Her only crime was that she was Mrs. Henry Johansen.

On Saturday evening, October 12, Kirsten and I dined alone at her home in Kristiansand and she made the farewell evening even more memorable by giving me as a special keepsake the beautiful gold watch her husband had carried for years. I have never played or conducted a concert since without that watch in my pocket.

I went to Oslo by overnight train, expecting to fly to New York on Sunday evening. It was a piece of luck that the plane was delayed until Monday morning. By remaining that Sunday evening in Oslo, through my good friend Dick Bennett, who was the representative of American Overseas Airlines in Oslo at the time, I happened to meet a young American businessman, Tom Swindoll. Sometimes a chance meeting can be of the most crucial importance. This one was. Later on, in 1949 when a battle, yet to be described, raged in San Francisco over Kirsten's return to the opera there, Tom Swindoll, who had moved to San Francisco, came forward voluntarily and made public important information on her behalf, all based upon firsthand knowledge from his stay in Norway.

I spoke with Kirsten two or three times from Oslo by telephone. Already she was lonely and depressed, fighting the desperate feeling that there never again would be a bright day and that she would never get her passport. I, who had always been the impatient one, now found myself counseling patience. Finally, on Monday morning, October 14, I flew off from the Oslo Airport, and after a hard trip finally landed back at La Guardia Airport in New York at one thirty on Tuesday morning. And of course there was my Peggy at the airport to meet me.

There was no time for any relaxation. I came back to America convinced that it would be but a very short time until Kirsten would be able to leave Norway and that everything must be well arranged for her future.

My first move was to call Captain Rieber, who immediately invited me for luncheon. We spent two hours together during which I reported to him in detail everything that had happened while I was in Norway. I hope the reader will understand my pride when at the end of this first meeting with this remarkable man he said to me: "Mac, you don't belong in the music business. Tell me what your income is annually—come to work for me tomorrow in my oil business, and I'll start you out at double your salary!" I have often thought what a mistake I made in not taking him up on that offer.

My instructions were to keep in constant touch with Captain Rieber, and for many weeks thereafter I heard from him every three or four days.

Meantime, the correspondence between Kirsten and myself resumed at the former pace, a letter back and forth every three or four days. Of course I told her that I had met with Captain Rieber and that he had said we were not to worry, especially about money. It was a reassuring feeling to know that a strong and able person was standing by. On October 24 she wrote me that it was terribly empty in the house since I had left—her depressions were harder to fight without me there to cheer her up. Mr. Rolf Christensen, who had been the Norwegian counsel in New York, wrote her, and this pleased her. He assured her of his friendship and told her to believe that she had many friends. Coming as this did from an important Norwegian, and a diplomat, it meant much to her. She also had an offer from La Scala and asked me to make the decision for her—Yes or No! On October 31 she wrote me again that La Scala was pressing and she said: "There is one place left in the entire world that I would just love to sing at and that is La Scala. I don't think I could finish my career without singing there. Have wired Horwitz impossible to make decision now, but please ask them to wait!"

I had decided that she must not accept any more engage-

ments until she was sure of getting out of Norway and able to
fulfill them. It would be ruinous to keep accepting offers and
then have the terrible responsibility of explaining the failure to
honor commitments. I wrote her this, and she acquiesced almost
like a child. But how hard it was for her to have to continue
refusing such offers. Again she was filled with depression over
still not having her passport.

Presently I was offered an engagement to join a company that
starred the great Bobby Clark in a revival of Victor Herbert's
Sweethearts, and I went to Chicago to take over the conductor-
ship of this show. I wrote Kirsten on November 20 to tell her
where I was and told her again that Captain Rieber called every
few days.

On November 29, again from Chicago, I was overjoyed to
write her: "Peggy telephoned me very early this morning that
your cable had arrived and no more wonderful Thanksgiving
present could have been made. [She had cabled that her
passport—principal symbol of her troubles—had been issued to
her.] I have spoken this morning with Captain Rieber's secretary, Mr. Croke, in New York. Captain Rieber is today in Mexico City, but Mr. Croke is calling him and will communicate
back to me. A representative of his will call you in Stockholm,
and may I advise you again not to be shy in asking for all the
money you need. You will now be out and must live and move
in a manner to demand respect of a person in your position."

Her cable did not tell me exactly when she expected to leave
Norway, but gave me the Strand Hotel in Stockholm as her
expected destination. Almost a week of anxious waiting went by
before I heard from her again, and then the news came to me
first by way of a Chicago newspaper. Kirsten had written me
two hasty letters from Norway before she left, but they had not
yet arrived. On December 5 I returned to my hotel from the

Opera House in Chicago, where we were playing *Sweethearts,*
and there in the evening paper was a picture of Kirsten with the
caption that she had left Norway for Sweden and was planning
shortly to come to America. When I went to the desk, there was
a cable waiting for me from the Carlton Hotel in Stockholm
saying: "I AM HERE WITHOUT FUNDS. PLEASE DO SOMETHING."

I immediately put in an overseas telephone call, and within a
few minutes she was on the wire. She told me over the telephone what she had written from Norway which had not yet
reached me. Stake had driven her and her sister to the Swedish
border, where they had been met by Henry Johansen, Jr., who
had driven them the rest of the distance to Stockholm. But she
had been permitted to take only a few kroner (I believe thirty)
out of Norway. I said to her: "Kirsten, stay calm. Everything
will be taken care of."

I called Captain Rieber at once in New York. He said: "Mac,
call Kirsten back and tell her that tomorrow morning my representative in Sweden will be at her hotel to meet whatever needs
she may have."

But that was not enough for a man like Cap, as I came to call
him. Not only did Kirsten have my second call that night, but
she also had one from Cap himself, and the following day in
Stockholm twenty-five hundred American dollars was delivered
to Kirsten with the promise of more whenever she said the
word. From then on Captain Rieber kept in touch not only with
me but also with Kirsten herself. She was a famous woman, but
she was at that time a badly beaten human being desperately in
need of help. This wonderful man was there to provide just that
need.

Not very long after that, when Kirsten's return to America
was imminent, Cap and Ruth insisted on making arrangements
for her to have an apartment at the Hampshire House, one of

the most luxurious hotels in New York. Despite the fact that her own American bank account had been freed, she was in poor financial condition, and I told Cap that Kirsten could not afford such an expensive apartment. He simply laughed at me and said: "You don't think I would let her *pay*, do you?"

And so the first three or four times she was in New York the early months of 1947, she stayed in comfort thanks to Cap's generosity.

Insecurity was a new experience for Kirsten. In previous years she had known plenty, and in later years she was to know plenty again. But in the first years after the war she did not earn as she had before, and it was a long time before the case against Henry Johansen was finally settled and all of her own affairs were put in order. But what friends Captain Rieber and his daughter Ruth were! Many many times we turned to them. Ruth always went to hear Kirsten sing. I don't think Cap ever did, at least not in the postwar years—he was not what could be described as an avid music-lover. He did care very much about Kirsten's success as an artist, but he cared far more about her name being restored to its clean place. When her spirits were low, and mine too, it would be Cap, in his rugged way and with his objective wisdom, who knew how to help us right ourselves. And he had no axe to grind. He wanted nothing for himself.

Some years later, when Kirsten was on her feet again, she said to me one day: "Edwin, I must repay Captain Rieber that money."

I told her that that was an item she would have to handle herself. She telephoned him and asked him if he would take her out to luncheon just alone. It took a lot of courage, for so shy a woman. He agreed, of course. The morning of the appointed day I went to the bank, got twenty-five new one-hundred-dollar bills, put them in an envelope, and gave them to Kirsten. When

Cap called for her, she tried to give him the envelope. He refused to take it and told her she was a "silly girl." The next day I took the money back to the bank, and then and there the matter was dropped.

I have always been thankful that I was able to spare Kirsten the knowledge of her disastrous financial situation during that period. I used to tell her that she couldn't go out and buy a yacht, but I never let her know how really terrible things were. At one particular concert in Carnegie Hall I remember thinking, as she stood there acknowledging the tremendous applause of a packed house, what a surprise it would be to many in the audience if they knew that early the next morning I would be going to the bank to make sure she had funds to cover her current expenses. No one, not even Kirsten, knew the real situation. I felt it a constant challenge to spare her every worry I could.

But now back to December 1946. She wrote me on December 7 from Stockholm how wonderful it was to hear my voice again —Cap has telephoned as well, cabled, sent his representative, and so on, and she had the world's wealth in her pocket. And on December 9, still in Chicago, I wrote her: "Yes, the same shop on Michigan Boulevard is open and you know I cannot resist the enclosed for you." It was another handkerchief and from the shop where I had bought one on her first trip in 1935. This was another little personal habit kept up through all the years, and she loved the various handkerchiefs I had bought for her all over the world and always carried one of them when she was singing a concert.

Her next letter was dated December 16 and she was still in Stockholm. That very day she had received four letters from me at once. She was disappointed to hear of Marks Levine's attitude and was interested to learn that her "first manager," George Engles, was going back into business. Gerard Semon had been to see her and she had been diplomatic. And then she asked me if it would be possible for me to meet her in London. I would have swum the Atlantic. And then, "Did I tell you that Sigurd Hall [her first husband] with wife and son paid me a visit the last day in Oslo? It was very nice." Then the word that she would go to Zürich for Christmas and take with her the ten-year-old son of Henry Johansen, Jr. The next word would be from the Dolder Grand—our old point of contact in Zürich.

Now we were on the way. Kirsten's first letter from Zürich was dated December 26. She was happy to be there, and having the young boy with her was an especial pleasure. The road seemed smoother now, and Frederick Horwitz was having some success in settling engagements. La Scala was arranged for, and she was to resume her operatic career with her most famous part—Isolde. First there were to be some concerts, fortunately all orchestral. She asked for suggestions for the programs. It was like the old days.

Chapter IX

1947–1948

SPORADICALLY the American press still carried derogatory stories, but the violence of the immediate postwar months seemed past. It pleased me to know that concerts in both Paris and London would take place before her return to America. The reactions of those cities could be watched carefully—they had suffered directly in the war, as we had not.

Meanwhile, George Engles had come to Chicago earlier to confer with me and we had decided that Kirsten would return to America under his management. She wrote me on January 5, 1947, of her satisfaction with this arrangement, and no small part of her pleasure was that Helen Mobert, who had been her devoted friend and had handled publicity so wonderfully well in the earlier years, would be associated with Mr. Engles. And she wrote me continually how happy she was to be hearing steadily from Captain Rieber. Normally she would have taken such contacts in stride. Kirsten had always been rather careless and, too often, indifferent to her friends. Her interest now was a good sign—for intuitively I felt that she might well need supporters, many of them, if troubled days were ahead.

On January 10 there was a letter from Zürich which was not only interesting, but professionally important. A Mr. Walter Legge had taken her out for supper. Legge is without doubt one of the real geniuses of the recording business. He was an important director of His Master's Voice, RCA Victor's London affiliate, and this personal meeting was part of his attempt to snare Kirsten again for HMV. Characteristically, Kirsten did not remember having met Legge before the war—they had been together with Sir Thomas Beecham.

It was almost frightening in those days how she insisted on referring everything, even of the smallest importance, to me. At such a distance I was immediately thrust into negotiations with Legge and his associates. Meanwhile, very shortly after, she had gone to London for her first postwar visit and had been indirectly approached by an important rival recording company. I counseled her to renew and maintain her old associations. Kirsten, mainly at my insistence, did return to HMV and Victor at that time and remained with them until the expiration of her last contract in 1955.

Her first postwar concerts took place on January 18 and 19, 1947, in Cannes. Grace Moore was in the audience, and with her husband gave Kirsten a lovely party afterwards. It was only a few days before the shocking death of that lovely American artist at the Copenhagen airport. Kirsten reported that she now was being treated like a queen and said she was thankful that her trunk of costumes, packed by the faithful Jennie of the Metropolitan, had arrived. All was now in order for her Isolde in Milan. What details she wrote in those days! Her letters were six and seven pages long—unlike the Kirsten I had known before and was to know again later.

At about this time there came some ominous indications of events to come later. Horwitz had started negotiations regarding

With Father James Carroll, Samoa, June 3, 1938

Aboard the *Tatsuta Maru*, August 1938 (Edwin McArthur, Henry Johansen, Flagstad, Marks Levine, Captain Ito)

At Paramount Studios, Hollywood: (a) with Adolph Zukor, George Burns, and Gracie Allen; (b) with W. C. Fields and Harlan Thompson

a tour of South America with an agent named Ernesto De Cuesado. He was concentrating particularly on her first engagement at the leading Opera House of South America, the Teatro Colón in Buenos Aires. On January 26, 1946, Horwitz and De Cuesado called on me in our apartment in New York and settled, subject to Kirsten's acceptance, an excellent contract that guaranteed a more than satisfactory financial return. I cabled her as follows:

WRITING FULL DETAILS OF EVERYTHING TO DATE SUNDAY. MOST OF TODAY SPENT WITH HORWITZ AND SOUTH AMERICAN AGENT PERFECTING DETAILS OF YOUR CONTRACT. MAY I SIGN CONTRACT FOR YOU. HAVE YOU ENOUGH MONEY. RIEBER AND I CONCERNED ABOUT THIS. PUBLICITY ABOUT YOUR COMING VERY GOOD AND ALL OVER THE COUNTRY. DEAREST LOVE. EDWIN.

But on February 16 I had to write a terribly difficult letter. Horwitz had called on me again to say that there had been protests, apparently from one or two of the conductors in South America, and that the whole tour was off. He was afraid to tell Kirsten himself, but I was not. Hard as it was, she would have to face up to reality. In writing her this dreary news I also predicted that one fine day South America would come crawling. And they did. The following season, 1948, Kirsten did indeed tour South America, and it was one of the great triumphs of her career. At that later date she deliberately made fantastic demands, all of which were met.

But that this original rejection happened in 1947, just prior to her return to America, was a body blow. Even if she did not appear to realize it, I certainly did. But meanwhile there had been further discussions with HMV and some very cordial conversations in New York between Constance Hope and me. Constance, by then, was in an important official position with Victor, and as an officer of HMV's American affiliate, she did everything possible to develop and maintain friendly relations. More and more I thought how fortunate it was that Kirsten had been persuaded not to make a break with this important company.

The next important event was Kirsten's re-entry into London. The late Dr. Berta Geissmar, the former manager of the Berlin Philharmonic and secretary to both Furtwängler and Beecham, was now connected with the London Philharmonic. (Kirsten and I had both known this brilliant woman during prewar days at Covent Garden). Dr. Geissmar wrote me that it brought tears to her eyes to hear this great singer again—Madame Flagstad had not faded in the slightest. And despite a few faint hints of possible trouble in London as well as in Paris, she was given the warmest of receptions. This was all fully covered in the American press.

Following the London concert on February 6 in Albert Hall, Kirsten went off to Milan for her first performances at La Scala. She had now finally realized her dream of singing in that great opera house, and told me herself how grand it was to be singing opera again. Then the London Philharmonic persuaded her to return for one more concert just before she sailed to America.

Meanwhile, Stephen Spiegel took over matters of her visa, and with all her documents in order, she finally sailed for New York aboard the S.S. *America*. On March 9, 1947, I received a radiogram from her aboard ship. It said: "HAPPILY ON MY WAY LOVE TO PEGGY AND YOU."

I should say here that if there had been even the slightest indication of what awaited Kirsten on America's shores, I would have exerted every influence possible to dissuade her from returning to the United States. Such a decision would not have been the result of any cowardice. It is just that I do not believe that any decent person should have been subjected to such torture. But we could not and did not know. And once we were embroiled in it, there was no turning back.

Just at that time I had a two-week engagement of concerts with the St. Louis Symphony and therefore was not in New York for her scheduled landing on Friday, March 14. When her sailing date had been definitely fixed, I had suggested that I cancel my concerts and remain in New York, although my engagement in St. Louis had been made a year in advance. But Kirsten herself had insisted that I go ahead with my plans. Besides, George Engles and the faithful Cleone Pottenger were well set to handle the details of her arrival. Peggy remained in New York to meet the boat.

It had previously been decided that there would be no mention of already arranged concerts for the spring until the formal press conference on Saturday, March 15, in New York. That decision was only one item of practically everything we said or did which was deliberately misinterpreted or completely distorted. At what must have been a most unpleasant press conference, she announced that she would sing concerts in America the following month. She was immediately accused of having given false information the previous day when the question had been asked by reporters at the ship. According to original plan, she actually had been saving the announcement for the first press conference.

Also, Arturo Toscanini's daughter Wally had given Kirsten a beautiful scarf autographed by the maestro. She happened to have it on when she landed, and her detractors immediately publicized this as an attempt to use Toscanini's name to clear her own. Kirsten told me herself that she had great difficulty later on when she met Wally (Countess Castelbarco) again in Milan in making an explanation, but it seems to have been graciously accepted, and I know that the two remained warm friends.

Then there was a thorough airing of what became for a while a genuine *cause célèbre*. This revolved around a statement by Emil Stang, the Chief Justice of the Norwegian Supreme Court. Mr. Stang had given Kirsten a statement dated September 12, 1945, which in translation is as follows:

It is hereby testified that Kirsten Flagstad during the entire period of the last war has shown a steadfast patriotic attitude.

Kirsten brought the original of this with her when she came to America. Apparently she and Mr. Stang differed as to the origin of this statement. Kirsten declared that Mr. Stang offered her the statement unasked and said Mr. Stang had personally expressed his hope that it might be of service, assuring her that she was at liberty to use it anywhere and in any way she saw fit.

For reasons which we never understood, Mr. Stang subsequently made public certain qualifying observations. Mr. Bendixen wrote me some time later that the political pressure from his colleagues had been great on Mr. Stang. In any case it is worth printing his second statement in full as it appeared in Oslo's *Aftenposten* on January 28, 1947. The following is a true and faithful translation of the original clipping, sworn to by a licensed translator in Oslo.

My Pronouncement too comprehensive states Emil Stang

The Chief Justice of the Supreme Court of Norway today made the following statement through N.Y.B.:

"When the newspapers contained the statement, that I had given Kirsten Flagstad a testimonial testifying to her firm patriotic attitude during the war, I was ill in bed with pneumonia and bronchitis, and could only confirm this statement.

"I now wish to state, that I did not know Kirsten Flagstad personally before her return from the U.S.A., however, I have known her family for a number of years. There was then much ill-natured gossiping about Kirsten Flagstad. According to the rumours circulating she was to have associated with the Germans, given performances in Germany, etc. On making inquiries I found that this was not true. Ever since she returned to Norway she has without flinching kept the musical front. She was invited to sing in Norway, Denmark and Germany, but refused categorically. She was held in high esteem both as the world-famous singer and as the wife of Henry Johansen; however, she always preserved a firm patriotic attitude.

"After the liberation of Norway Mrs. Flagstad applied for a passport to go to the U.S.A. and on that occasion asked me for the usual certificate of national conduct. This certificate I was pleased to give her.

"I now understand that Mrs. Flagstad is criticized for her conduct in the U.S.A. prior to her return to Norway, and naturally I cannot express any opinion as to her conduct in that country. I do not know if there is a substratum of truth in the accusations against her. I now realize that my former pronouncement was too comprehensive. It ought to have been expressly restricted to her conduct in this country, as my knowledge of her is confined to this period.

Oslo, January 27th. 1947"

. . .

This second statement if printed and read in its entirety was
not particularly damaging. But the unfortunate part about it
was that only a very few words of it were printed in the *American* press. On March 16, 1947, *The New York Times* printed a
special from Washington which said:

The Norwegian Embassy today had no comment on the arrival
in this country of Kirsten Flagstad, opera and concert star, except to point to its statement of Feb. 6. This statement was to
the effect that Emil Stang, Chief Justice of the Supreme Court of
Norway, had modified the testimonial he had given Mme. Flagstad, emphasizing that he should have stated explicitly that he
referred only to her stay in Norway and not her attitude in the
United States, of which he had no knowledge.

There obviously had been absolutely nothing wrong with
Kirsten's behavior in the United States before her return to
Norway. But her enemies would seize upon anything, and the
mere fact that Emil Stang had felt it necessary to qualify his first
testimonial was enough for them to spread the unsupported
impression that Kirsten was guilty of all sorts of heinous
crimes.

The columnists and radio commentators, led by Walter
Winchell, had a field day. For three straight Sundays that
March and April, Winchell filled his listening public with the
most amazing tales, and practically every day his column had
references to Kirsten Flagstad. On two occasions during this
period he devoted his entire column to her. And he was not the
only one. Some of the information, tragic as were its implications, was really quite funny. In the *New York Daily News*, of
January 25, 1947, Ed Sullivan in his column "Little Old New
York" wrote:

Flagstad, whose husband was a $26,000,000 quisling of the
Nazis, first fell into Norwegian disfavor in April, 1940, when she
gave a concert at Washington at which she sang only German
songs, with Nazi bigwigs in the audience.

Of course there were those who came to Kirsten's defense and
some of her friends unfortunately found themselves victims of
similar attacks. Geraldine Farrar, Gladys Swarthout, and the
venerable Walter Damrosch received Winchell's mudbaths for
taking her part. In contrast, George Sokolsky wrote two provocative columns in her defense, and elsewhere others like the
music critic of the *Chicago Tribune*, Claudia Cassidy, spoke out.
But we were in an all-out war and the voices of quiet sanity are
never heeded in such times. Allen Sven Oxenburg, the impresario, in an excellent letter printed in the New York *Herald
Tribune* on April 20, 1947, stated the case fairly and clearly. To
him it was only logical that inasmuch as our own State Department had granted Flagstad a quota visa and entry into our
country, we should accept that higher judgment of her integrity.

What was Kirsten Flagstad doing all through this? She and
Peggy had dined her first night in New York with Captain
Rieber and Ruth. Next morning she had been through what
she described to me as the "ordeal" of the press conference. "I
am sure, Edwin," she told me on the telephone, "that I will be
misquoted and misunderstood. Please don't ask me to see the
press again."

I talked to her the evening following a Winchell broadcast—
she had heard that one. I don't believe that she ever listened to
him again and I am very sure that she never read his column.
And I will be eternally thankful that despite the urging of many
well-meaning friends, she refrained from ever trying to answer

him or the other columnists and detractors. And how beautifully time proved them all to be wrong. That it was hard to take, there is no denying—especially when one realizes that an attempted character assassination of this kind may have had as its final motive an increase of readership.

After three or four days in New York, Kirsten set out for Bozeman to visit her "little family." Meanwhile, I completed my engagement in St. Louis and had arranged to meet her in Chicago so that we could return to New York together. It was wonderful to see her so refreshed. Out there in Montana they had not even turned on a radio or seen a metropolitan newspaper and the family had been all but oblivious of the ugly nonsense.

The beginning of her singing schedule was drawing close, and already we were getting the warnings of terrible things to come at her concerts. Some managers had refused to present her at all. But there were those, always to be affectionately remembered, who would not shrink. Among these were a great lady in Milwaukee, Mrs. Myra Peache, and Harry Zelzer of Chicago. But Harry also had his troubles and reported to me that the sale for Kirsten's Orchestra Hall concert April 11 was going very badly. With this in mind, I asked Kirsten to invite Claudia Cassidy to lunch during our stopover in Chicago. Miss Cassidy accepted at once, and together with Harry, we had a good two-hours' conversation covering our growing dilemma. A few days later Miss Cassidy wrote a really great piece in the *Chicago Tribune* and it is to the credit of Chicago music-lovers that they preferred to take her word rather than that of the Winchells of the world. Pickets shamefully paraded outside Orchestra Hall— our first experience with them—but the auditorium was packed with a wildly enthusiastic audience.

The return trip from Chicago to New York was Kirsten's first experience with protection by detectives. There had been many terrible and threatening letters, and we were growingly concerned for her personal safety. As we boarded the *Twentieth Century Limited,* we were unobtrusively guarded, and on arrival the next morning at Grand Central Station, we were similarly met. Kirsten thoroughly disliked this and protested. But for some time we had to continue it. Despite all of the threats, not once was she physically attacked, possibly because of this precaution. In any case, no chances were taken.

During Kirsten's first weeks in America the realization broadened in her mind that the friendship and support she had counted upon were not about to materialize. Despite the controversy of the past, she really expected that the Metropolitan Opera at least would welcome her back to America. Edward Ziegler was ill, and it was understandable that she would not hear from him. Earle Lewis, the other assistant general manager, did telephone her and greet her as a personal friend, but no word at all came from Edward Johnson. George Engles had sent Johnson an announcement of her return and had received no reply whatever. It quickly became apparent that Kirsten could expect no support from that quarter—not, for the moment, even a word of welcome. It also hurt her very much that Engle's attempts to arouse interest in San Francisco were ignored and pointedly. Also, it would have been of inestimable help if the New York Philharmonic had invited her to appear with them. Any one of these institutions could have withstood a temporary storm to help the innocent woman to whom they owed so much. It took another management to re-open the door for Kirsten's career in San Francisco; it took a completely new regime at the Metropolitan to re-open the door there; and the Philharmonic, for whom Kirsten had generously sung a pension fund concert in 1941—without a fee—timidly

waited until the battle was over before inviting her again in
1951.

Kirsten's first American concert was scheduled for Easter Sunday afternoon, April 6, in Symphony Hall, Boston. Mr. Engles
had arranged with George Judd, the conservative and eminent
manager of the Boston Symphony Orchestra, to handle the local
management. Mr. Judd's name itself added great prestige to
the occasion. But before even this short tour could begin, another blow fell. At a meeting of the board of governors of the
American Guild of Musical Artists (AGMA) on March 28, 1947,
the following resolution was passed:

*Be it resolved that in view of the serious statements made in the
press concerning Mme. Kirsten Flagstad, the Board does not
feel warranted in restoring to Mme. Flagstad the privileges of
full membership in AGMA. Nevertheless, in view of the fact
that such charges have not as yet been substantiated by any official body of our government, of Mme. Flagstad's native land or
any government, the Board will grant to Mme. Flagstad a working permit, subject to revocation, with respect to her engagements in this country.*

Kirsten was crushed. Although several of her former colleagues had stood by her, she was now being officially repudiated by her own profession. And, of course, this got into the
press and further poisoned the situation.

We went to Boston on Saturday, April 5. The following,
Mr. Engles, Mr. Judd, and I went to Symphony Hall to see
that everything was in order. The hall had been searched beforehand. Nothing dangerous was found. The house was practically sold out, and that afternoon the entire audience rose to its
feet in welcome as she walked on the stage. It was a glorious

success. Virgil Thomson of the New York *Herald Tribune* made a special trip to Boston, and even this dedicated anti-Wagnerite came out with a particularly enthusiastic piece. The following day Kirsten was again radiantly happy and was particularly encouraged at the large number of her colleagues—among them the American tenor Frederick Jagel—who had come back-stage to see her. So the start was good.

We went on to Milwaukee, but there things were different. The posters outside the Pabst Theater had been defaced with swastikas and violent graffiti, and Kirsten sang to a mere handful of people. Engles was making the tour with us, and in every city, he went to great pains to arrange a secret entrance and exit at the hall. Not once did Kirsten have to go through a picket line. All we knew of them were the pictures in the newspapers. Then we went on for two or three other concerts in the Midwest. Attendance was shockingly poor and the financial loss was flattening. We were beginning to realize the true power of the press.

But the main event was still ahead. Sunday afternoon, April 20, was to be her first appearance in Carnegie Hall, New York. In those days the Philharmonic gave regular concerts on Sunday afternoons in Carnegie Hall, but their season was finished and the date was available. As soon as the concert was announced, Walter Winchell in his column on March 24, 1947 wrote: "Her Carnegie concert, by the way, will be given on April 20th—Hitler's birthday! . . . If she is given U. S. citizenship, will you war vets see to it that the court house flag is at half mast, please?"

We were open-mouthed—how can one begin to deal with this kind of imaginative malice? But, as if we cared, we did learn from this the date of the monstrous criminal's anniversary.

Carnegie Hall was sold out almost as soon as the concert was announced. Again we had the experience of being accompanied by detectives, but thanks to the friendliness and ingenuity of the manager of Carnegie Hall, John Totten, we again were spirited into and out of the hall without passing the pickets. But it was unpleasant to hear them screaming on West 56th Street, right outside the artists' room of the hall.

I went to the window and looked out at the motley and pathetic crowd, and I think realized for the first time the frightening power of mob hysteria.

When Kirsten walked out on that stage—strikingly gowned in black with a collar of white lace—she was regal in her assurance and poise. The standing reception from her public then was the most memorable experience in a gallery of hundreds of fine occasions in our long career together. There were all her loyal friends, and to her joy she knew that among the crowd were such dear and close colleagues as Geraldine Farrar, Elisabeth Rethberg, Gladys Swarthout, Karin Branzell, and Marion Telva.

The applause that greeted her lasted for minutes. I remember saying to myself: "Is she real? How can she sing, knowing that outside a frantic and ignorant mob is protesting her very presence?" And I also wondered how she could live up to the audience's expectations in the face of their unbelievable welcome. But sing she did, and immediately removed any possible doubts of her greatness.

Later, Marion and Elmer Jones (she the former Marion Telva of Metropolitan Opera fame, he the president of Wells Fargo) gave a lovely supper party for her in their New York mansion. All her friends were there. I remember that I was sitting next to Elisabeth Rethberg and she said to me: "Edwin, I have waited for years to see in reality what Lilli Lehmann always described as 'the perfect.' This afternoon it was that. The audience, the artist, the gown she wore, the way she walked on the stage, the way she acted, the applause, the program and the way she sang it—it was the whole thing." It was a great tribute from a great singer and colleague.

But the worst experience of all still lay ahead. We had been warned that terrible things were in store for us at the Academy of Music in Philadelphia on April 22—but no one could have believed that what did happen that night would ever take place. There were the most disgraceful and unforgivable demonstrations inside the walls of that great old hall. Rowdies were literally thrown out right during the recital. The police were everywhere in the auditorium and stink bombs were thrown. Over and over again there were shouts of "Nazi!" Fist fights broke out in front of our eyes. Kirsten stood quietly by the piano each time a disturbance erupted and then continued when all was still. She finished the entire program. We drove back to New York the same night and not one word passed between us the entire trip. When we were back finally in her apartment she said: "I am sorry to do this to you, but I am determined to win. They just can't do this to me!" That was everything that really was Kirsten Flagstad.

There was one bright moment after that terrible night in Philadelphia. The following Sunday, April 27, we went to Charlotte, North Carolina, for a matinée concert. In that friendly Southern city, Police Chief Frank N. Littlejohn announced publicly that there would be no disturbance. "We positively are not going to permit any disorder, and if anybody thinks he is coming down here from Philadelphia or anywhere else to start anything—for one reason or another—then he'll have another thought coming." He was referring to reports from Philadelphia that the placards the pickets carried at the concert there were being sent to Charlotte. There was no disturbance that Sunday afternoon.

After the terrible Philadelphia episode, many spoke out publicly in the press. Walter Damrosch violently protested the treatment of this woman and offered to accompany her at her next recital. Miss Farrar, Madame Branzell, and two other fine singers, Paul Althouse and Julius Huehn, joined the protest. Kirsten was not entirely without friends.

But the battle still was not won. The concerts, with the exception of those in Boston, Chicago, and New York, had been financial catastrophes. We were a sinking ship. I reached out for help in every direction I could think of. Cheever and Andrea Cowdin had already shown their friendship and support. One day Andrea had taken Kirsten and Peggy to a prominent public restaurant for lunch. Afterward the headwaiter had advised her that he thought it unwise for her to entertain Flagstad publicly. Andrea was furious and vowed never to go to that restaurant again.

Peggy and I were not spared either. Friends of long years standing would cross to the other side of the street to avoid speaking to us. Rhea Silberta, a prominent musician who had actually introduced me to Peggy, turned her back on me at the corner of Seventh Avenue and 57th Street when I sought to greet her. It made us sad, but did not for the slightest moment deter our campaign to clear Kirsten's name completely.

Cheever Cowdin as a prominent businessman could have felt it inopportune to associate his name with so controversial a figure. But, like Captain Rieber and Elmer Jones, he and his wife stuck by us. How I longed for some of those whose names were continually in the columns to speak out in defense of Kirsten. A good friend suggested that I approach Helen Hayes, whose name and position were unassailable. But I had never met Miss Hayes, and how would it have been possible to ask a total stranger for support? Kirsten had not as yet met Katharine

Cornell, who later, after the trouble was over, became her close friend. If Miss Cornell and others had for a moment realized what public support would have meant, I feel sure they would have spoken out.

There was only one more concert left—in Cleveland—before she was to go to Europe again. I could not play for that concert because by that time I had to be in St. Louis for the Municipal Opera Season and I was very happy indeed that an old friend and colleague, the late Edward Hart, agreed to go and play that concert for her in Cleveland. Ned was a fine accompanist, and for the rest of Kirsten's career in America he played many concerts where I could not go. Finally, on May 24, she flew off to England. She again sang with the London Philharmonic in Albert Hall on May 29 and then went on to Zürich for an engagement at her beloved Stadttheater. She wrote me from Zürich saying, "How happy I am to be in this peaceful calm, and yet how I long back to America, despite our desperate struggle."

It was good to have her long letters again. She had a particularly fine time at the London concert and wrote that "the Third Act *Walküre* went brilliantly with thirty-five Valkyries, a good Wotan and Sieglinde and myself in exceptional good form!" She had hoped, too, that Stake and his wife would be able to visit her in Zürich, but Sundför had not given up, and now was preventing Stake from getting his passport.

She returned to America by ship in July. After a few days in New York, she went for a lovely visit with Mrs. Morris (Katherine Hall's mother) at her estate in Morris, New York, and then went to St. Louis for a visit with Peggy and me. I was particularly eager for her to see what we did at the Municipal Opera there. The theater is the largest of its kind in the world, seating over 12,000 people. For twelve weeks each summer we give a series of musicals and operas in spectacular fashion. In 1947 I was in my third season there as Musical Director. Kirsten arrived on Sunday, August 3, and that very afternoon came to the orchestra rehearsal of our next production, Victor Herbert's *Naughty Marietta*. That night she attended our performance of Planquette's *The Chimes of Normandy*, an operetta that had a great vogue many years ago, but is seldom done today. I had completely forgotten how many times Kirsten had done it herself in earlier years. She was particularly delighted to hear and see it again. It produced in her a visible nostalgia that lasted for days. Toward noon the next day she came over to our open-air rehearsal platform and I had the great pride of introducing her to our young company. They all sat around on the floor as one of the greatest singers of history, quite informally, sang for them. She later asked me for the names of each of our company and before she left St. Louis she had signed a photograph for each of them.

From St. Louis she went to Montana and a reunion with her "little family." They took her off for some real American "roughing" in a typical Western mountain cabin where she lived for a while the authentic simple life, helped Else with the cooking, and forgot for a time the cares of her complex life. At this time it was very heart-warming that Else and she were so close to each other.

Now the season was about to begin again. We hoped and prayed that at least the worst harassments would not be repeated. But resistance was still met at every turn and Mr. Engles could persuade only a few local managers to take the gamble of presenting Flagstad in concert. It was really a horrible situation. In these postwar years she was already in tremendous demand in Europe, where the war had brought nearly total devastation. If there had been the slightest shadow of guilt in her life, she could never have survived there as an artist. But in America, where we had been untouched by bombs, tanks, or a Nazi occupation, she could scarcely even get a hearing.

This irony was emphasized by a translated excerpt from Oslo's *Aftenposten* of the previous June 6 which Kirsten received at about this time. The statement is an illustration of the progress of the European attitude toward her—most significantly the attitude of her own country—and is worth reprinting here in full:

Translation   *Extract from "Aftenposten"*—17.6.47.

THE PERSECUTION OF KIRSTEN FLAGSTAD.

———

It is now more than two years since the Liberation and even those of our artistes on whom the longest period of quarantine was imposed for their conduct during the war, are now back at their work.

Even more unjust and unfair is the fact that the persecution of Kirsten Flagstad has not yet ceased. There are no complaints against her either by the police or by the department dealing with collaborators with the enemy. The statements which have been made public about her are for the most part torn from their sequence and have thereby been seen in a false light, so that the account given absolutely does not agree with the facts. On the other hand, all the overwhelming expressions of human sympathy and enthusiasm for her art which have poured in to her from the world press have been systematically withheld here at home.

We appeal to our countrymen to stop these unworthy attempts to undermine Kirsten Flagstad's name and reputation.

Oslo, 13th June, 1947.

A few engagements were booked for the fall season of 1947. Among them were two of importance. For many years a wonderful couple, Mr. and Mrs. C. H. Crandon, have headed the Civic Music League in Miami, Florida, and they were determined to weather the storm and present Kirsten. They had all sorts of protests from many groups and there was a good deal of controversy in the press, but the concert did take place on October 30. Mr. Crandon wrote to the headquarters of Civic Concert Service in New York that the concert was simply magnificent and had been probably more enthusiastically received than any given in Miami for the past ten years. Kirsten wrote me before we met that she was particularly happy in Miami and was also very pleased with a local musician, Annie Laurie Lee, who had accompanied her in fine style.

Now came the happiest postwar occasion yet. Even if the opera companies would not have her, the Chicago Symphony Orchestra and its distinguished musical director, Artur Rodzinski, determined that they would. On Sunday afternoon, November 16, 1947, at the Civic Opera House in Chicago she returned to the American operatic stage in a fully staged all-star production of *Tristan und Isolde* under their auspices. Singing opposite her was the great Swedish tenor, Set Svanholm, and in the cast was her favorite Brangäne, Karin Branzell. It was another great triumph, and unlike the concert appearance the previous season in Chicago, there were no pickets.

At this point there was another pleasant surprise. The London impresario Harold Holt cabled asking if she would fly over to appear at one concert with Sir Thomas Beecham and the Royal Philharmonic Orchestra in Albert Hall on November 24. Svanholm was also to appear. The concert was for the benefit of the British Empire Nurses War Memorial and was under the patronage of Her Majesty the Queen. It was a rigorous journey to make for just one appearance, but Kirsten was proud and happy to do it. Here again was evidence of an affectionate and warm welcome in, of all places, London, which had so recently been subject to the physical terrors of the war.

But on Kirsten's return once again to America, still another bitter blow fell. The Southern impresario Marvin McDonald had booked two concerts: one in Atlanta, the other in Savannah. Eventually he bowed to local pressure groups and requested cancellation. We had to agree. I still remember Kirsten on the telephone, almost in tears, saying, "Edwin, we really needed those concerts and the money!"

Two Carnegie Hall recitals were planned for that season, the first one on Monday evening, December 22, 1947. The pickets were back, but their numbers had shrunk and they were much less noisy. The house as usual was sold out. Unbeknownst to me, Frederick Horwitz had taken two tickets for the evening to S. Hurok's office and these had been passed along to O. O. Bottorff. Bottorff had been Max's partner for many years and together they had a close affiliation with the Hurok attractions. Mrs. Bottorff and a friend attended the December 22 concert and the very next day "Bott," as I knew him, telephoned me and asked me to come to see him. I was quite sure of his reason and declined. But after a couple of hours of thinking it over, I changed my mind. When I got to his office, the Christmas party of their firm was in progress and in the confusion of these festivities I was able to slip into Bott's office unnoticed by anyone. He told me of his wife's enthusiasm over Kirsten's recital the evening before and then said: "Edwin, let's be frank. We know perfectly well that Madame Flagstad's business is going badly. She should be back here under our management."

He spoke nothing but the stark truth. We were on the brink of disaster despite the fact that Kirsten was sailing in three weeks for a long season at Covent Garden and later was booked for an extensive tour of South America. But the United States continued to be important. I had been bitterly hurt by Marks Levine's neglect of Kirsten, apart from our own personal differences. Beyond that, others closely associated with Max, some of them friends of many years, had completely ignored us during this dreadful period. I must say in fairness, however, and perhaps in defense, that the trouble of the preceding months with Max had been at least a three-sided matter. Kirsten herself was not completely blameless: she too had been truculent and stubborn about a number of matters of common concern. But at that moment we were literally searching for a bone.

Bott and I talked for about an hour, and I finally consented to see Max. Bott called him at his home and, after telling him I was there, persuaded Max to return to the office. It took him about ten minutes to get there, and during that short time I made one of the most difficult, and for Kirsten, important decisions of my life. When he walked into Bott's office, I simply said: "Max, there is no use to discuss the trouble and differences between Kirsten, yourself, and me. They have concerned only the three of us. But here and now I say to you in Bott's presence, that one hundred percent, the entire fault of all these differences has been mine alone."

Never was a more profound falsehood spoken. But I knew with whom I was dealing, and I felt that this was the only possible solution. Neither Kirsten nor Max would have given an inch without accusations back and forth. I doubt if either at that time would have accepted any responsibility for anything that had happened. It was a very hard thing to do, but it was the only way of solving the most difficult situation. It hurt me to have to do it, but I have no regrets whatever.

Max accepted without comment what I had said. I picked up the telephone on Bott's desk, called Kirsten at the Stanhope Hotel, and said: "Kirsten, you have ice and there is also Scotch in the cabinet. Call downstairs and have some soda water brought up. In half an hour I will be in your apartment for a drink and I will have with me Marks Levine and O. O. Bottorff."

This is a verbatim quote of myself—I can never forget that. I hung up before she could even answer. The three of us went up Fifth Avenue in a taxi, and when we walked into the apartment, Kirsten and Max kissed as though nothing had ever happened. There were a few surprisingly mild words over past differences, and within a short time it was settled that Kirsten would cancel her contract with George Engles and return to the management of Marks Levine. I am quite sure that in the immediate days to follow, Max had some hideous second thoughts over his quick decision. But the affiliation was resumed. I fulfilled the odious task of breaking the association with George Engles. He never forgave me, and for that I was sorry. I am convinced he did the best he could, but unfortunately for Kirsten he was not able to put it over.

Almost immediately the outlook became brighter. The San Francisco Opera Company and several established concert managers in America had been entirely unwilling to discuss Kirsten with George Engles, but now they seemed willing to do business. This is not to say that it was all a bed of roses for Max. He had his troubles too in the days ahead. But the roadblocks were definitely removed.

The January 17 following this episode Kirsten sailed for Europe on the S.S. *Queen Mary*. I remember that the great conductor Erich Kleiber came to her cabin to pay his respects, and though they had not met before, his visit had great meaning for her. We had heard reports that he had been among those who had protested her in 1947 in South America, and this made his gesture of support more than welcome. He became one of her staunchest admirers, and after they had worked together, she came to think of him as one of her favorite conductors.

The European tour at the beginning of 1948 was to take Kirsten to Britain, Paris, Zürich, and Milan. In my opinion, the one really important concert of the entire tour was one that she gave in London, the first of several appearances there for the United Jewish Relief Appeal. The core of the world's revulsion against Nazi Germany is tied up with the fate of European

Jewry, and if Kirsten had ever been guilty of any of the charges
made against her, public reaction would have to lead finally to
this area. It would have been ridiculous, of course, to accuse her
of personal anti-Semitism—the pattern of her associations both
in America and Europe was well known and simply would not
allow the charge. But there might remain the idea of ultimate
moral complicity in the crime, had there been any shred of truth
in assertions that she had collaborated with the Germans.

In light of all this, Kirsten felt particularly tentative and shy
when she was approached by A. Shusterman, an officer of the
United Jewish Relief Appeal in London. She was especially concerned lest she be accused of making an empty gesture to extri-
cate herself from a difficult situation. But after meeting Mr.
Shusterman she accepted, and on July 7, 1948, sang a special
recital in London, to be followed the next year by another. Mr.
Shusterman issued a statement of "My Interview with Kirsten
Flagstad" and I quote the final portion herewith:

I wish to express on behalf of our Committee our grateful
thanks to Madame Flagstad for her generosity, and the great
help she is giving by her name and her world-famed artistry to
enable the U.J.R.A. to carry on its work of making possible the
continued maintenance of some of these 75,000 children, most of
them orphans, whose parents perished in the death camps. God
Bless you, Kirsten Flagstad!

I myself met Mr. Shusterman in London a year later, and over
the tea table he told me frankly that the Jewish community
there was aware that Madame Flagstad had been accused of
being anti-Semitic. But they simply did not believe it. And I
have in my possession a remarkable file of correspondence in
praise of Kirsten from Mr. Joseph Leftwich, the Director of the
United Jewish Relief Appeal.

Not unexpectedly, when a later concert was planned, there were those who objected. But Mr. Shusterman and Mr. Leftwich were convinced of Kirsten's integrity and stuck to their guns. Kirsten again emerged the heroine.

Chapter X

1948–1949

FOLLOWING the European trip, Kirsten was scheduled to make an extensive tour of South America. During this period a serious misunderstanding and temporary break developed between us. If we had been together for a face-to-face talk, it would never have happened. From the beginning she had asked me, and I had agreed, to go with her to South America. She was to do a series of concerts all over the continent after her opera performances at the Teatro Colón, and I was to conduct a performance of *Tristan und Isolde* in Caracas with her as Isolde and the great tenor Max Lorenz as Tristan. There would be orchestral concerts in certain places which I would conduct, and of course I would be her accompanist at all of her recitals. I looked forward to this trip, even selfishly. Who would not want to see all parts of the world and make music continually with Kirsten Flagstad at the same time? There was never any discussion of my conducting opera in Buenos Aires. Erich Kleiber was the conductor that year for the whole Wagnerian repertoire. But the rest of the schedule had been arranged as a sort of "joint" tour.

As the winter went on, I began to wonder if it would be practical for me in my own career to undertake this trip. Among other questions was the fact that we could never seem to get a definite commitment as to the number of concerts or even their possible locations and dates. Also, although I would have been paid for the concerts I would be conducting, Kirsten would herself have had to assume the financial burden of my being with her. She had always done this before and would have done so again. But I knew her financial situation far better than she knew it—and was aware that she should not and actually could not afford it.

By this time my own career in America was progressing well. Also, despite the fact that Max was again handling business very well, it was in her better interests that I remain behind to look after many details.

I kept postponing a decision, and that was a mistake. Kirsten always had the impression that I would surely journey from New York to meet her in South America, where she would go directly from Europe. I finally reached the decision not to go, and on April 25, 1948, I wrote her in detail the reasons for it. In various meetings in New York, De Cuesado had seemed to make it plain that he had a conductor other than me that he would prefer. In this instance, I was definitely not being imposed, and his attitude irked me. But inasmuch as he felt this way, and had probably been informed of the conditions of the past, I wrote Kirsten that I thought it very unwise both for her and for me to repeat the embarrassing situation which had arisen at the Metropolitan years before.

If only when one has to write such a long letter it were possible to gauge the frame of mind the receiver will be in when he reads it. Also, the letter had to include important information on some other matters—some good, others disappointing. The letter happened to reach Kirsten at the wrong time. After considerable delay she wrote me a letter I have always wished that she had never felt she had to write and that I would not have had to receive. I had betrayed her, she said. She would never have signed the South American contract at all if she had not been sure I would be there with her. Why had I waited so long to tell her? Only a month earlier she would have canceled the entire tour.

Then, having unburdened herself in this heartbreaking way, she went on to assure me that she believed after all I had made the correct decision. She had realized finally that she was a lone woman with no one to take care of her, and she was learning to get along by herself and would continue to do so.

Words could not describe my despair when I got her letter. I wrote her immediately, simply repeating my reasons with even fuller explanations.

Now she understood and very quickly she wrote back that she could see its impracticality from my point of view, although it would have been so much nicer if I were there with her. She also told me how much, even more than ever, she needed me to look after matters for her. And in a letter written a little later aboard ship just before landing in Rio de Janeiro she wrote: "To whom should I speak my mind freely if not to you and *only* to you? I need to have you to confide in. I cannot carry my thoughts inside me and grieve and worry. I never in my wildest dreams ever doubted your wholehearted loyalty and friendship."

And then in that same letter this startling piece of news:

230

"Edward Johnson has been in Zürich and came to both performances and came to see me—sent me roses and embraced me
with tears in his eyes. He was very enthusiastic. I was nice,
Horwitz asked me to, and later at a party at Reinshagen's we
talked a lot but never any business, so that is that."

During the months of separation, I had one particular day
with the Melchiors which Kirsten used to get me to recount over
and over again. They had chosen to ignore Kirsten in the years
after the war, and this had saddened her greatly. The only
explanation could be that their behavior was "temperamental."
Like so many others, they seemed to feel that continued association with such a "controversial" person would be too great a risk
for the safety of their own skins. She never saw them after that
parting in Grand Central Station in New York on April 18, 1941,
and it was years after the war before she even heard from them
at all.

A whole year after Kirsten's return to America after the war, I
had been engaged to conduct a concert with the St. Louis Symphony with Melchior as soloist. The date was March 20, 1948,
and happened to be his birthday. Following the morning rehearsal, I lunched with the Melchiors and two or three others in
the coffee shop of the Hotel Jefferson in St. Louis. I recall the
conversation just about word for word, and I hope the reader
will trust my memory if I set it down in the form of dialogue.

MELCHIOR: "By the way, Edwin, how is Flagstad? I have never
heard from her."
MC ARTHUR: "Oh come now, Lauritz. Why do you refer to
Kirsten as Flagstad? You have always called her by first name."
MELCHIOR: "Well, I never heard from her when she came back
to America last year."
MC ARTHUR: "Lauritz, do you think we should discuss this here?

There are people at this birthday luncheon who are strangers to such a discussion."

MELCHIOR: "No matter."

MC ARTHUR: "Well, Lauritz, since you insist, I must tell you that Kirsten was very surprised and somewhat hurt that neither Kleinchen nor you communicated with her."

MELCHIOR: "Well, you know what the situation was."

MC ARTHUR: "*What* situation, Lauritz? There is no situation when a friend is in need."

KLEINCHEN MELCHIOR: (*really embarrassed*) "Let's not talk about it more now."

MC ARTHUR: "Oh yes, we must finish now we have started. Let me tell you something. If you, Kleinchen, had lost your husband as Kirsten did hers, I feel quite sure Kirsten would have called you. Henry Johansen was a good friend of yours—in fact I remember when you took friendly advantage of your closeness to considerable profit in making some foreign exchange in Paris several years ago. You should have communicated your friendship to her when she came back to troubled days, and innocently, too, if you had the friendship in your heart which you now choose to profess."

The conversation ended there. Amusing—interesting—and sad.

I flew by late afternoon plane on November 17 to New Orleans. When I checked in at the hotel, there was a message from Kirsten saying that a rehearsal of *Tristan* was in progress and would I go directly to the auditorium. As I walked in at the stage entrance, the remarkable sound of her voice flooded the whole place. She and Frederick Jagel were in the midst of the great Second Act duet. I stood there in the wings, and soon Kirsten saw me and waved.

The first of two performances took place the next evening. But meanwhile we spent hours catching up on everything. Although her South American tour had been hard and the travel demanding, she felt that it had been worthwhile. De Cuesado had assigned a representative to travel with her everywhere and that had been a help. She was exultant over her triumphs at the Teatro Colón, and I was struck once again how necessary applause was to her.

She had also been very good about keeping an accounting of her finances. I had given her the strictest instructions in this department. Ten months was a long time, and a professional schedule involving so many different countries posed problems of returning proper tax information. By now she was a legal resident of the United States and naturally filed tax returns for the entire world here. I kept the complete record I provided her accountant, Joesph Henry Ide, that year, and with the information from so many different countries and such different currencies, it proved to be an interesting document. Kirsten had herself kept close account of the taxes she had paid in each country, a remarkable detailed account of expenses, and had even translated the various currencies into American dollars.

The personal contact between us immediately cleared up the misunderstandings of the previous months and we moved into discussions of the future. But I felt instinctively that she had an impatient urge to tell me something really more important than anything else. Finally, with a twinkle in her eye, she said: "Well, Edwin, I can't keep it secret any longer and I haven't written you about it. I have a new and devoted friend!"

I literally gasped—"A boy friend?"

"Oh heavens no, not that," she replied. "But a very attentive one who means a great deal to me."

"Well, who is it?" I demanded.

"Bernard Miles," she said. She had met him the previous winter in London, and they quickly had become fast friends.

Bernard Miles, his attractive and talented wife, Josephine, and their children became very important to Kirsten, and in her later years superseded even Else and ourselves at least in the amount of attention Kirsten gave to those close to her.

Bernard Miles was not a new name to me. He already had a brilliant reputation as an actor I well remembered for his performance with Noel Coward in the superb war picture *In Which We Serve*. From at least one angle, the friendship of Kirsten and Bernard was a curious one. He is a violent anti-Wagnerian. When later, in 1949, we met for the first time, he and I had a strenuous argument on the subject of Wagner and his operas. But he was and is a man of considerable musical knowledge and taste. I regret his influence on Kirsten in the last years of her professional life for reasons I shall go into later. But the Miles family provided a haven of comfort for her in years when desolate loneliness was generally the order of the day. And for me it was a satisfaction, in the beginning at least, that a new interest had come into her life.

During those months Kirsten and Bernard corresponded voluminously. In a relatively short time she was quoting Bernard's opinions with increasing regularity, and very soon she began planning her schedules in Europe more and more around her visits to the Miles family in London. That first evening in New Orleans she invited me to spend the following April in Europe with her, where again I could play in Albert Hall in London. There was also to be a recital in Zürich. And then she said: "You will meet Bernard and his family and see for yourself."

We returned to discussions of business. None of us could be satisfied with the state of things in America even then. After I had carefully reviewed with Kirsten the artistic as well as financial rewards of her previous ten months in Europe and South America, I wondered if she would not then and there say: "Let's call it a day."

But she did not. I reported to her that Max had ascertained the desire of the San Francisco Opera to have her, even in the 1948 season, only to discover that she was not available. But he had already started informal discussions for 1949. Although she had written me angrily before of her determination not to return to San Francisco, she had not meant it and now hoped a season there might yet fall to her. It eventually came about, but formidable difficulties had to be overcome even there. The final settling of that contract was laborious, and it is to Marks Levine's credit that it was finally arranged at all.

I questioned her for more details of her visit in Zürich from Edward Johnson with an eye to future possibilities at the Metropolitan, but she could tell me no more than she had written. She did speak of inquiries from both Salzburg and Bayreuth for 1949. I believe the inquiry from Bayreuth never reached the point of a definite offer—she never sang there after 1934. But Salzburg was another matter, and when she told me that the proposal was to sing *Fidelio,* and with Furtwängler, I asked her how could she hesitate for a minute. And then her reason: "Edwin, remember the story of *Fidelio.* Leonore succeeds in rescuing her husband from prison. In my own life I was not so successful."

It was hard for me to reply to such a statement from her. Kirsten intuitively understood her roles, although, as we have seen, some critics chose to praise her more for the opulence of her vocal delivery than for psychological penetration. She did have an intuitive grasp of the part of Leonore, just as she had for all of her parts. But it surprised me that she would compare the heroine's situation to her own life. In the opera Leonore not only struggles to gain the freedom of her husband, who is, she hopes, alive in the dungeon, but also is a very conscious part of the political drama—quite a contrast to the case of Kirsten and her own husband.

I let the whole matter drop for the moment. Eventually, of course, the performances at Salzburg materialized, with results to be described shortly.

In the early days of December 1948, Kirsten received a charming letter from Tallulah Bankhead, whom she had not met as yet. Miss Bankhead enclosed a communication from the Honorable Nathan D. Perlman, chairman of the fund-raising committee for the Foster Parents Division of the Labor Zionist Committee. The letter was an appeal for a contribution from Kirsten. Kirsten immediately sent Miss Bankhead a donation and explained that it would have been more had she not already given to the same cause by her singing in Europe. Miss Bankhead wrote back and asked permission to send Kirsten's letter on to Winchell: she wanted him to know of Kirsten's activity overseas. She also said she had been one of those fortunate enough to hear Kirsten's memorable performance of *Tristan und Isolde* with Dr. Rodzinski in Chicago.

Miss Bankhead was playing in New York that season in a revival of Noel Coward's *Private Lives*. Her part, Amanda, required her to sing "Some Day I'll Find You." The qualities of Miss Bankhead's voice are well known, and when Kirsten told her that she intended to go to the play, Miss Bankhead begged her above all to ignore her singing.

Peggy and I went with Kirsten to the theater, and it was a delightful production of one of Coward's most charming plays. Afterwards we all went up to Kirsten's apartment for what we had thought would be a quick nightcap. When Peggy and I

The Chicago Opera *Tristan und Isolde*, November 24, 1939
(Giovanni Martinelli, Flagstad, Edwin McArthur)

At RCA Victor Recording Studios, Hollywood, November 11, 1939, with
Edwin McArthur and Lauritz Melchior

were riding home in a taxi through Central Park, I looked at my watch and found it was six thirty the following morning. It had been an entertainment in itself to watch the two women, each trying to get the other to talk about her career. Kirsten was much taken by Miss Bankhead's rough magnetism and her warmhearted anger at the antagonists Kirsten was still facing. They were certainly poles apart in their personalities, but they were quickly congenial.

One day shortly after in her apartment, I found her positively exultant. Mrs. August Belmont had invited her to dinner. One would have thought she was to be presented at court—her excitement was like a young girl's. After midnight the evening of the dinner, she telephoned me when she got back to her apartment. "Guess what, Edwin," she said rhapsodically, "Edward Johnson was there and toasted me with champagne."

I said: "That's just fine, dear Kirsten. I'm happy for you and we'll talk it all over at lunch tomorrow."

But next day when I asked her if Johnson had sent up a Metropolitan contract that morning, she had to tell me sadly that he had not. He never did.

Kirsten spent that spring in Europe. I was scheduled to join her in Amsterdam in the early days of April. When I got there, she did one of the thoughtful little things of which she was capable when she felt like it. On my arrival at the airport in Amsterdam the morning of April 2, there, to my astonishment, was Kirsten to meet me. She had driven out from the city, untypically, only on my account. When I told her that, much as it was appreciated, she need not have gone to that trouble, she said: "You don't think I'd let you arrive without being here to meet you, do you?"

Those days in Amsterdam are happy recollections. There were performances of *Tristan und Isolde* conducted by Kleiber and the Tristan was the superb tenor Max Lorenz, who had been a colleague of Kirsten's in the early Bayreuth days. On occasion Max had been to America, but his career never quite caught fire in the United States. His position as one of the greatest in the European opera houses was unchallenged, however. Kirsten adored him and loved singing with him. Max and his wife Lotte were among her very dearest and most devoted friends during her later years, and often she would write me of her pleasure in looking forward to an engagement simply because Max was to be her tenor. Those opera-lovers who did not hear this combination of Flagstad and Lorenz missed something unique. To be sure, it was different from the Flagstad-Melchior duo. Each had its own distinction. Melchior's voice had perhaps a more "dramatic stature and ring," but the sympathetic appeal and suave beauty of Max Lorenz's instrument blended wonderfully well with Kirsten's clarion delivery. And they were extraordinarily handsome together on the stage. It was curious that Kirsten's closest friends among her colleagues were again her tenor and his wife. Max and Lotte would have been her friends in any case, but their renewed warmth during this period, when Kirsten had been neglected so shamefully by the Melchiors, seemed to make the association even more binding.

We went from Amsterdam by air to London on April 7 for the recital in Albert Hall the next night. Then I met for the first time Kirsten's most loyal and energetic fan in England. Of course she had plenty of them here too; some of them became insufferable pests, and it used to be one of my unpleasant duties to keep them out of the way. Then again, like all prima donnas, she feasted on their adulation. But the leading fan in England, and I believe the most devoted in the world, Joyce Reah, was in a class by herself. She absolutely adored Kirsten and waited on her hand and foot. When we arrived at the Savoy Hotel, there was Joyce with a leather bag in which were glasses, bottles of liquor, and countless other simple necessities for Kirsten's comfort there. Joyce was a friend, but behaved almost like a menial servant. I believe she would have swum the English Channel if Kirsten asked her to. But with dear Joyce, as with all of the other fans, she never seemed to know when to stop.

It embarrassed me on many an occasion when Kirsten was actually brutally rude to such well-meaning people. And, as a matter of fact, her unpredictable bad manners and indifference were not confined to people like Joyce Reah. Just at this time her good friends Andrea and Cheever Cowdin had been trying unsuccessfully to get tickets to the Opéra in Paris and had sent a message to Kirsten that they would be very grateful if she would arrange the matter. She sent a very curt message in return that she was not a ticket-broker! This to two of her most loyal supporters in the darkest days! But now, at least in Europe, she did not need them, and she was playing the prima donna. It is no wonder that Andrea never gave Kirsten another thought and I could not blame her when she complained bitterly to me over the telephone about such behavior. I even tried in this particular case to remonstrate with Kirsten, but dropped the matter when she turned on me in a particularly unpleasant way. "Why?" one might ask. It is a question that can never be answered.

The concert in Albert Hall was lovely and I thoroughly enjoyed being back in London again—my first visit after the war. Albert Hall is by no means the best concert hall in the world, but I always loved playing there and thinking of the great personalities who had been on its stage. Kirsten had made me promise her in America that I would take her out for supper alone after that concert. That was always a pleasure for me, and I like to remember the elegance of that particular night. Kirsten had by then discarded the somber clothes she wore during the first postwar years and on this occasion wore a striking gown of blue brocade. She looked the queen indeed. I was in white tie and tails and really felt like somebody when we were ushered to our table at the Savoy. Presently on the dance floor we noticed the great actress Flora Robson. At that same moment she had seen Kirsten. The two had met through Reggie Allen many years before in Los Angeles. Miss Robson came over to the table for a few pleasantries and compliments and it was good to see how Kirsten appreciated the tributes paid her by other greats of the theater. Her reaction as usual was like a very pleased child's.

The following day, April 9, was one I looked forward to eagerly. Bernard Miles and his wife, Josephine, were in a town quite some distance from London called Stroud, making a film on location in which they were both playing important parts. Bernard was also directing. Kirsten and I were to go there for the weekend. We left by car early in the morning and arrived in Stroud in time for luncheon. I immediately liked Bernard. He was charm personified and gave me a genuinely warm welcome.

After luncheon we went to watch the filming for several hours. That night Kirsten with me at the piano gave an informal recital for all of those involved in the making of the picture. Already Kirsten was involved in discussions with Bernard about a pet project of his: the founding of the Mermaid Theater, now an important part of London theatrical life. The weekend was a happy one, and I could only be pleased that Kirsten had found such warm friends.

I remained in London for six days and Kirsten went alone to Milan, where I joined her the following Friday, Good Friday. On Easter Sunday we went together into the great cathedral in Milan and as the organ pealed forth in that magnificent edifice,

Kirsten grabbed my hand tightly and whispered: "Isn't it just too grand?"

The rehearsals of *Die Walküre* at La Scala were interesting under Victor de Sabata, and the orchestra was one of the finest I had ever heard. She had the added happiness of her sister Karen Marie's being there to sing one of the Valkyries.

Right after Milan we went to Zürich and I had the thrill of playing a recital for her in the famous Tonhalle. We stayed at the Dolder Grand (the hotel where she had always lived during earlier visits to Zürich and from where she had dramatically contacted me during the war). And I had the opportunity to meet the very wonderful friends in Zürich who had been such a comfort to Kirsten in hard times.

Then on to Paris where Kirsten and Max Lorenz sang *Tristan und Isolde* together again and where, on Kirsten's instructions, I had an important conference with Horwitz regarding her future plans. Already Salzburg for that summer was in order and we had the good news from Max Levine that he had finally arranged the details of her engagement with the San Francisco Opera Company.

When I left Kirsten at the Grand Hotel in Paris on May 1, everything was again healthy and happy, and as she questioned me carefully as to my own satisfaction over what Horwitz was doing, all I could answer was that to my mind not only was everything in Europe in splendid order, but that finally even affairs in America were bright.

Still—not the Metropolitan Opera. She kept on professing her belief that it would never come, but in her heart I don't think she believed what she was saying. I feared only that her singing days might be finished before the invitation to return there would come.

Meanwhile, the case against Mr. Johansen's estate was progressing in good order in Norway. It was not completely settled yet, but the pressure of personal matters had been greatly relieved. Kirsten was working, she was happy, and that was practically all that mattered. In Europe her financial affairs were in good order, and I was sure that they would eventually be straightened out in America. In any case, she was not in need and was able to stand on her own. Else and her family had made a visit home to Norway and that had made her happy, although she had not been able to be there to greet them. Back in America, Else and Arthur had moved to Madison, Wisconsin, which made it considerably easier for her to visit them while she was in the United States. I flew home from Europe after a beautiful month with a sense of calm relief that the dark days of trouble seemed really a thing of the past.

Our correspondence resumed with ominous warnings of illness. On July 8, 1949, she wrote me from Zürich that her arm continued to cause her terrible pain. And then her first mention of psoriasis, that terrible infection of the skin from which she was never to be free again. She was looking forward to Salzburg and would do her best to see as many of her friends as she could. This she had promised me when we were in Paris. Becky Hamilton was there and was acting as her faithful chauffeur all over Europe when her business permitted. She had heard, too, that Sundför had had a nervous breakdown, news that did not at all upset her.

At this point there was another contretemps involving the Metropolitan. Max, obviously with the astute intention of arousing constructive interest, cabled Kirsten to ask if she would be available to sing the three Brünnhildes and Kundry for the Metropolitan the following year. He knew as well as she did that her time was already completely booked and that she would have to say "No." Kirsten cabled in reply simply that she was not available. She had naturally assumed that Max's cable had originated in an actual inquiry from the Metropolitan. Max apparently had made this gesture on his own initiative, and Edward Johnson immediately denied having made any approach whatever. What had started as a good move on Max's part boomeranged badly. It got into the press and Kirsten was castigated for having said "No" to the Metropolitan and for having now betrayed those who had been fighting her battle alongside her.

Chapter XI

1949–1950

T H E L A T E S T Metropolitan discussion was a mere puff of smoke compared with the fight that now broke out in San Francisco. The simplest way to relate the happenings of the crisis is to reprint my cable to Kirsten, an excerpt from my following letter to her, and a relevant letter to her from Captain Rieber.

My Cable

St. Louis, Missouri—July 27, 1949

KIRSTEN FLAGSTAD

FESTSPIELHAUS

SALZBURG, AUSTRIA

ALTHOUGH I KNOW IT IS DIFFICULT FOR YOU TO UNDER-
STAND THERE ARE MANY GOOD REASONS WHY I HAVE NOT
COMMUNICATED WITH YOU THESE PAST TWO WEEKS STOP
A FEW DIRTY INDIVIDUALS HAVE MADE MATTERS DIFFI-
CULT AND CONFUSING BUT WE ARE ALL HAPPY AND YOU
SHOULD BE HAPPY TO KNOW THAT WE HAVE FINALLY
WON THE BATTLE AND I HONESTLY BELIEVE THERE WILL
BE NO MORE TROUBLE STOP YOU HAVE MANY MORE
FRIENDS THAN ANYONE COULD REALIZE. STOP LOVE AS
ALWAYS.   EDWIN

From My Letter—St. Louis, Missouri—July 28, 1949

The United Press carries a story today all over the country of
your enormous success in Salzburg and the tremendous ovations
accorded you, and as always, this makes me very happy. You
are quoted in the same release as having stated that you have
been invited for a series of performances by the Metropolitan,
but because of previous commitments, you have declined the
invitation. I think this has made a fine impresson.

The past two weeks have been the unhappiest of my life. On
Wednesday, two weeks ago, Max telephoned me from New
York that he had received word from San Francisco that a certain post of the American Legion there had lodged a protest
with the directors of the War Memorial Opera House, and that
there was to be an open hearing on the question of the San
Francisco Opera Company being permitted to present you in
their season. You must understand clearly that the San Fran-

cisco Opera Association does not control the War Memorial
Opera House. They merely rent it as tenants. The Board of
Trustees of the Opera House itself is made up of another group
and control the auditorium itself. The directors of the Opera
Association, and in particular the business manager, Mr. Posz,
did not feel too much concerned over the proposed hearing, and
felt quite confident that when all the facts of your case had been
presented, and especially your enormous success in this country,
and in California last year, that the entire matter would be
dropped. Quite the contrary was eventually the case. You and I
know the type and background of those who are your enemies,
and apparently they decided to make this the "last stand." The
result was that the Trustees of the building voted at this meeting to ban you from the Opera House.

Now, here comes an important thing which you *must understand*. The whole question became an issue of national prominence, not so much about you as an individual, but the question
of democratic rights in a democratic country. Of course, our
friend, Walter Winchell, was on the air immediately in an endeavor to vindicate himself. What reports you have heard of his
broadcast, I do not know, but I made a point to listen, and he
was nowhere nearly as bad as before. The San Francisco press
unanimously took your case as the most prominent challenge of
the day. The San Francisco public at large rallied unanimously
to your cause. Every Labor Union involved in the presentation
of opera in San Francisco protested the ban. Your own AGMA
sent a telegram to the Board of Trustees of the Opera House,
completely supporting you as a person and as an artist, and
threatening to boycott the building if the ban stood. The Mayor
of San Francisco immediately called subsequent meetings. The
Board of Directors of the Opera Association announced at once,
(and this received nationwide notice) that if you did not ap-

pear, it would be forced to cancel its entire season. It has stuck to this decision. The battle has raged for two solid weeks. There have been front page stories in practically every newspaper in the country, including a large article in the New York Evening Sun with your picture a week ago Saturday.

Captain Rieber telephoned me at once, and he advised me the same as Max, that it would be better not to communicate anything to you until we knew definitely where things stood. There are several reasons for this, the first being that I was hopeful you would be so occupied with rehearsals in Salzburg, and so far removed from this unnecessary unpleasantness, that perhaps you would not hear about it at all until it was all over. Secondly, the situation changed so rapidly from day to day that it would have been completely impossible by cable to have kept you informed. Thirdly, and perhaps most important, I have been so thoroughly convinced that because all of the decent people in the community of San Francisco were so horrified by the behavior of a small minority, that eventually the stupid ban would be lifted and we would come through clean.

In the meantime, Captain Rieber himself had occasion to go to California, and I know he has worked in your behalf, as he telephones me every two or three days.

Max telephoned me this afternoon from New York to say that he had been informed that the season would proceed as planned, and I feel that more than ever, we have been vindicated and justified, and the important thing for you is to realize that decent people in this country are not going to be dictated to by a minority.

We will therefore plan for your arrival, as scheduled, around the fifth or sixth of September and within a few days I will finally get you off the program for your season.

Captain Thorkild Rieber's letter dated August 3, 1949

Dear Kirsten,

I am just back from San Francisco where I arrived about the time that all the "noise" with respect to your appearance at this Fall's opera season broke loose.

I do not want to tell you that I am responsible for the situation having been cleared up. However, all the principal people connected with the Opera Association, and for that matter with the War Memorial Opera House itself, happen to be very close friends of mine of long standing, and as a result I was called upon by the President of the Opera Association, Page Monteagle, Herman Phleger, Attorney for the Opera Association, Robert Miller, Ex-Mayor of San Francisco, Roger Lapham, Acting Mayor George Christopher (the Mayor was off on his vacation) and a dozen others.

As you can well imagine, it gave me a great deal of pleasure as well as satisfaction to set the San Franciscans right about everything that you had to go through because of a few vociferous swine in this country and in your own. The San Franciscans decided that they were not going to be pushed around by any pressure group, and by giving a little time to the situation and arranging for one of the Directors of the Opera Association to get out of town, making himself unavailable for the final vote, the whole thing was cleared up on Monday night.

Now, Kirsten, I think this has been a most fortunate occurrence for you. I believe that all of your enemies are licked for good and all and that on your arrival in San Francisco you are going to be treated by everybody as the lady and great person that you are; and of the many successful appearances you have made all over the world, the one in San Francisco is going to be right at the top.

I am sending a copy of this letter to Edwin McArthur in St. Louis, with whom I have had several telephone conversations and who I know has sweated blood for you.

I know that things are going well with you, and Ruth, Tex and I are looking forward to your arrival in this country.

All the best!

Sincerely,
Cap

Mme. Kirsten Flagstad
Festspielhaus
Salzburg, Austria

Kirsten was not spared the ugly news in Salzburg. She had even read a false account that her San Francisco contract had been canceled. Fortunately, Becky Hamilton was with her at the time; she needed support. On July 25, Becky wrote a complete and very fine explanation of Kirsten's situation to her good friend Robert Watt Miller, one of the most important members of the San Francisco Opera board. The matter of course was all settled before Becky's letter reached California, but I am sure that Mr. Miller was pleased to have this reassurance.

On July 30, Becky wrote me that Kirsten had been beside herself until my cable had come. What a state of mind for her to be in and before the all-important performances of *Fidelio*.

Kirsten arrived back in New York on September 9, went for a short visit to Else and Arthur in Madison, and then traveled on to San Francisco for her re-entry into the musical life of that city. Her first performance was again Isolde on September 30, and the reports were that she was received with unprecedented affectionate acclaim. Was the battle over? We thought so, but there was still one more battle ahead which none of us could possibly foresee.

During all this time the controversial storm over Kirsten continued at a furious pace. Public figures were jumping on and off the bandwagon by the dozens. Mary Garden gave a press interview on the subject. Miss Garden was always vocal about what she believed and thought, and at the time her praise was particularly welcome. I wrote to Kirsten in California on October 2, 1949: "Mary Garden certainly gave you a lot of fine publicity. It made all the papers, two of which I enclose."

Kirsten had several concerts on the coast that autumn, but I purposely did not go out there. It was better for me to stay clear of everything that spelled San Francisco Opera. To be sure I had many friends in that wonderful city, but I had been such a controversial person when Kirsten had last sung in the opera there that I myself preferred to stay out of sight. The only hardship for her was the necessity of rehearsing with different accompanists, and although she wrote me that they were all fine, she repeatedly told me how much she missed my being with her.

After the season in San Francisco and Los Angeles, I arranged to join her in Denver and to play a short tour of six or seven concerts in that part of the West. I flew out to Colorado and Kirsten flew from the coast the morning after her last performance with the opera company. Driving in from the airport in Denver, she gave me a welcome piece of news. It had been her intention to sing only the one season in San Francisco. But the day before we met, Mr. Merola had called on her and asked her please to return for another season. It would have been a great mistake for Kirsten to refuse and I was pleased when she told me that she had accepted. She could be fair too. She had acknowledged her great desire to sing in San Francisco again and she did not forget the battle the San Franciscans had waged for her. At the same time however, she told me she had written Horwitz that she would decline an invitation to return to Salzburg in 1950.

"Why?" I asked her.

"Do you think I really should go again?" she asked. "It will cost me a vacation in Norway."

I was blunt with her: "You'll be sorry if you don't. Another year your voice may be gone!"

And so she notified Horwitz that he could accept 1950 in Salzburg. She went there and had another notable success in *Fidelio*.

That little tour around Denver was a very happy one. She was never very comfortable on trains. Now she had gotten used to airplanes, but her favorite means of travel was always the automobile. She loved to sit in the front seat next to the driver. My good friend in Denver, Ira Rothgerber, had a big new car that he lent me for our entire stay and I drove Kirsten to all the engagements she had to fulfill. I remember that as we drove from Denver down to Colorado Springs she fairly gasped at the massive beauty of the Rocky Mountain range. It brought her much-needed relaxation.

Back in New York in December (she was shortly to leave for Europe), there was a most important secret meeting in her hotel. It was Edward Johnson's last season as general manager of the Metropolitan, and Rudolf Bing had already been announced as his successor. All this time, Max had been in constant touch with Bing about all the artists under his management, and naturally there had been extensive discussion of Kirsten's return to the Metropolitan. Reggie Allen was now an assistant general manager of the Company, and in the background played an influential part in the decisions made. It was determined that to avoid any speculation whatever, the matter of Kirsten's return to the Metropolitan would be kept a dead secret until Bing's formal announcement. At that time, it was already known to us, Kirsten herself would not be in the United States.

In any case, Max brought Bing to Kirsten's apartment in the Stanhope Hotel late one afternoon. Kirsten had insisted that I be present. She was immediately struck by Bing's straightforward and cordial approach. He must have known the difficulties of the past and we felt sure that Reggie himself, although not present at this meeting, had briefed Bing on the behavior of Edward Johnson. Bing made no reference at all to that situation. He simply told Kirsten that he would like to have her at the Metropolitan and asked if she would return.

"What would you like me to sing?" she asked.

Bing said that Bruno Walter was to be there to conduct *Fidelio*, that naturally there would be performances of *Tristan und Isolde,* and that he would like to present two cycles of the *Ring*.

Kirsten asked Bing directly what about his plans for the American soprano, Helen Traubel, particularly with regard to the *Ring* cycles. When Bing gave her to understand that he had planned for Kirsten to sing them both, she declined firmly and told him that one cycle would be all she would agree to sing. She made it very clear that she admired Miss Traubel, who in her absence had functioned with great distinction as the leading Metropolitan soprano in the German repertoire. She would not be put into the position of brushing her aside.

She made only one request of Bing: that she return to the Metropolitan in the part of Isolde. She correctly thought that her public would be pleased. The meeting was most pleasant, and when Max and Bing departed, both Kirsten and I almost collapsed with satisfaction—understandably, I think.

She left for Europe two or three days later and kept her word that she would await Bing's public announcement before telling a soul about all this. I myself told but one person—Peggy. There were some leaks, however, the origin of which we never knew. But in any case, at the end of January 1950, Bing held a formal press conference to make his announcements for his first season, and in *The New York Times* of January 31 there was a front-page story under the headline FLAGSTAD RETURN TO THE MET APPROVED. The article was written by the then music editor Howard Taubman, and he went into considerable historical detail about the Flagstad case, pro and con. Bing made it clear at that time, as he has ever since, that he was to be the boss. He established that if there was to be any shooting, it had better be aimed at him.

Before the announcement, Bing had not negotiated with either Helen Traubel or Lauritz Melchior. In the same issue of *The Times*, Miss Traubel's manager, the late James Davidson, complained bitterly on behalf of Miss Traubel. Melchior immediately got into the act, making preposterous demands on Bing such as a deadline for his contract to be renewed (all this reported in the papers). If not, he said—also according to the newspapers—he would not sing again at the Metropolitan. Bing was absolutely masterful. He again made it clear that he was the boss and very quickly it became known that Melchior would not be singing at the Metropolitan after that season. And, as a matter of fact, he did not. This was regrettable. Melchior was still in full command of his powers, and it would have been appropriate if Kirsten's return to the Metropolitan could have been the occasion of her being together again with him.

The Traubel affair eventually cleared, but not until after a good deal of dirty linen had been hung out publicly. And it was only natural that again Kirsten's enemies would try for another field day. At the time she was in Barcelona singing opera. On January 31 she wrote me that she had been called by a news service in London for her reaction to the Metropolitan announcement and the statement, later withdrawn, that Traubel would not sing there any more. Bing's words had not yet reached her, and she was depressed that she was again the center of a dispute, in spite of his well-laid plans and her own concern to honor their agreement of secrecy.

In this letter, having covered this unpleasant bit, she went on to a long list of typical Flagstad comments in methodical order, even itemized. She liked the idea of copying the beautiful blue velvet gown for our coming orchestra concert in Carnegie Hall on April 12. The previous December she had had made an unusually stunning gown of royal blue velvet. People actually gasped when she walked on the stage. Shortly after, she wore the same gown at a concert in Covent Garden, and my London friends wrote me that they thought for a moment when she appeared that the Queen herself had walked onto the stage.

Well, copies are not always successful. The replica for the spring concert was not of velvet, but of green taffeta and without doubt was one of the most horrible dresses ever seen on any stage. The audience gasped this time too, but from fright.

The case in Norway having been settled, both sides were appealing the decision and Stake was optimistic. Kirsten wrote how she loved Barcelona—the Opera House was beautiful and had the handsomest audiences she had seen anywhere.

"I have consented to be available Sept. and Oct. 1951," she continued. This was her commitment to Bernard Miles's Mermaid Theater for the first of her memorable performances of

Purcell's *Dido and Aeneas*. From then on we were to arrange all other engagements to accommodate this enterprise. Much correspondence continued, and feeling that she had had enough, I purposely kept much of the renewed gossip and dirt from her.

We were now facing what turned out to be the last of all our battles, after which there would be nothing more to fight for or to win. On March 9, 1950, the Norwegian newspaper in Brooklyn, *Nordisk Tidende,* printed a remarkable editorial in its columns. March 12 I wrote Kirsten: "What do you think of the enclosed from Nordisk Tidende of this past Thursday? Cap Rieber translated it to me over the telephone today." The English version of this editorial follows:

It Is Time to Put a Stop to This

From Oslo it is reported that Chat Noir's Variety Show has included Kirsten Flagstad in its gallery of persons which the show derides. The excellent Norwegian critic, Paul Gjesdal, in "Arbeiderbladet" draws the lines strongly against this. He says that it is about time to put a stop to such persecution.

We are tempted to shout that it is also time here in America, where Kirsten Flagstad's new contract with the Metropolitan Opera for the coming season—spring 1951—has resulted in evil-minded attacks against Kirsten Flagstad and against the Metropolitan's new manager, Rudolf Bing.

Radio commentator, Walter Winchell, has hurled out a pure lie, namely that Kirsten Flagstad was singing in Germany during the war. Billy Rose, who writes the column, "Pitching Horse Shoes," for a long list of newspapers, came out with such coarse insinuations against Manager Bing that "New York Herald Tribune" through its legal department was advised against printing the column. When Mr. Rose consequently announced that he would not renew his contract at its expiration in May, the "Herald Tribune" cut his column on the spot.

It is not true that Kirsten Flagstad sang in public within occupied territory during the war. There were several Norwegian artists who, with the blessing of the Germans, sang and played and conducted during the war years, and most of those continue to sing and play and conduct to this very day. The fact that Kirsten Flagstad did not let her voice be heard during the long years of the war is of the greatest importance in the case.

It is true that Kirsten Flagstad went to Norway after her home land was occupied by the Germans. Her departure caused no apparent commotion or indignation in American circles at a time before America had entered the war.

In *"Nordisk Tidende"* of April 17, 1941, we find the following item:

It is announced that the famous opera singer, Kirsten Flagstad, is soon to leave for Oslo. The trip is laid over [*sic*] Lisbon on the Yankee Clipper. This contemplated journey was announced from the Metropolitan stage by Lauritz Melchior, the Danish opera singer, last Saturday night after she had sung Isolde in "Tristan."

Kirsten Flagstad gave a little speech to the audience. "My dear friends," she said, "I am very happy to be able to take this trip home, but I know that I shall be still happier the day I return. I thank you all."

Kirsten Flagstad is expected back in New York again by September. Her contract with the Metropolitan Opera has been renewed. Her last trip to Norway was during the summer of 1939.

The war developed differently than many had expected. The Germans kept on gaining ground. In the fall of the same year

(1941) came the episode of Pearl Harbor and the United States entered the war.

After the war came the great trials of the traitors in Norway. They have lasted five years. There were ninety thousand Norwegians who belonged to the Nazi Party, including Henry Johansen, Kirsten Flagstad's husband, who was conspicuous as a war profiteer. He died before his case came up in court.

In Norway there are many strong spokesmen now in favor of stopping all persecution against those who did not stand on the side of the Allies.

In a leading article in "Aftenposten," under the title "Justice and Mercy" it is mentioned that "The years of the occupation are now water over the dam. People are dominated by a strong desire that there must be a stop to all this."—"The field that has been plowed by justice, needs a hand to sow mercy upon the furrows."

In connection with much of the human mess of the war years in Norway we are reminded of the strange funeral speech by the priest in Ibsen's "Peer Gynt." Lines like these emerge in memory:

> "He was short-sighted. Out beyond the circle
> of those most near to him he nothing saw.
> To him seemed meaningless as cymbals' tinkling
> Those words that to the heart should ring like steel
> His race, his fatherland, all things high and shining,
> Stood ever, to his vision, veiled in mist.
> It is not ours to search the heart and reins;—
> That is no task for dust, but for its ruler;—
> Yet dare I freely, firmly, speak my hope:
> He scarce stands crippled now before his God!"

During the war there were Norwegians of all possible shades, and outside Norway—right on Manhattan and in Brooklyn—

there were many relatives of the man, who Ibsen so sympathetically buried in the last act of "Peer Gynt." Five years after the war we can afford to say with the priest: "It is not ours to search the heart and reins; that is no task for dust but for its ruler."

Out of this war,—political excitement came—came Kirsten Flagstad with all her official papers in order. In connection with her visa her national loyalty was certified. And the St. Olav's decoration which she received from King Haakon in 1937, has not been revoked.

When she visited Norway last year, she was elected honorary member of the Norwegian Musical Society. Former honorary members of this society include the violinist, Arve Arvesen, the pianist, Fridtjog Backer-Grøndahl, Hildur Andersen, the Danish composer, Haakon Borreson, the Finnish composer, Jean Sibelius, and the conductor, Harald Heide.

Kirsten Flagstad has after the war been singing in London for the British Royalty, and we all have to admit that England had something to do with the war. In the British Isle [*sic*] she has also held concerts for the benefit of Jewish refugees.

It is almost laughable to listen to the hysterical tone which certain self-appointed moral guardians here in America are using. But the sad part is this—that they create sensation at the cost of truth. It is time to put a stop to this.

Kirsten Flagstad is an artist and a phenomenon which hardly occurs even once in a century. "She is our time's Caruso," says Manager Bing at the Metropolitan. In people's memory, in the history of music, on the gramophone recordings, she will live—long after a Walter Winchell's and a Billy Rose's high-salaries gossip is forgotten and buried.

Kirsten Flagstad will in years to come reach still further heights at the Metropolitan—on the stage where a few years ago she won lasting fame and where she rightly belongs.

Again she will create such miraculous moments when she

opens the mystic spring of music that we feel the eternal now
in her art—an art that lasts and that speaks its own language to
the heart—above the booming cannons and the market shouts
of peddlars and the sensations of the day.

In the letter with this enclosure, I went on to say: "It is
difficult, if not impossible to write you of the happenings here
and I am only sorry that you have seen some of the unfortunate
clippings. I have had two meetings myself with Mr. Bing, who,
you may be sure, is standing firm and you should also be sure
that every day you are gaining more and more friends and the
other side is continually losing."

Following Bing's press conference I wrote him on February
6, 1950:

The past ten days have afforded us all a great deal of interesting reading in the newspapers.

You are to be highly congratulated for your remarkable and
clear handling of the situation.

I doubt if there is anyone who knows Kirsten Flagstad anywhere nearly so well as I do. And I can assure you that when
she has read the clippings which I have just sent to her in
Europe, she will be highly pleased and grateful to you for your
attitude concerning her return to the Metropolitan.

He acknowledged my letter cordially on February 7 and, after
thanking me for my words of commendation, made clear he felt
the trouble was only beginning, but that he expected we would
see it through. I had to smile at the word "beginning." It was
beginning for him perhaps, but for us it was an old story.

Shortly afterwards, Bing telephoned me and asked me to
come to see him at the Metropolitan. When we met, he told

me of some of the troubles he was having and asked me to fill him in on the background of the controversy. I did. I knew pretty well what he must be facing and I admired his courage in the situation. A few days later he telephoned me again and asked me to call for another conference. This took place on March 3, 1950. He greeted me this time with a report of complaints he had received from Norwegian officialdom in Washington and then brought up the old and dreary subject of the concert programs Kirsten had sung there in 1940. I had thought that this exasperating matter finally had been laid to rest by my testimony in Norway. Bing went on to say that he considered this particular controversial program in exceedingly bad taste under the circumstances in 1940, and that whoever had made it up had been anything but wise. Without hesitation I confessed that I was the person who had not been "wise" and assured him that he had not heard the whole story. I continued that in a vain attempt to clear up the whole thing, Kirsten had issued a formal statement on the subject when she first came back to America in 1947. Naturally the statement never got a fair play in the papers, but I promised to Mr. Bing that I would send him a copy. Then he suggested that if Kirsten would write him a personal letter of explanation and confidence, that would be most helpful. I proposed that he call in his secretary, and that very day, March 3, 1950, in his office I dictated a letter which I assured him Kirsten would be willing to put into her own handwriting. It was as follows:

Dear Mr. Bing:

I was very happy to receive your letter, and I have been deeply sorry the last few weeks to hear account of the trouble which has been placed at your door in connection with my engagement next season at the Metropolitan.

I would like to say first that I am deeply appreciative of the stand you have taken regarding my engagement and as you are new in your position, it would not be possible for you to know my feeling in the enormous case which has been built up around me.

Throughout my entire life, both as a person and as an artist, I have only tried to behave in an honest and straight-forward manner, and it has been extremely difficult for me to face the accusations which have been heaped upon me. I have even at times been accused of being a disloyal Norwegian, and whereas there have been occasions that Norwegians at home and in various parts of the world have been unkind and unsympathetic to me, it has always been inconceivable to me to think that anyone would accuse me of disloyalty to my beloved homeland. I have tried repeatedly in public interviews to state that my main reason for going home from America in 1941 was for the purpose of being with my own Norwegian family and people. It has always distressed me that even the activities I participated in for Norwegian causes in America were always completely ignored.

Despite the bitterness of my critics, I love to come and to sing in America and I can tell you that I am looking forward to singing once again at the Metropolitan Opera House and you can count on me to do everything in my power to make your first season a fine success.

With cordial regards, I am

I waited while Bing's secretary typed the proposed letter. He then gave me a copy, which I still have, but asked that I wait a few days for him to give it more thought before I sent it to Kirsten.

On March 5, I wrote Bing again, as follows:

. . .

Mr. Rudolf Bing
Metropolitan Opera Association
Broadway at 39th Street
New York City, New York

Dear Mr. Bing:

The enclosed is a copy of a statement released by Madame
Kirsten Flagstad some months ago.

The facts stated by Madame Flagstad are true. The same
information was part of sworn testimony given by myself in
Norway in October, 1946, in response to questions precipitated
by reports of a derogatory nature from His Excellency, the Norwegian Ambassador to the United States, Mr. Morgenstierne.

With the exception of certain benefit concerts in which Madame Flagstad participated, two specifically for Norwegian relief, none of her recitals or concerts were arranged with any
regard for nationalism or politics.

We did not consider Madame Flagstad's program on November 27, 1940 in Washington D. C. incorrect. And we do not now
consider it wrong.

It is indeed unfortunate that His Excellency, the Norwegian
Ambassador, was embarrassed at this concert, but his embar-
rassment was in no possible way any responsibility of Madame
Flagstad or of anyone connected with her.

With kind regards,

                    Cordially yours,

                    Edwin McArthur

With this letter I enclosed a copy of the famous statement
which follows:

. . .

Statement by Kirsten Flagstad

I wish to make clear the actual facts about the concert I gave in Washington D. C. in 1940 when—it has been charged—I sang an all-German program and the Norwegian Ambassador "was embarrassed by the presence of the German Chargé d'Affaires."

During the thirteen months between January 1940 and February 1941 I was engaged five times to sing in Washington. On January 23, 1940 I sang my usual concert program in Constitution Hall, including a group of Scandinavian songs. On February 14, 1940 I appeared with the National Symphony Orchestra and my program included a group of songs by Norway's famous composer Grieg. I again sang with the National Symphony Orchestra July 31, 1940 when an all-Wagner program was requested. My third appearance with this orchestra within ten months took place November 27, 1940. My part of the program consisted of the aria "Leise, leise" by Weber, a group of Strauss songs and two arias from Wagnerian operas. On February 11, 1941 I sang a concert in Constitution Hall, and my program included Grieg's "Haugtussa" song cycle.

It has been stated that the Norwegian Ambassador, Mr. Morgenstierne, was embarrassed at the November 27, 1940 concert when he found himself in the box next to the German Chargé d'Affaires. Neither Mr. Morgenstierne nor the German Chargé d'Affaires was my guest. Both apparently purchased their tickets at the box office, the same as the rest of the audience. I never met nor had any contact with the German

Chargé d'Affaires or any representative of the German
government in the United States.

Bing obviously gave careful consideration to the letter I had
dictated in his office and which I had assured him Kirsten would
be willing to write. But it was not quite as strong or as apolo-
getic as he wished. On March 7, 1950, he wrote me and sent me
a draft of a letter that he felt would serve his purposes more
completely as coming from Kirsten. I knew immediately that
Kirsten would not be willing to write such a letter, and on
March 13, I had to write him as follows:

Since our meeting in your office on March 3rd, I have naturally given considerable thought to the subject of our discussion.
Thank you for your letter of March 7th with the enclosure of
suggestion.

I trust you will not be too disappointed when I tell you that
after completely reviewing the matters of the past few years I
cannot recommend to Madame Flagstad that she write a letter
such as you suggest. Throughout the years and months, as has
now been publicly stated in Nordisk Tidende, she has been
the victim of vicious and false accusations. She has maintained a
magnificent dignity and any sudden change on her part would,
in my estimation, not represent Flagstad sincerity.

I would like to take this opportunity, however, to tell you that
if at any time I can be of service to you, please do not hesitate
to call upon me.

Chapter XII

1950–1952

A N D   W H A T   O F   Kirsten during all of this? She was singing all over Europe and, when she received my letters of explanation, cabled me: "HAPPY ABOUT YOUR LETTER BUT UNHAPPY
PUBLICITY."

She arrived back in New York on April 8, 1950, from Milan,
where she had the most marvelous time singing the entire *Ring*
at La Scala with Furtwängler conducting. The first concert following her return was an orchestral concert in Carnegie Hall on
Wednesday evening, April 12. This was the first time New York-
ers had heard her with orchestra since 1941. We put on that
event ourselves—that is, no impresario took any responsibility. I
conducted the orchestra, which numbered ninety-five men,
mostly from the Philharmonic. It was an all-Wagner program.
As usual, the house was sold out, but to our shock and surprise,
even after all that time, Carnegie Hall was surrounded by
screaming pickets. Again we had to be spirited into the hall, and
I must say my heart was heavy. But her reaction was nothing
more than mild annoyance, and in the green room before going
on the stage, she asked me with a hearty laugh if those silly

people parading up and down outside didn't have anything better to do with their time. As usual, the faithful Marion and Elmer Jones entertained afterward, and that particular party was like a celebration of victory.

We then flew to San Francisco on the 14th and gave two concerts in the War Memorial Opera House on April 16 and 19. In the opera house from which she had been temporarily banned the previous year, she was now welcomed back and treated by everyone with the utmost affection and respect. I was glad to be there to see it. We went down to Santa Barbara for another recital on the 21st and had the pleasure of being house guests of another dear and loyal friend, Ganna Walska, the internationally famous woman who in addition to her own career has for years been one of the world's really great and generous patronesses of the arts. The following day we lunched with another old friend, the great actress Judith Anderson, and then continued on to Los Angeles for a Sunday matinée on April 23.

That afternoon as we approached the Philharmonic Auditorium in Los Angeles, I was horrified to see parading up and down in front of the hall another line of pickets. Fortunately, I knew the hall well and directed our chauffeur to take us to an unused side entrance. We slipped unnoticed into the auditorium. When Kirsten came out on the stage that afternoon, the entire audience rose not only in tribute to her, but also in protest against what was going on outside.

This was the very last time in her life that pickets ever appeared. I must say her detractors put up a long, fierce battle. But they were warring against an honest and decent woman, and it was always our conviction that they would lose.

In some of those concerts on the Pacific Coast that April, business was very bad. Even in Oakland, where she had previously had a packed house, she sang to a mere handful. But victory of a more important kind was really achieved on that trip, and it was an indescribable satisfaction to me that I could be there with her when this last physical evidence of protest appeared. There were to be threats in the future, especially when she returned to the Metropolitan the following January. But the real end of the battle came in California that April of 1950.

We had one very pleasant experience on that trip too. When we were in San Francisco, Kirsten was asked if she would go to the United States Army Post at the Presidio to sing for American servicemen. She accepted at once, and nowhere ever was she more cordially received and honored than she was that day by General Albert C. Wedemeyer and the men under his command.

There was one more day of interest while we were still in California. It will be remembered that in 1940 she had recorded in the RCA Victor Studios in Hollywood her favorite song cycle, Grieg's *Haugtussa*. Now, in 1950, long-playing records were a reality and she was prompted to record the cycle once again. So those ten years later we went to the same studio one afternoon and made the new recording. In 1956 when I went to London to make records for English Decca with Kirsten, she recorded the cycle again. It is of especial interest to connoisseurs of her art to listen comparatively to the three recordings of the same songs made at such intervals.

I left her in California in May to go to St. Louis and did not hear from her again until the end of the summer. By then she was in Europe once more. She eventually sent me a long letter from Salzburg with a typical beginning:

. . .

1 9 5 0 – 1 9 5 2

Salzburg Aug. 22nd, 1950

Dearest Edwin! If only thoughts could substitute letters, then you would have had many from me. I have no excuse, only my arm has been bad again, but have waited to get the programs from you and the English songs.

She had had the most wonderful time in Norway and had finally gotten all of her belongings from America. It had been a pleasure for her to unpack all her things and get them arranged. "I had things which I had entirely forgotten," she observed. She had been in Oslo for her birthday and gave the family party at the house of her stepson Frederick. The day she wrote me she was singing her fifth and last *Fidelio* in Salzburg, and she wrote me later that she thought she had been better this year even than last time. She was going back to Norway after the Salzburg Festival and would come directly to America from there. No mention now of trouble or concern about the future. Prayerfully all that was past.

When she got here, she immediately went off for a series of concerts in various parts of the country and her second postwar season in San Francisco. She was also able to spend Christmas with her children, who were living in Madison. But all thoughts were of course on her coming return to the Metropolitan. She wrote me on January 7 from Ames, Iowa, to arrange hotel accommodations for the Dusenberrys, who were also bringing young Sigurd with them. Tickets for the Metropolitan performances would be scarce, and we were to be grateful that Francis Robinson at the Metropolitan had put aside several pairs for Kirsten's use.

A few days before the return to the Metropolitan came a happy surprise. Kirsten had a telephone call from Mr. Anneus

Schjoedt, the same great lawyer who had been of such help in Norway. Mr. Schjoedt was in America on business. I called him at once, and it was a great satisfaction that we were able to secure for him four seats for Kirsten's first postwar performance at the Metropolitan. It was fortunate that he was here to witness firsthand the affection and esteem awaiting her from her loyal American public at the Metropolitan.

When she returned to New York some ten days before the Metropolitan, she was in superb vocal form, but in a tense and difficult frame of mind. She chose to turn even upon me. I am not always innocent of course—perhaps I had been *too* active and "possessive," as I had been described in some quarters. But when Kirsten wanted to put the brakes on even a person like me, she did not know how to do it graciously. Even the simplest things that had been routine for years annoyed her. She seemed to want me out of the way. She curtly instructed me to stay out of the disposition of her tickets. And when I told her of course that Marion and Elmer Jones were planning their usual party following the performance, she told me to tell them not to bother—she had other plans. I was deeply hurt by this. Not only had Marion and Elmer already invited all of Kirsten's close friends who had stood by during the terrible days, but also Geraldine Farrar, living in quiet retirement in Connecticut, was planning to make one of her extremely rare visits into New York and to the Metropolitan to hear Kirsten again. It was so terribly wrong of her to so rudely brush aside those who had shared the long ordeal with her.

But I followed instructions to the last detail, even though I knew in my heart that Kirsten did not mean everything she was saying or doing. No question, she was nervous about the Metropolitan. She had no need to be nervous. But she was human too, with her share of frailties.

Edwin McArthur's Metropolitan Opera debut, February 17, 1941

Elisabeth Rethberg, Flagstad, Geraldine Farrar, Marion
Telva, Peggy McArthur, Silvermine, Connecticut, April
1947

Karin Branzell, Flagstad,
Rose Bampton, New York,
February 1952

Now a stream of threatening letters began over her return to the Metropolitan. I succeeded in keeping most of them from her, and she never saw or knew of the worst. I am glad of that. One woman sent a letter threatening to throw acid in her face as she entered the stage door. I was not really worried, and because, as I have said, the worst had been kept from her, she was completely unconcerned.

I decided that this time, following instructions, I would stay out of the way completely. When Max telephoned me a week before the date and asked if I had plans for getting Kirsten to the opera house as I had always done before, I told him simply that this time it was up to him and the Metropolitan and I would have nothing to do with it. Peggy and I went to a dinner party and arrived at the opera house about twenty minutes before the performance was to begin that memorable night. It was January 22, 1951, and the opera was *Tristan* as agreed. As soon as we had entered the house, I searched out Reggie Allen and he took me backstage to Kirsten's dressing room. It was a strange feeling not to be entering the great building through the stage door for a Flagstad performance and to be in the strange position too of being taken back to her dressing room. She was like a racehorse waiting for the starting bell. It gave me a glow of warmth to have her tell me that she would have been heartbroken if I had not come to her before she once again stepped out on that stage.

It was obvious that the management was concerned that night. It appeared to be no accident that Thomas Murphy, at that time Police Commissioner of New York City, was prominent in the audience. Even when Reiner was conducting the prelude, the less obtrusive house lights were left on and burned so until the curtain had risen and Kirsten had sung her first phrases. Voices in the audience called out "Welcome home" as she began. There were no pickets and no acid was thrown in her face at the stage door.

I really remember very little of that performance. All evening I was living through the anguish we had endured. In my mind I returned to the year of crisis before Kirsten had left that stage to return to a Europe flaming with war. The long separation had left a void never to be filled. I thought of the volumes of correspondence we had carried on right after the war, my own trip to Norway and the difficult days in the Norwegian Court of Law, and, most tragic of all, the years of strife we had gone through together in America. A woman of less courage and clean faith could not have won against such a dirty campaign. But she and I, affectionately supported by a handful of unforgettable friends, had carried on.

"Tonight," I told myself, "it is over. There will be no more threatening letters—no more pickets—no more vicious stories."

She was there on the stage where she had had her greatest triumphs in the palmy earlier days. She had been forced to the lowest depths. And now she was back again victorious, and I think it is only natural that I had tears in my eyes when, after the final scene, Kirsten came alone before the curtain for one of the greatest ovations ever witnessed in that house.

Shortly before her return to the Metropolitan a letter came which left her open-mouthed with astonishment and amusement. Ten years before, it will be recalled, she had contributed her services to the New York Philharmonic at a Pension Fund concert. The Philharmonic was now asking her to repeat her generosity. This organization, like many others, had stood aside and allowed the battle to be won before acknowledging her existence. The request has always seemed to me the rankest of opportunism, among other things. But I am glad that Kirsten let bygones be bygones. She accepted, and, with Bruno Walter conducting, appeared again for the Pension Fund with the Philharmonic in Carnegie Hall on February 5, 1951.

At this very same time began a friendship of great warmth and affection which was to last until Kirsten died. In the first postwar years in London she had met and become very friendly with the famous English playwright and composer Ivor Novello. Kirsten told me about her new "fan" and she was proud of Novello's interest in her now important new enterprise, Bernard Miles's Mermaid Theatre. Novello, by virtue of his great prominence in the theatrical life of London, brought many assets to the theatre, so Bernard himself told me. Novello visited America every year, usually at the height of the theatrical season. When he was here in the winter of 1951, he asked Kirsten if he might bring his good friend Katharine Cornell to meet her.

I confess that I was cross with Kirsten that she didn't invite me to tea the day of the meeting. I would so like to have met Novello and would have been as thrilled as she to have met Katharine Cornell. Shortly after this, Miss Cornell and her famous husband, Guthrie McClintic, invited Kirsten, Else, and Arthur to dinner.

At that time Kirsten met Francis Robinson, Assistant General Manager of the Metropolitan for the first time and she also came to know someone else who was destined to become an important part and interest of her life, the well-known playwright Nancy Hamilton. Thus began an affection which for Kirsten's remaining years became one of the most important of her life. Katharine Cornell and the brilliant circle of people Kirsten thus came to meet and know provided a new and vital interest of a kind she had never before experienced. It was only unfortunate that there were times when she could see and think of only her new friends and neglected the old ones. Even Captain Rieber and his daughter were forgotten, as were many others. These melancholy observations are only to show that, like everyone else, Kirsten had her failings, despite the foolish claims of those who idolized her, and also that she was stubbornly determined to have her own way.

Katharine, Guthrie, and Nancy entertained Kirsten royally and not only brought the interests of their fabulous careers into her life, but also created for her a new audience within her own world. In later years, when she would literally allow months to go by without writing a line to either Else or myself, she would say to us: "Why should I write you? There is nothing new to tell and besides I am sure of your affection."

That was very true. But nonetheless it was increasingly galling for even us to be dismissed in favor of newer friends. Not that we were ever really "dismissed" of course. Events in later years proved that, as will be seen.

The 1951 season at the Metropolitan was a triumph for Kirsten in every way. I think most of all she enjoyed doing *Fidelio* there again and with Bruno Walter, but needless to say, even more important than making music was her wholehearted satisfaction that she had won the battle.

Eventually the time came when Max had to know something about her plans for the following season. The three of us— Kirsten, Max, and I—decided to repeat a custom we had formed years before: dinner at Lüchow's whenever plans were to be discussed. At that year's dinner she definitely and firmly said to Max that she was going to sing only that season at the Metropolitan and that nothing would make her change her mind. Even Max did not agree with her that night and tried to point out the folly of the decision. For one thing, as she had agreed to sing two seasons in San Francisco, she should at least do the same for the Metropolitan. But she was fiercely determined on this point and gave him permission to arrange the following season only if the Metropolitan was left out.

It goes without saying that it was difficult and unpleasant for Max, but a very short time later he had booked a very solid tour of concerts. Then, in face of that, Bing succeeded in persuading Kirsten to reverse herself and return for a second season. I am not sure that Bing's intention was to have Kirsten for only the five performances of Gluck's *Alcestis* (in English) that were ultimately arranged. It has always been my impression that in holding out this bait—she had been eager to do the work again for some time—he had hoped to have some more performances of Wagner.

Kirsten told me that she was weakening in her decision about a second season at the Metropolitan, but she told me as well that if she did go back it would only be for *Alcestis*. I urged her not to do this second season on such a condition. First of all, I was tired of her habit of changing her mind; secondly, I felt that after she had given such a firm decision to Max and he had finally without any resistance been able to book a wonderful tour, it was grossly unfair to put him in such a position. But mainly I thought *Alcestis* was a completely unsuitable vehicle for Kirsten's operatic farewell at the Metropolitan. I felt then, and feel still, that she should have said good-bye to her New York public in one of her great Wagnerian parts.

About this time we were scheduled for a recital in Pittsburgh. On the train she invited me into her drawing room for a drink and told me rather flatly that she had gone alone that evening to Bing's office at the Metropolitan. She had formally agreed to return to the Metropolitan for five performances of *Alcestis* the following season. When I asked her how she expected Max to adjust the already committed bookings, she shrugged it off with an air that he would have to meet her wishes. Typically Flagstad! That Max had his difficult times, complete to a highly unpleasant correspondence with Bing, was of little consequence to Kirsten. And a few days later when Max wired her and me of the difficulties he was having and asked her consideration and support, she simply stepped aside and left him to work it out.

But now we were in England again. Kirsten had another Albert Hall concert on April 17 on this 1951 trip. This was followed by another and more enlightening meeting with Bernard Miles. The Miles family was at home in London, and the day we arrived we went out to their big house in St. John's Wood. I remember that they had the most wonderful huge old grand piano and we were able to rehearse.

On the property in the back was a large barn which in earlier years had been St. John's Wood School. Already Bernard had aroused Kirsten's interest in the founding of the Mermaid Theatre and had described to her his plans of transforming this very barn into an authentic Elizabethan theater. The work had not yet been started on the building, and although he carefully explained and described the plan, I must confess that I could not picture how it would be. I have only regret that I did not see the theater when the project was realized. Reports had it that it was quite charming and that the plays, opera performances, and concerts were excellent. The theater was small, seating less than two hundred persons. Bernard's plans sounded wonderful, and I could only be pleased that Kirsten was to have this diversion.

But never in my wildest dreams would I have believed that day in 1951 that Bernard Miles would succeed in persuading Kirsten to make his little theater the setting for her final farewell to the operatic world some two years later.

The mock contract drawn up by the Mermaid Theatre for Kirsten is an amusing document, and Bernard Miles so described it to me himself. But Kirsten took it very seriously and publicized it widely. Her compensation for singing consisted of living quarters with the Miles family and generous portions of "stout." The signatures were "sealed with a kiss." All very nice and affectionate as a private and personal document. But I thought it very silly to make it known to the public at large.

Kirsten sang three seasons—1951, 1952, and 1953—in Bernard Miles's little theater. She had publicly announced that her final performance would be there on September 28, 1952. But Bernard was clever, as others had been before him, and he got her to change her mind. The third season of the Mermaid Theatre was in a new locale, The Royal Exchange in London, and there during the celebration of Queen Elizabeth's coronation, Kirsten finally made her farewell to the operatic world on July 5, 1953. For the record, a permanent Mermaid Theatre is now one of the most important theaters in London. It is down in the City of London at Puddle Dock, and its present enormous success is a kind of tribute to the memory of Kirsten Flagstad, who was so important a person in its founding.

That season of 1951, to the regret of the Covent Garden management and of the London public, she made her farewell at that great opera house in *Tristan und Isolde* on June 30. After twenty-one curtain calls she spoke to the audience: "I want to take things more easily; please forgive me."

At least she gave Covent Garden the consideration of a few farewell remarks, a graciousness that she later denied the Metropolitan Opera and her American public.

Triumphs of every sort still came to her. On September 5, after I had returned to America, she made her reappearance

275

as a singer in Norway, an event of the highest meaning for her. The audience completely lost all restraint and gave her a shouting reception. The Oslo newspapers on the following day were rapturous in unanimous acclaim. She wrote me that she was as overjoyed that this had happened while her mother was still alive as for her own sake.

Then in a letter from London dated October 4, 1951, after thanking me first for a birthday handkerchief I had sent, she wrote that the entire case in Norway had been settled out of court and that all conditions have been agreed. The long ugliness was finally over.

Her season in America was to start with a concert in Englewood, New Jersey, on January 7, 1952, but she was determined to come early enough to have at least a short visit with Else and Arthur and little Sigurd in Madison. On December 21, 1951, she wrote me: "Oh Edwin—I am longing to see you. It is such a long time. I hope Peggy dear is well and happy, please give her my love. Lots of love and devotion to you! Kirsten."

She was to arrive at Idlewild Airport early on the morning of Sunday, December 30, 1951, and I had discovered that if her plane was on time we could have an hour together before I put her on a plane for Madison. The plan worked, and she let it be known that the winter season of 1952 she was about to begin would definitely be her last in the United States. I knew that in December 1953 she would retire, after forty years of singing, and I earnestly hoped she would now keep her word. She had always said she wanted to retire before it was too late, and somewhat to the annoyance of certain friends and fans I had encouraged her in this. I am glad that she did not join that depressing throng of artists who appear long after they have lost their powers and are remembered for sadly inadequate farewells.

During the heavily booked season three important events were to take place in New York City:

1. Her final song recital in Carnegie Hall on February 1.

2. Her three concerts with the New York Philharmonic Symphony on March 20, 21, and 23, with Bruno Walter conducting. In addition to singing with the orchestra, she was also to sing the five Wesendonck Songs of Wagner accompanied by Dr. Walter at the piano.

3. Her farewell performance at the Metropolitan Opera on Tuesday evening, April 1.

The night that we drove to Carnegie Hall for the season's recital I had no reason to expect that it would be different from all the former occasions we had had there, unless, possibly, it was to be more pleasant. Kirsten seemed very much her usual self. But at the end of the recital, before the encores, she raised her hand and announced that she would make a few remarks. Unfortunately, they were not recorded, but I assure the reader he may trust this paraphrase:

A year ago I announced definitely my retirement. Then Mr. Bing suggested five performances of *Alceste* at the Metropolitan, and as a woman I reserved the right to change my mind and am looking forward to those five performances. I am also happily anticipating three concerts next month in this hall with the New York Philharmonic conducted by Dr. Bruno Walter. I must say, however, that the highlight of every season in my career has been my annual Carnegie Hall recital for my own faithful and affectionate audience—you. Tonight is a very special recital, for after long and careful consideration, I have decided that this will be my last in Carnegie Hall and in New York City. I am going to say "good-bye" at the end of this concert with three songs, but before singing these songs, I want to pay one particular tribute. There are many to whom I would like to express my appreciation, but you will understand that time does not permit mention of all. However, to the one who for seventeen years has been my faithful accompanist for almost a thousand recitals and so many orchestral and operatic performances as a conductor, but—even more than as a musician—has been an unbelievably faithful and loyal friend, particularly in these latter years when I have been so alone, who has shown a devotion, loyalty, and affection far beyond what any woman could ever hope for or expect, I must take this opportunity of paying public and affectionate tribute to Edwin McArthur.

I was overwhelmed. I had always made so many decisions for Kirsten, written so many of her letters, and told her on so many occasions what I thought that she should say, that I was nonplussed by her having done this completely on her own. I could scarcely get up from the piano bench to acknowledge the applause of the public and then step over and kiss her on the brow.

The three songs as the finale—all by American composers—were not important musically, but they were very important for the meaning that Kirsten gave to the words. The first was my own "We Have Turned Again Home," with a touching text by Charles Hanson Towne. The first line of this song reads: "Heart, oh my heart, we have turned again home." The way she sang it suggested the coming days of retirement were a turning home to rest and peace. Then came Oley Speaks's song "Morning," almost a signature song for her by this time. She concluded with Ernest Charles's charming little ballad "When I Have Sung My Songs." Its text had particular meaning for that occasion: "When I have sung my songs to you, I'll sing no more." Then she took countless curtain calls, and as usual we were outside halfway down the block having our car stopped for the invariable shot of brandy while the audience in Carnegie Hall was still on its feet roaring for one more song.

The farewell performance at the Metropolitan took place on April 1. Peggy was at the Opera house in time for the performance. I was there early, having taken Kirsten down, and I remember dining quite alone that evening in the Sherry Room. I wanted to be alone and not to have to talk to anyone. It was in that very restaurant that Kirsten had given her great party for the entire personnel of the Metropolitan when she had celebrated her twenty-fifth anniversary as a singer. It was in that room that she herself had been present at the farewell party for Lucrezia Bori. It was there that I had myself been host to her and to Frances Alda. It was there that her husband and I had had many long talks and had smoked many cigars together. It was her final night as a singer in the grand old opera house, and on that particular night it was good for me to be there alone with poignant memories.

She had expressed such satisfaction with the casting Bing had arranged for this production of *Alcestis*. She herself had suggested that the young American tenor Brian Sullivan would be excellent. And Brian did sing four of the five performances. This was another indication of her continuing interest in American artists. In earlier years she had shown a keen interest in the great baritone, Julius Huehn, and in many other American singers as well. Later she was often to speak with enthusiasm of the singing of two other Americans in the *Alcestis* cast, Lucine Amara and the late Ann Bollinger.

Also in *Alcestis* there were several beautiful children to whom Kirsten had become attached. Around four o'clock the day of this final performance she telephoned me and said: "Edwin, I must remember those sweet children. Please do something for me about it."

I went to a confectioner's near our house and arranged a fancy basket for each. That night they were all brought to her dressing room and it was touching to see her affection as she distributed her little remembrance to each with an embrace. I would like to think that they all kept the baskets in memory of the great lady.

When the performance of *Alcestis* was finished, a large part of the company, headed by Mr. Bing, directors of the Opera Guild, and officers and board members of the Metropolitan Opera Association came onto the stage to honor her. There was a large table with various mementos which I later described as "Kirsten's Metropolitan hardware." The principal speech and presentation came from George Sloan, chairman of the Association. Brian Sullivan graciously took Kirsten by the hand and brought her to the center of the stage. But as I sat there in the Metropolitan and listened to Mr. Sloan and watched the proceedings, I was quite sure what was going on in Kirsten's mind, and I remember very well what was going on in my own. We had been through days of triumph and we had been through days of tragedy which would have been greatly alleviated if that very same Mr. Sloan and that very same Metropolitan Opera had come forward with a friendly and helping hand in the grief-laden days of trouble. It is so easy to be fair-weather friends. It is not so easy to be friends in time of sorrow and it is to the discredit of the Metropolitan Opera Association that Kirsten Flagstad was allowed to wage a bitter battle which could have been avoided had they given her their support. It might have been better if Kirsten later on had not expressed her real feelings about that night. But she spoke the truth, I think, when she said that she had no feelings whatsoever of sentiment or

regret at leaving the Metropolitan. Kirsten made no response to
Mr. Sloan's remarks, and it has often been said that the reason
was that she was too shaken emotionally. That most certainly
was not the case. She was indeed proud and happy to have sung
two more seasons at the Metropolitan. But it was only natural
that she was bitter that those in that institution had left her to
fight her desperate battle alone. The curtains fell without Kirsten's saying a single word.

As had been my custom for years, I went backstage to her
dressing room and we had a final drink of brandy with Jennie
Cervini, the much-beloved wardrobe mistress. We gathered together her many bouquets of flowers and all of the "hardware,"
and, with the aid of two amiable stage doormen, forced our way
through a crowd of several hundred people, both happy and
sad, who waited for her at the exit. We got into the limousine,
and my Peggy had a special supper at our house. That night we
had only Kirsten's relatives—her daughter, her son-in-law, her
brother-in-law and his wife—and ourselves.

One of the things that final night of which she was extremely
proud was the visit she had backstage from the Honorable
Trygve Lie, then Secretary-General of the United Nations.
When she told me about it, I was reminded of an item which
had appeared in *Newsweek* on July 21, 1947:

NORWAY—UNPOPULARITY POLL

Last week, the editors of a Norwegian weekly conducted a private poll to determine the most unpopular
of their countrymen, excluding quislings. Two ladies
won hands down: Sonja Henie and Kirsten Flagstad.
Also ran: UN Secretary-General Trygve Lie. Norwegians rightly or wrongly blame Lie for promising
bases in Spitzbergen to Russia.

I pointed this out to Kirsten, and we agreed that she was in excellent company.

After the final Metropolitan performance two recording sessions for Victor were scheduled which turned out to be among the happiest recording experiences she had anywhere. At her February concert in Carnegie Hall she had sung for the first time Schumann's incomparable song cycle *Frauenliebe und Leben* and had surprised everyone, myself included, by the beauty and subtlety of this performance. She asked if she might record it. Naturally, Victor was delighted and used the occasion to record many other songs.

The success of these sessions was owing very much to the patience, tact, and graciousness of Victor's director of classical recording, Richard Mohr. He brought a personal enthusiasm to his work which had always seemed lacking in his predecessor, Charles O'Connell. He was demanding both technically and musically, but his quiet, sincere admiration for Flagstad was more than apparent. I have often thought how much happier her American recording history could have been if Richard Mohr had been in charge earlier.

There was still another happy memory of this last season here. When Else, Arthur, and Sigurd came for those final weeks, Katharine Cornell and Guthrie McClintic entertained them lavishly for a weekend at their country home. Along with the Reginald Allens, Francis Robinson, and two or three others, Peggy and I were invited to go for supper. When the car came to our apartment to pick us up, I took along a small briefcase, unnoticed by anyone. When we arrived at the McClintic home, the party was already in gay progress. There was a huge fire in the fireplace and everything was warm and cozy. We new arrivals were immediately offered the expected glass of champagne. But before we took a sip I said: "Now Kirsten, before we go any further, I think it would be nice if you would sing *Haugtussa* for Katharine and Guthrie and all of us here."

Kirsten cried out: "Oh, I can't possibly. And besides, we haven't the music."

I could have played them from memory, but I was taking no chances. "Oh yes, we have," I said. I had slipped the score into my mysterious and unremarked little briefcase.

Kirsten could not protest.

Those fortunate to be there that Sunday will never forget the way Kirsten, standing by the piano, gave a little story in her own simple way to summarize the Norwegian text. I had played that cycle with her many many times in public and private, but I cannot remember that she ever gave quite so poignant a rendition of it as on that Sunday afternoon.

Easter Sunday afternoon, April 13, 1952, Kirsten sang what proved to be her actual farewell recital to America. It was in Orchestra Hall, Chicago. Else, Arthur, and Sigurd came from Madison, and Kirsten thoughtfully invited Cleone Pottenger to come from California for the weekend. The day before the concert, Kirsten again entertained that great lady from the *Chicago Tribune*, Claudia Cassidy, whose support had been so loyal and constant. On the Sunday afternoon, as usual an hour before the concert, I went to her hotel suite for what we thought at that time would be our last rehearsal together for a concert— and for my last official private rendition at the piano of "Lovely to Look At." All through the years her generosity had been indescribable. It is a wonder I was able to play that afternoon concert at all after her having insisted there in her apartment on pressing a check for $5,000 into my hand as what she said was "a far too little material token of love and appreciation."

Once again the concert was a delight, and again she made a short farewell speech, this time designed specifically for her

Chicago public. They had always been particularly dear to her. Then we flew back to New York, and two days later Peggy and I took her to the airport, where alone we saw her off for Europe. We hoped of course that our plans for a meeting the following year would be successful, but we never realized that her voice would ever be heard again in America.

Chapter XIII

1952–1962

WHEN KIRSTEN had arrived in New York in December 1951, she had pointedly failed to tell me of her latest and most grandiose family plan. She had conceived the idea of having Arthur and Else move to Norway: Arthur would become a member of the firm of Henry Johansen, Ltd., with the specific responsibility of looking after Kirsten's interests, and would at the same time build a career for himself as a businessman in Scandinavia.

When I heard of this plan, I was speechless with astonishment. It was inconceivable to think that a typical Western American boy could be transplanted to a place like Norway and thrust into a business about which he knew nothing, and which, moreover, would be conducted in a language entirely incomprehensible to him.

Kirsten's motives for the proposal seemed clear. Her career was coming to a close, and like all divas, she had feasted for years on public adulation. I am sure that she had a desperate fear of loneliness and boredom in her later years. Having her daughter and family close at hand in Norway would conveniently solve this problem for her. But even then I felt strongly that the Dusenberrys' own happiness and welfare were being completely ignored. On several occasions during the winter I raised the question with her, but in the same way as she had succeeded in persuading Else and Arthur that everything would be just wonderful, she persuaded me that the plan would work, or that there was at least some hope it would.

Else and Arthur did not agree immediately. It was Else who at first emphatically said "No." Already she was proud of being an American, and she balked at the thought of leaving the United States. I also believe she wanted her son to be brought up as the fine American boy he is. But Kirsten painted a rosy picture of the future, and it must not be overlooked that she also held important purse strings. She had always been generous to Else and Arthur, and there was no reason to believe that she could not and would not continue. For weeks the young couple talked of nothing else, and finally, and I believe reluctantly, agreed to move to Norway.

And so they broke up their home in Madison, sold their belongings, and, after a visit with Arthur's family in Montana and a few days with Peggy and me in St. Louis, sailed in the latter part of July. They were to have a visit first with Kirsten at her home in Kristiansand and then very shortly Arthur was to take up his duties. All sorts of promises had been made to them, not the least of which was that happy living quarters would be secured, despite the Norwegian housing shortage at that time, and that their general standard of living was to be measurably raised.

When their boat arrived in Kristiansand, Kirsten and Stake came out in a motor launch to meet them. Else's grandmother had come down from Oslo for her first glimpse of her great-grandson as he was growing and to give the children a special greeting. Everything was serene—but only for a matter of days. Within the week, Kirsten was complaining bitterly of the playful noise her grandson made in the garden. She then announced without warning that she was leaving shortly on an extensive tour of concerts and that they would not be seeing her for a long time. When Arthur tried to find out when he was to begin his work, the replies from the firm were evasive. Kirsten left. After six weeks of waiting at Kristiansand, the Dusenberrys finally moved north to Oslo. But the bare problem of shelter had not been solved, and although Kirsten herself had an apartment in Oslo which was then unoccupied, the Dusenberrys were not permitted to stay in it. Kirsten never did make any explanation of this. Finally, they were taken to a house where they saw themselves installed in a three-room shack heated only by stoves which Else had to stoke herself. They were miles from the city, and as a final insult, there was not even indoor plumbing.

Arthur quickly discovered that the possibility of any future in the firm of Henry Johansen, Ltd., was remote. We have never found out who, if anyone, openly opposed his being considered as part of the business, but there was no doubt at that time that Kirsten's plan was meeting resistance. Meanwhile, she herself seemed content to leave her "little family" to shift for itself.

To her dismay, Else found any direct contact with her mother completely impossible. Everything had to be arranged through

Stake. That had been the order when she was a child, but now that she was a grown woman it was stupid and unbearable. I believe that Else and Arthur might have stuck out even this situation if Kirsten had shown anything like a warm and motherly affection for them. But she was off, incommunicado, in other countries and Else, naturally, was filled with consternation over the entire project.

Finally the Dusenberrys decided they had had enough and determined to return to America. Else wrote her mother of this decision. Kirsten received the letter in London, I was told. She was in the midst of her tour, and the first that I heard of the matter directly from her was in a letter from Lisbon on November 18. She had been shocked to learn that her children wanted to go back to America. She wrote me she had not answered the letter, but had spoken twice with Else on the telephone—"but only on the surface, so to speak, and I feel I must only keep quiet and let them do what they want."

Before they left Norway, a near-tragedy occurred which seemed to epitomize this whole disastrous episode. A fire broke out in the Dusenberrys' house and young Sigurd was seriously burned. The scars did not heal for many months, and he was still in bandages when we had them in our home that November. They were a crushed and broken family. But they were a determined family too: from then on their lives were going to be their own. Else, with bitterness and finality, declared that her mother, no matter who she might be in music, would never again have the chance to rule and ruin her life.

Before starting out again for Madison, they spent hours with Peggy and myself in our apartment. We let them talk it out, and I tried my best to piece everything together. I knew that Kirsten was singing all over Europe, and I thought of how sad she must be too. At the same time, I could not help but feel that this time she was completely to blame for this wretched fiasco, although of course she would never have admitted it. But for all that, my heart went out to her. She was still facing the responsibilities of a career, after all. When the earlier break with Else had come in the nineteen thirties, Kirsten still had had her strong husband to care for her and to comfort her. But now he was gone. It seemed that her life would *never* be free of strain and grief. Even at this time some shreds of political antagonism against her cropped up. And now again a rupture with her own family.

So that I would have the Dusenberrys' story clear in my head, I asked Arthur to write me the details as systematically as he could. After he had done so, and after I had also received several heartbroken messages from Kirsten, I wrote her that it was apparent that there had been a great misunderstanding. I proposed that I fly over to meet her in Europe for the Christmas holidays and go over the whole affair with her. I really was the only person in the world who had the confidence of both sides.

On November 28, 1952, I wrote her:

> I think it is tragic for you to have a rift between yourself and your very own children and grandchild and I would propose to do everything possible to mend the hurt feelings.
>
> I really question in my own mind if you know exactly what the situation was and is in Norway as concerns your very own interests and I would like to satisfy myself that you are on the right track.
>
> According to your schedule you are finished in London the 14th. Could you go to Zurich then and have me meet you there? If you would rather, I could come to London, but personally I would rather see you in Zurich at the Dolder Grand.

Kirsten disposed of this idea with a curt cable to the effect that she and Stake were unaware of any misunderstanding. She

288

asked me to write details of my discussion with Arthur and Else.

I am glad that I did not attempt to put into writing the details of my conversations with Else and Arthur. It would have been difficult if not impossible to set down such emotions, and some of their tales of what had gone on in Norway should never be recounted. I have always been sorry that Kirsten did not allow me to attempt a reconcilation that winter. But Kirsten Flagstad had many curious characteristics and among them was a massive unwillingness to admit that she might ever be wrong. In her heart she must have known that she was at least partly to blame for the family break. But she simply would not face up to it. It was easier for her to brush it aside and to feed on the sympathies of those who offered them.

But deep down in her being she loved her daughter, her son-in-law, and of course her pride and joy, Sigurd. A few months later, after her formal retirement, she came again to America. She arrived in New York aboard the S.S. *Oslofjord* on December 9, 1954. Naturally, I met her at the boat. Meanwhile, Else and Arthur had moved out to Phoenix, Arizona, where they still live, successfully and happily established. After only a short stay in New York, Kirsten left to visit her "little family" for the first time in their new surroundings. She and I never discussed the Dusenberrys' regrettable Norwegian episode, and I do not think she and Else ever talked about it, either. The crisis was over, and the matter was never to come up again.

These personal tragedies were hard, but Kirsten never seemed to succumb to private grief. And fortunately there were still new and interesting things for her to do. One of her major satisfactions was that Richard Strauss had chosen her to give the world *première* of his now famous "Four Last Songs," the only condition being that there be a first-class conductor. The "first-class

conductor" was none other than Wilhelm Furtwängler, her favorite of all. The *première* of these lovely, autumnal songs took
place at a concert in Albert Hall, London, on May 22, 1950. She
had always had not only the greatest admiration for Strauss, but
a pleasant professional memory of him as well. In 1933, when
singing her first season at Bayreuth, she had been chosen as the
soprano soloist for a performance of Beethoven's Ninth Symphony and Richard Strauss had conducted the performance.

She had never sung any Strauss opera parts, and that seemed
not quite right to her. In the spring of 1952 she decided to ask
Horwitz to arrange some concerts in Germany, where, except
for the two seasons at Bayreuth, she had never sung. Then she
decided to use the occasion of her Berlin appearance to sing
some Strauss operatic excerpts and did two big sections of *Elektra*. She wrote me on June 8 that "Hamburg went fine, interesting audience. But Berlin was more thrilling."

She then went to Helsinki for a great Sibelius Festival, and
for the occasion had learned some songs she had never sung
before. She wrote me that "the great event was the visit to
Sibelius yesterday. He had asked to see me. He is nearly 87 and
he is unbelievable. We were there in his cozy home for nearly
two hours and we talked about everything. He hears perfectly,
reads without glasses, walks briskly, only his hands are shaky.
His memory is excellent. In all, that was a wonderful experience
and well worth the long trip to Finland alone."

For a long long time she had discussed the plans for her
formal farewell in Oslo in December 1953, and the plan always
had been that of course Peggy and I would be there. Now our
preparations for our trip began to assume their final form. We
had talked about this all in America, and to make the celebration impressive, Kirsten had planned three public concerts: two

recitals with piano and a final concert with orchestra. In a letter of April 7 she wrote that plans were taking final shape and gave me details so that we could arrange our trip: "The recitals in Oslo are December 4th and 8th, with my finest collaborator at the piano!! Naturally! Nationaltheatret has been booked for December 12th, as well as the orchestra. The Oslo Philharmonic with extra musicians. Olav Kielland is the conductor, as you suggested. At the final concert I think of singing: Strauss's Four Last Songs and *Elektra*—Orest-Orest. Grieg: Haugtussa, with you at the piano. And Wagner: Liebestod." For the two recitals, could I please send some suggestions? It would be hard to decide what to leave out of such a vast repertoire.

Peggy and I were on pins and needles at the thought of this trip. And I must say I floated with pride that I would be with Kirsten Flagstad when she was to say good-bye formally to her long, glorious career. It would be forty years to the day of the occasion and it would be on the same stage where she had sung her first notes as a professional.

But now still another blow fell, and it struck Peggy and me too. Early in August the Norwegian papers carried articles regarding charges and accusations Kirsten had made against Messrs. Morgenstierne and Sundför in a book that she wrote jointly with the American music critic Louis Biancolli, *The Flagstad Manuscript*. Even at this late date, the accusations had found their way into the press, and the two men eventually had made public their defenses against her assertions. It seemed that Kirsten's victory might well be illusory even now. The press observed that it would be interesting to hear Kirsten Flagstad's answer to the rebuttal that each of the men had made. Fortunately she kept still. But it was all terribly unpleasant for her again. At once she canceled the plans for her farewell concerts and wrote me sadly on September 10 that we were not to come. Again she turned over in her mind the idea of leaving Norway for good.

This last outburst turned out to be a bit of a tempest in a teapot. I have only the deepest regret that we did not go over anyhow. Eventually Kirsten was persuaded to give at least the big orchestral concert on her fortieth anniversary day. By then the trouble had completely died down and she was given a tremendous farewell. Afterwards there was an enormous party of over a hundred and everything ended in triumph. But the occason had gone sour for her and she wrote me that her heart had not been in it. For her sake it probably was better that Peggy and I were not there.

Then our contact for some months was confined to correspondence. She wrote that Dr. Furtwängler had been delighted with the new recording of *Tristan*. She was so very unhappy over the publicity that arose from her not having sung the two high C's in the second act. It was, according to her, to have remained the deepest secret. That anyone thought such a thing could have been kept quiet was pretty naïve. Actually, she had not been singing those two tones for several years, and I would have thought it just as well to leave them out completely. Another great singer, Elisabeth Schwarzkopf, sang them for her on the recording, and I would defy anyone who did not know it beforehand to detect this substitution. In any case, it was no crime, but there were those who chose to blow the matter up beyond any reasonable proportion. But the sale of the album was not hurt, and it eventually proved to be the most important of all Flagstad recordings, her most mature performance of her most celebrated role.

Later came the good news that she was coming to America

for a visit, and as a private person. She made the visit, but, as it turned out she arrived as a very public person. In the spring of 1954, Arturo Toscanini had retired and the great NBC Symphony had been thrust out of existence. That is, it went out of existence as far as the National Broadcasting Company was concerned. But, as many of us remember, the musicians themselves refused to disband and determined to carry on under the name of the Symphony of the Air. Early in the autumn of 1954 they gave their first concert in Carnegie Hall. They were without a conductor, as a gesture of respect for Maestro Toscanini. Presently I was asked if I would inquire if Madame Flagstad would be willing to come out of retirement and sing a concert with the courageous group. At first I refused point-blank even to ask her. Frankly, I thought the answer would be "No" and I did not want to be in the position of being refused. But eventually I was persuaded and on October 26 I wrote her a carefully worded letter explaining the situation of the orchestra and reminded her of the fact that the NBC Symphony was one orchestra with which she had never been invited to sing. I wrote this letter with great misgivings. My last paragraph read: "Please forgive me if I have suggested a terrible thing about this concert, but I just feel it is something worth thinking about."

She wrote me on November 20, 1954, that she was terribly flattered by the invitation, but, to put it bluntly, "I don't know for sure if I can still sing such a concert *and* Wagner!" It was almost a year since her farewell, and she had hardly sung at all, and then nothing at all heavy, she continued. We were to wait until she arrived here in New York and then at our house she and I would decide if she could still do it.

When she arrived that December 9, she dined alone the first night with Peggy and me. We devised and rehearsed the pro-

gram that she eventually sang the following March in Carnegie
Hall. There was no doubt that she could still sing. It had been
agreed with the Symphony of the Air that not one word was to
be said about this proposal. I had not even told Max Levine.
But the minute she said "Yes" I went personally to break the
news to him. Together with two representatives of the Symphony of the Air we called on Kirsten at her hotel two days later
for final formalities.

Max generously offered to manage the concert without fee.
That was in itself a joy. Miss Jeannette Green of NCAC, Max's
firm, had managed practically all of Kirsten's New York recitals
in the past, and she knew that with Miss Green running things,
everything would be in order.

There remained the problem of finding a suitable date. She
made one condition: it must be on a Sunday night. Katharine
Cornell was playing in the theater that season in New York, and
by that time Kirsten would not under any circumstance have
sung a concert at which Kit could not be present. March 20 was
found available in Carnegie Hall, and with this complete settlement of the program (which to my joy I was invited to conduct), she went off to visit her family in Phoenix.

The advertisement appeared in a few days, and within a matter of hours the house was completely sold out. The orchestra
asked me if we might schedule a repeat performance. This time
I telephoned Kirsten to ask her and she said: "I haven't anything to wear! But I'll have something made. Only I must tell
you that I have to sail on the 24th."

We found that the then unusual hour of 5:30 p.m. was available in the hall on the 22nd. When the second concert was
announced, it too sold out. Kirsten sang as gloriously as ever.
She looked radiant and extraordinarily youthful, and the public
once more acclaimed her as the greatest singer of her time. It

was the first time that she had sung Wagner publicly since her farewell some fifteen months earlier. One would have thought she had never stopped.

From her contribution of her services, The Symphony of the Air realized thousands and thousands of dollars. She was elected an honorary member of the orchestra. The second concert was the last time in her life that she sang the great pages of Brünnhilde's "Immolation Scene," and with that great artist and that great orchestra I had the precious and well-remembered privilege of being on the podium.

At this point, all Kirsten's affairs in Norway having been settled, there were no future bookings to be thought of and everything was happy between her and her "little family." There remained only one matter to dispose of—her future in the recording business. She was bitterly unhappy with the way her records were being promoted and also disappointed that HMV had not scheduled more recording for her. It was difficult then and impossible now for me to form a convincing opinion of the controversy—which, besides matters of promotion, involved both repertoire and scheduling. I heard only Kirsten's side, and her side as told me by particularly busybodied fans and friends. I have always felt that if Max or I could have sat down across the table from the officials of HMV, every difficulty could have been ironed out. In any case, I hated to see her contract with them come to an end, for even though her singing before the public was finished it was perfectly clear that she still possessed her amazing ability. She obviously was able to meet all the requirements of recording (in which one does not have to face the public). In an attempt to sustain and heighten Walter Legge's interest, I sent him the reviews, which were quite ecstatic, of the Carnegie Hall Symphony of the Air concerts. He wrote me a most cordial reply on April 29, 1955, and pleaded

with me to use my influence with Kirsten to let bygones be
bygones and make herself available for the recordings he then
said HMV was anxious to make. But I knew from conversations
we had had that Kirsten was counting the days until that affiliation would be finished. I was sorry then, and, if only for old
times' sake, in many ways I am sorry now.

By then Kirsten was back in Europe. Out of the blue came a
delightful surprise—a letter from Miss Jeanne S. Heslop of the
Decca Record Company in London dated November 16, 1955,
informing me that Madame Flagstad would in all probability go
to London early in the following year to make a recital record
for them and inquiring if I would be available to come and
accompany her. It was exciting news, and the first word I had
had that any negotiations at all were in progress with a new
company. Naturally I was available and immediately wrote to
say so.

I also wrote at once to Kirsten for more details. She wrote me
on November 24 that she had really not wanted to do it (events
proved later that she did not mean this), but that it was really
Bernard Miles who had persuaded her and who had handled all
of the negotiations. Subsequently Bernard arranged my engagement and wrote me as well that he was glad I was coming over,
for I could then help him to arrange proper payments of Kirsten's royalties! Despite my regret that she had broken with
HMV, I could not help but congratulate Bernard for the manner
in which he had handled the new arrangements, and naturally I
was delighted at the opportunity to record with Kirsten again.
In her letter of November 24 she wrote: "Do I need to tell you
how thrilled I am to have you to play for me again!!!"

She was coming to New York shortly after January first, and
we could discuss repertory in detail then.

But again the disturbing news of her health. She had been

back in the hospital for eighteen days of treatment, and her skin trouble and other complaints had not responded well. But how happy she was right at that time over a new project—*Götterdämmerung* was to be produced for broadcasting in Oslo, with Set Svanholm as Siegfried. She wrote how wonderful it would be to sing it again, and with Svanholm, and went on to say that he and she would be of help in maintaining the true Wagnerian tradition. It is to the credit of the Decca Record Company that eventually they took the tapes from those Norwegian broadcasts and issued them as discs.

The coming recording sessions for Decca continued to dominate my thoughts. I was tremendously pleased that Kirsten had said she would record only if they would have me over from America. And I am very proud that the only other accompanist on records with her throughout the years of her great career was the incomparable Gerald Moore. Not only did Kirsten find pleasure in making music with Mr. Moore, but my disappointment at not being with her on the occasions when he recorded with her in Europe was soothed by her having such a distinguished pianist. As a matter of fact, it would have been much easier for Decca to engage Mr. Moore instead of me: he was right there in London. But Kirsten felt that she would probably be recording songs for the last time, and in addition to the fact that we had done so many of the songs together, relieving her of the necessity of extra rehearsal, she did feel a sentimental reason for having me for the occasion.

Before the recording session, Kirsten made another trip to the United States to visit Else. We spoke by telephone and she told me with great excitement that she had flown over the North Pole to Los Angeles and then on to Phoenix. When she came east from Arizona, it was with the warning that she wished to see absolutely no one. When she arrived at the airport, I suddenly realized that her illness was graver than I had feared. But as yet we said nothing about it.

Almost immediately she left for Norway. She wrote me on March 5, 1956, confessing finally that she had been really ill and was even then only going from day to day. But a few days later we met for our recording sessions in London and she seemed in excellent health and voice again, and was in the best of spirits. We worked hard for several days, but it was decided then that Decca wanted more and we tentatively arranged another recording session the following November. I was to make two trips and eventually to be Flagstad's collaborator on a total of five new albums.

When I returned the following autumn for the final sessions, we completed the five records, and in the studios of the Decca Record Company in London on November 30, 1956, I played a song for the very last time for Kirsten Flagstad. It was Sinding's "Sylvelin."

An event of that last trip to London is worth a digression. After all those years, she had received at long last a letter from Lauritz Melchior. He asked her to forget the past and be friends. She translated it for me and practically shouted: "I will never forgive, I will never forget."

"Now, Kirsten," I said, "you should answer that letter, and if you like I will help you write what I think would be appropriate."

"Never, never," she said over and over again.

I went back to my hotel and drafted a friendly reply which said that perhaps it would be better not to start the old friendship anew. But she would not write it. Later, in 1960, Melchior went to Denmark to celebrate his seventieth birthday and Kirsten wrote me she had heard him sing Act I of *Walküre* over the radio and that it was "grand." Also, she had tried unsuccessfully to reach him by phone, but had sent him a cable instead.

"She is softening," I thought.

In any case, they did in fact correspond near the end, but never again met. In a tribute printed in the February 1963 issue of the British magazine *Opera,* he wrote:

It was a strange thought of God that two Scandinavians—a Norwegian and a Dane—should be the singing ambassadors in a wartorn world. I know that we both felt that we were selected to show that music and war have nothing in common, and we were thankful for our success.

Rather startling from a former colleague who had not seen his Isolde since April 18, 1941, in New York and had most expediently ignored her in the days of her anguish.

Kirsten still kept herself well occupied in Norway, singing dozens of church concerts, which had much interested her of late, and doing all the recording possible. Only on this latter item could I have disagreed with some of the advice she was getting, not only from Bernard Miles, but also from some of the directors of English Decca. Many of the recordings she made for them are great, and it is certainly doubtful that any other company would have been willing to devote as much time and expense to them even for a Kirsten Flagstad. But I am also sorry for some of the things they persuaded her to record. John Culshaw, who was in charge of the recording sessions at which I was the accompanist, is an extremely able person, but I question some of his taste as far as Kirsten Flagstad was concerned. In the February 1963 issue of the magazine *The Gramophone,* he reported that in 1961 and 1962, when Kirsten really was dying, they were negotiating for her to record Brahms's *Alto*

Rhapsody and the Waltraute of *Götterdämmerung*. These are both for mezzo or contralto, and all I can say is Thank God that she never did them. To have commemorated the name of one of the greatest dramatic sopranos in history with a repertoire so blatantly unsuited to her would have been an act of reckless folly, musically speaking, and also would have proved an insult to her memory.

This leads me to put forth a frank and firm opinion of the real Flagstad as we can know her today only from recordings. This is not merely for those of us fortunate to have heard her alive, but most particularly for the generations who can know of her voice and art only from her recordings.

Her recorded performances of art songs are frequently very persuasive, notably her subtle *"Frauenliebe und Leben"* of Schumann. Perhaps the best of all her recorded songs were those in Norwegian, particularly Grieg's. Her voice always seemed to take on a different color when she was singing in her native tongue. Many of the more dramatic songs of Schubert, Brahms, Hugo Wolf, and Richard Strauss seemed made for her as well. I have never heard Strauss's *"Befreit"* and Schubert's *"Dem Unendlichen"* so gloriously sung.

But for the real Flagstad, one must hear her in Wagner. The breadth, power, and brilliance of her extraordinary vocal instrument found their natural element in her big Wagnerian roles, and in her execution of them the composer's intent and the artist's delivery were uniquely matched with a rightness and "inevitable" quality rarely, if ever, equaled in history.

I would be much happier if she had never been persuaded to record operas at the other end of the stylistic spectrum—*Dido and Aeneas* or *Alcestis*. Also, the recorded song cycles of Gustav Mahler were completely out of her natural sphere. Selections of Beethoven and Weber made in 1937 with Ormandy are impres-

As Kundry in *Parsifal*, Covent Garden, London, 1951

As Alcestis, Metropolitan Opera, 1952

As Dido in *Dido and Aeneas,* Mermaid Theatre, London, 1951

sive. But it is in the music of Wagner that she really belonged, and without question, the greatest recording of them all is her complete *Tristan und Isolde* with Furtwängler.

On February 4, 1953, we were utterly delighted to read in *The New York Times* that Kirsten Flagstad had been named director of the new Norwegian State Opera the day before in Oslo. Her appointment to that public post seemed to make her final victory complete, as if she needed any further vindication. She wrote me details on February 9, saying she had been offered the "job" by telephone on January 29, had accepted on February 2, and had been appointed February 3. This letter came from London, where again she was recording some Sibelius songs with orchestra. Shortly she would be in America and would give me all the details, and as usual she asked for my help.

On February 18 she wrote me again from London: "This is to inform you that my dear mother passed away quietly at 7 P. M. today. . . . I am not going home, but will proceed with my plans and will see you in a few days."

She had seen her mother but a few days earlier in Norway, did not feel the need to go back, and shortly came to New York again.

She was eager to see opera now, and during this visit went several times to the Metropolitan. Francis Robinson was indeed a most cordial host. He provided her with tickets always and entertained her at dinner in the opera house. She unbent more than in earlier days—she would even smile at admirers in the opera house when they recognized her. I twitted her: "Kirsten, you're getting so really soft and gentle in your old age!"

She wanted to see some Broadway musicals too, and was particularly excited by *My Fair Lady* and *The Music Man*. One evening at the Metropolitan she met Meredith Willson, the composer of the latter, and expressed herself exactly as she always had: "Thrilled."

She asked me to suggest American operas and operettas to produce in Norway. I gave her four: *The King and I* and *Carousel* of Rodgers and Hammerstein; Deems Taylor's *Peter Ibbetson;* and a new opera by Vittorio Giannini, *The Taming of the Shrew.* She liked them all and, if she had remained as head of the State Opera, would have mounted some of them.

She returned home, and there began to be depressingly long stretches with no word whatever from her. I did not give it too much thought because it was more than apparent to me that Kirsten was not a well woman. It only disturbed me periodically to learn that, while she was neglecting Else and me, to say nothing of many other old and devoted friends, she was continuing a staggering correspondence with casual acquaintances and complete strangers. She told Peggy and me once during this period that in one calendar year she had written over six hundred letters. I was cross with her. "Why should you?" I demanded.

I found it upsetting to walk down the street and get intimate bits of news from virtual strangers on the corner. But this was Kirsten Flagstad: she acted under her own rules, and no one else's.

On December 20, 1958, she did write me some details of her life at that time. She planned to open her first season with Eugène d'Albert's *Tiefland,* the opera in which she herself had made her debut. It was scheduled for February 16. She had found a charming nineteen-year-old girl for her own part, Nuri, and said: "I have great hopes for her."

She proudly sent me pictures from the newspapers of the grand opening under her direction, and I actually wept when I read the accounts of Madame Kirsten Flagstad's giving the State

Opera's official welcome to His Majesty, King Olaf, and making the official opening remarks at this national occasion. She was the very same woman whose name had been besmirched up and down that same country but a few years earlier.

On September 15, 1959, I received the most alarming letter yet from her. She told me frankly that she had not been well for half a year and described in great detail her ailments and the various treatments attempted. No one except my Peggy knew until after she died that I understood the seriousness of her illness those last years.

In December 1959, she informed me that she was to fly, over the Pole again, to Phoenix and hoped that I would come out to see her. She could not stand the thought of New York. And so of course I went and spent several particularly wonderful days at the end of that month with her. Except that she had evident difficulty in getting comfortable because of pain in her hip, she seemed bright and gay, and we had hours upon hours of "family" conversation. We also reverted to earlier habits and had a number of energetic arguments.

She had hoped to go to San Francisco to visit Caroline Esberg, but Mrs. Esberg came to her instead, and that pleased her.

But I returned to New York after that visit with the heaviest of hearts and said at once to Peggy: "Kirsten has cancer!" There could no longer be any doubt in my mind of it.

She came once more to Phoenix in the early days of March the following year (1961), and again announced that she would not come to New York. Nancy Hamilton had gone to Norway the previous Christmas, so that I could not quite understand Kirsten's burning desire to see her again so soon, but then there were Katharine Cornell and Guthrie McClintic, whom she wanted to see so much. At the time, I made one of my great

mistakes. That particular period was very busy for me, and it
would have been difficult for me to go again to Phoenix. But I
knew that she planned to spend a few days with Katharine
Cornell and Nancy Hamilton on Martha's Vineyard, off the
coast of Massachusetts, and I could not understand why she
should not visit Peggy and me at our home in New York. We
had two or three rather difficult arguments on the subject by
telephone. Although I knew that she was not completely well, I
did not know until we finally saw her the day she flew to Europe that her illness was actually fatal. Had I realized that the
end was near, I would have canceled everything and gone to
Phoenix to be with her. But at that particular time I thought
that she was being a stubborn Norwegian and I resented the
care with which she made her plans to visit Martha's Vineyard
but could not seem to arrange to be with us. Finally, Arthur
interceded and a plan was fixed. She was to have driven down
to New York, or rather to the McClintic residence at Sneden's
Landing, near New York, on April 13. Then, having spent the
night there, she would come to our apartment in the city to
spend the day with only Peggy and me. We promised faithfully
not to tell one soul that she would be there. Afterwards we
were to have taken her to Idlewild Airport for her departure,
late in the afternoon, for Copenhagen. At about 7:00 p.m. on
the 13th the telephone rang, and it was she. We assumed naturally that she had made the trip with Katharine Cornell and was
near New York as planned. To our surprise and sorrow she told
us the weather that day was so bad they had been unable to
cross to the mainland from Martha's Vineyard and that they
were still there. What were we going to do? Our plans went
right out the window. What eventually happened was that they
left Martha's Vineyard the following morning and drove the five
or six hours to Sneden's Landing. From there she went on to

Idlewild to meet Peggy and me for what should have been a two-hour visit. We were there in good time, but her driver lost the way. When Kirsten finally got there, we had a scant half hour left. We had one drink together, a last embrace—and Peggy and I were the last of her friends in America to see her alive as she boarded the plane for her last trip home.

Months went by in silence. The last letter I ever received from Kirsten was dated September 20, 1961. Again she was in the hospital. She had had to give up her directorship of the Opera. (She had told me in Phoenix during that visit in 1959 that she might have to.) The doctors had told her that it was too much for her. She had sent off to me her fabulous collection of the tapes of all her recordings and told me of having made the translations into English herself of all her songs, mainly to please Nancy Hamilton.

As 1962 approached, Else and Arthur periodically received messages on the subject of another possible visit to America. Always it had to be postponed. I was in constant communication with the Dusenberrys. Finally, on June 5, 1962, Stake wrote me confidentially of the seriousness of Kirsten's illness, and with his letter in hand, I tried repeatedly to persuade Else that she must go before it was too late. But Else knew her mother and was reluctant to cross her. Kirsten had kept saying, "Come later."

However, when September arrived, the Dusenberrys decided that they would go. Else telephoned her mother and then wrote me on September 13 that Kirsten had said it was much too soon for them to come even now. They had then arranged that they would go for a reunion in Norway at Christmastime.

Meanwhile Kirsten was to go back into the hospital, but was certain that she would be out again by Christmastime. Else had no alternative under the circumstances but to abide by her mother's wishes. Even in her last days, Kirsten was still the prima donna.

On November 17 Else telephoned me from Phoenix to say that her father had died the day before in Oslo and that she was leaving the next day by air for Norway to attend the funeral. Else drank the full cup of sorrow in those days. When she arrived in Oslo, she realized at once that the end was not far off for her mother. Kirsten was almost constantly in a coma. As if by a miracle, she suddenly regained her full powers of communication on Tuesday, December 4, and talked long and with complete lucidity to her "Elselill." Then she had a farewell chat with the faithful Stake and slipped off, never again to regain consciousness.

Early on Saturday morning, December 8, 1962, my telephone rang and a young fan of Kirsten's, Bill Gallagher, told me he had just heard on the radio that Kirsten had died the night before. I immediately telephoned Arthur in Phoenix. He was hardly able to speak. Some days before he had received a letter from Else in Norway saying that the end was near. But Kirsten had given strict orders that no one at all was to be told until after her remains had been laid to rest. "Not even Edwin must know." The day Kirsten died, Else sent a cryptic cable giving the news to Arthur. Following instructions, he kept silent. I quickly advised him that it was all over New York by radio at that moment and would soon be all over the world. Only then did he telephone Else in Oslo to arrange that an official announcement be made.

I did not go to Norway for the funeral. Kirsten would not have had me do so. Bernard Miles had flown up from London to see her about two weeks before she died, and she had been with him for five minutes. Beret, her faithful servant from Kristiansand, who had been with her for so many years, went to

Oslo, but was not permitted to see her. I wonder if Kirsten would have seen me if I had gone. Yet, she knew where my affections were, and I will always know where hers were.

Kirsten's funeral in Oslo on December 14 was noted the world over. Leading those of the great who paid her honor was the very special tribute from His Majesty, King Olaf. Dozens of others came from every corner of the globe. And thus a great great artist and true Norwegian was laid to rest with national honors.

The tributes heaped upon her memory would fill volumes. One of the most beautiful was a broadcast that Francis Robinson made from the Metropolitan Opera House on the afternoon of February 9, 1963. He traced Flagstad's career briefly and played a number of her finest recordings. There were similar broadcasts in many countries throughout the world. She had left her life-size portrait, which she had proudly hung in her music room in Kristiansand, to her grandson. Sigurd in turn gave it to the Metropolitan Opera, and on December 12, 1963—fifty years to the day after Kirsten Flagstad sang professionally for the first time—I had the great honor of presenting it to the Metropolitan Opera Association on behalf of Sigurd and his family. It hangs in the Metropolitan now, and when the new Metropolitan in Lincoln Center is opened, it will hang there along with portraits of other greats in the glorious history of music.

This was the Kirsten Flagstad that I knew. A great lady—a great artist—a simple woman—a complex individual—sweet and bitter like all human beings—but above all, a true personification of uncompromising integrity.

APPENDIX

Appendix A

COURT TESTIMONY IN NORWAY

ON OCTOBER 10, 1946, I appeared for several hours as a witness in the Torridal County Court in Kristiansand S., Norway. The major part of my testimony consisted of direct testimony with a brief interruption of cross examination by the opposing attorney. The subject matters were almost exclusively financial and tax affairs. We were successful in having admitted into official evidence certain letters and statements that I had written and prepared prior to the actual court hearing. Some of these follow here:

My letter to A. L. Gullestad dated September 13, 1946
My letter to A. L. Gullestad dated September 20, 1946
My letter to A. L. Gullestad dated September 28, 1946
Type of programs sung in America
Arrangement of concerts for Norwegian Relief in America
Dinner honoring Wendell Willkie
Of telephone calls
American social life and parties
Arrangement of trip to Norway in 1941
Of publications

September 13, 1946

H. R. Advocate A. L. Gullestad
Kristiansand S., Norway

Dear Mr. Gullestad:
I am herewith quoting from the letter of H. R. Advocate Ingolf Sundför under date of June 24th addressed to you:

311

FLAGSTAD

"All accounts sent by Mr. Edwin MacArthur [*sic*] to Mrs. Flagstad Johansen during the years 1935 to 1941, both years inclusive."

I will at this time explain the routine of these accounts in detail. In October 1935, at which time Madame Flagstad commenced her first American concert tour on which I accompanied her as assisting artist and secretary, a regular routine was inaugurated which continued throughout her entire American career. Madame Flagstad was herself desirous of having me take care of all financial details connected with living expenses, hotels, and various other incidental expenses incurred both on tour and in New York. She herself made me various advances to cover these running expenses. (These advances amounted to Fifteen Hundred Dollars in 1935 and One Thousand Dollars in 1936. This total sum of Twenty Five Hundred Dollars was returned in cash by me to Madame Flagstad in the spring of 1937, and I know she brought this cash to Europe with her that year.)

The regular routine method used was as follows. Each week I would prepare a detailed account of expenditures. On this account would also appear an account due me for professional services rendered as accompanist for Madame Flagstad at her various concerts. This weekly bill was presented to Madame Flagstad. She herself "okayed" each bill and it was then sent to NBC Artists Service, which firm managed Madame Flagstad's career in America. NBC Artists Service in turn sent me a check for the total amount of each bill. The amounts thus paid to me, with the exception of the fees therein included for accompanist services, were in reality re-imbursements for expenditures, and were deducted by NBC when final settlement was made by them to Madame Flagstad.

Each year when it was time to prepare Madame Flagstad's

312

income tax return, a voucher report of each bill was sent by NBC to Mr. Joseph Henry Ide who prepared Madame Flagstad's tax returns during her entire time in America. The total of my weekly bills is included each year under the item of "expenses" as reported by Mr. Ide in returning Madame Flagstad's tax return.

At the end of each year, NBC Artists Service having no further interest in and no use for these weekly bills, returned them to Madame Flagstad. As far as I know, Madame Flagstad did not consider it necessary to keep these bills, and with the exception of three originals which were paid to me in 1941 after Madame Flagstad returned to Europe, and which I am attaching, I do not believe that any of the originals of these bills are in existence.

I wish to fully explain about the three originals, herewith attached, and referred to above. They are dated March 4, 1941— March 11, 1941—and April 4, 1941. NBC Artists Service declined to honor these bills in the regular manner, as their legal department had not determined if they would be allowed to do so inasmuch as payments of moneys involving Madame Flagstad at that time were controlled by the United States Federal Reserve, on account of her being a Norwegian National and Norway being an enemy invaded country. You will note that subsequently, the Federal Reserve Bank issued a special license covering these items, this license having been issued after Madame Flagstad's departure for Europe in April, 1941. I myself, acting on the Power of Attorney, drew a check from Madame Flagstad's account, according to the terms of the special license, and was thus re-imbursed for expenditures as explained on these bills.

In my file of copies of bills for the year 1941, it will be noted that a later bill, dated June 21, 1941 for One Thousand fifty four dollars and ninety nine cents, was paid me by NBC Artists Service. NBC Artists Service had by that time decided they were allowed to make this remittance to me. This item is referred to in a letter from Mr. Porrier of the NBC Artists Service to Mr. Ide under date of February 2, 1942. Mr. Porrier was in error, however, in referring to this bill as of the date of July 21, as in reality it was June 21st.

It is of importance to state that the routine of weekly bills covering Madame Flagstad's expenses was followed during her annual residences in New York City as well as on tour. With possibly a few unimportant exceptions, all of her bills in the Astor Hotel, the Dorset Hotel, and the Waldorf-Astoria, were paid by me in the regular manner and these items appeared on my weekly bills which were settled, according to routine, by NBC Artists Service. I mention possible exceptions. During the early part of 1936 I was not in New York and I believe Madame Flagstad paid some of her bills at the Astor herself. This explains certain checks, which appear on the transcript of the Central Hanover Bank, which I believe were payable to the Astor Hotel during this period in 1936. It is also a fact that in April, 1941, a check for Two Hundred Forty Two Dollars and forty two cents was drawn by Madame Flagstad to the Waldorf-Astoria. This item appears on the transcript from the Central Hanover Bank as well as the transcript from the Waldorf-Astoria Hotel which I have delivered to you today. I wish to repeat, that with these few exceptions, which in total amount to very little, all of Madame Flagstad's bills in New York were paid by me in the regular manner. I myself kept copies of these bills herein described until each current year was over. I too then, finding no further use for these accounts, destroyed my copies.

I make special mention of the fact that I kept the bills until the end of each year, as it explains clearly why I am now able to present copies of these bills for the years 1940 and 1941. Mr. Johansen always left me in personal charge of his wife in America. It was my regular custom to go into details, at least in a general way with him on the occasion of his trips to America or when I would meet him in Europe. When Norway was invaded in April of 1940, I realized that it would be impossible to communicate reports to Mr. Johansen about his wife and also that it would be some time before we would possibly meet. I therefore considered it wise to keep the copies of my 1940 bills and those through 1941 covering expenses which I paid for Madame Flagstad according to our regular plan.

In 1943 I myself went into a special service in connection with the Armed Forces of the United States and spent over eighteen months in the Pacific Theatre of War. Before leaving America, I decided to turn over to Mr. Ide such documents as he would be interested for Mr. Johansen to see when the war was completed and which I might unfortunately not return from the war to show myself.

The copies of my bills for 1940 and 1941 herein described are attached. I might add that they are typical of all bills which preceeded [*sic*] them in the earlier years, and I do state further that these copies are all that are in existence.

A confirmation of this routine followed can be obtained from Mr. Marks Levine and Madame Flagstad has this date addressed a letter to Mr. Levine requesting this confirmation.

Very truly yours,
Edwin McArthur

.   .   .

FLAGSTAD

H. R. Advocate A. L. Gullestad
Kristiansand S., Norway

Dear Mr. Gullestad:

Attached herewith is a statement which I have prepared entirely from recollection, of checks withdrawn from the account of Madame Kirsten Flagstad-Johansen in the Central Hanover Bank and Trust Company—Madison Avenue at 42nd Street—New York City.

This statement commences with a check which passed through the bank on March 17, 1936 and finishes with a check which cleared on May 21, 1941.

From June 1941 through January 1946, I was, according to regulations set down by the Federal Reserve Bank of the United States, required to make a monthly statement to the bank of checks withdrawn from Madame Flagstad-Johansen's blocked account. I am attaching herewith my copies of these monthly statements.

It will be noted in these last mentioned statements that there is a period during 1943 and a period during 1944 when no statements were made to the bank. This time in 1943 as well as the time in 1944 were periods when I was overseas in the services of the United States Armed Forces. During these periods, a standing order was left with the bank by myself for regular remittances out of Madame Flagstad's account. With few exceptions, the remittances consisted entirely of the monthly check allowance which was sent each month to Mrs. Else Dusenberry, Madame Flagstad's daughter, who resides in the United States.

Very truly yours,
Edwin McArthur

. . .

September 28, 1946

H. R. Advocate A. L. Gullestad
Kristiansand S., Norway

Dear Mr. Gullestad:

On September 20th I sent you a statement, made from recollection, of checks which had been drawn against Madame Kirsten Flagstad-Johansen's account in the Central Hanover Bank and Trust Company from March 17, 1936 through May 21, 1941. On this statement appear several items marked "Edwin McArthur for personal financing from Henry Johansen." You will further note that the total of the items thus marked is thirty thousand dollars. I will herewith below explain the sum total of these items. In 1938 Madame Flagstad went on a concert tour to Australia. I went as accompanist and piano soloist, and we were joined on this trip by Madame Flagstad's American concert manager, Mr. Levine, and by Mme. Flagstad's husband, Mr. Johansen.

We had gone to Australia expressly for the purpose of giving recitals with piano. But no sooner had Madame Flagstad sung her first recital in Sydney, did an urgent request upon the part of the public appear for her to sing some of her big operatic scenes with orchestra. This Madame Flagstad agreed to follow, but knowing my long desire to commence a career as an orchestral conductor, she made a condition that I be engaged for at least one concert in both Sydney and Melbourne. These concerts were arranged according to Madame Flagstad's wishes and I conducted my first concert in Sydney on July 13, 1938.

The rehearsal with Madame Flagstad and the orchestra for this concert took place on July 12th. Mr. Johansen was present at this rehearsal and afterwards he expressed himself as being very impressed with the work I had done and further said he would like to see me devote my time to the development of a conducting career. Being a practical man, he realized full well that such a pursuit would cost money. And he stated plainly to me that he wished to be financially responsible for whatever would be entailed.

Already at this time, in 1938, I had made an independent living for many years, and even before Madame Flagstad's arrival on the American musical scene, had been associated with only the first artists of the profession. It was not an easy decision to make that I should accept financial help from anyone and thereby feel myself obligated. But, knowing my desire for such a career, and further encouraged by Madame Flagstad's firm belief in my latest display of talent, Mr. Johansen pressed me.

We were sailing for America the early part of August of that year. We therefore had considerable time to discuss details during that three week voyage. It was agreed that I was to continue my association with Madame Flagstad as her accompanist and secretary, but that in order to have time to devote myself to study, I was to give up all my other work. This involved considerable loss of income, a fact of which Mr. Johansen was fully aware. In addition to the loss of this additional income, the expense of study was not small, and Mr. Johansen asked me to figure out for over a period of three years what would be financially entailed.

I gave careful thought to this and then told him that I felt three years a fair time to prepare myself and that if I could be assured of ten thousand dollars a year from him for these three years I could devote myself with full energy to my work and studies.

Madame Flagstad was fully aware of Mr. Johansen's intention to help me, as naturally he relied completely upon her judgement as to my musical potentialities. But she knew nothing of the financial discussions between us, and we were made to understand from the beginning that this was purely a personal matter between Mr. Johansen and myself.

A personal letter from Mr. Johansen and Madame Flagstad was composed and signed when we arrived in San Francisco the end of August, 1938. This letter stated their belief in me as a potential leader of orchestras, and the desire to be of practical assistance to me in the endeavor to reach my goal. The letter further states the amount to which Mr. Johansen would be committed and makes clear that this money is not intended as a loan, but further states however, that at some future time if I should feel able and inclined to return it, without interest, that will be left entirely to my discretion.

Mr. Johansen then personally advised me the manner in which I was to receive this money as I needed. I was instructed to write him personally to Norway and further to let him know my New York bank. He in turn intended to send me either his personal check or have transferred the desired amount to my bank in New York.

I made my first request in October of 1938 by writing a letter to Mr. Johansen in Norway saying I would like one thousand dollars at that time. In reply to this letter I received an immediate answer from him enclosing a check for one thousand dollars drawn against Madame Flagstad's account in New York and signed by her. In his letter, Mr. Johansen explained that since his return to Norway he had decided that because of the continual fluctuation of foreign exchange, it would be more practical for me to receive the money as I needed it from Madame Flagstad in America. He went on further to say that he expected me to make use of the full amount of his agreement with me, and that the fact that the money was reaching me from Madame Flagstad's account had nothing whatsoever to do with it. He explained this by saying that he would re-imburse Madame Flagstad in full in Norway, as financially this was his responsibility.

The last time I personally saw Mr. Johansen was in May, 1939. I remember as though it were yesterday, his questioning me at length as to my study and progress and I recall as though it were today his writing me a check at that time, in the Dorset Hotel in New York, for three thousand dollars and having Madame Flagstad sign it.

From time to time as I needed money, I would write my own checks and yearly figure them to total the agreed amount. Madame Flagstad always signed these checks that I wrote and never asked what they were for. It is with pride that I know she had utmost confidence in me in regard to everything.

The last item on my agreement with Mr. Johansen was drawn on Mme. Flagstad's account, cleared through the bank on December 5, 1940. It is in the sum of ten thousand dollars. Madame Flagstad's account was blocked at that time, but upon producing a copy of my personal letter of 1938 to the Bank, the Federal Reserve Bank of the United States issued a special license permitting the withdrawal of this ten thousand dollars.

I wish to state clearly once again, that this arrangement between Mr. Johansen and myself was of a very close personal nature. There are not more than a half dozen people, before the writing of this letter, that even know I ever received this financial aid in the pursuit of my career. And I wish to state again as well, that Madame Flagstad herself was not involved in any responsibility whatsoever in the financing of my career. The money was paid to me out of her American bank account purely for convenience and for practical negotiation. But it was Mr.

Appendix A

Johansen's avowed intention to re-imburse Madame Flagstad in full for the amounts paid to me.

Very truly yours,
Edwin McArthur

TYPE OF PROGRAMS SUNG IN AMERICA

Written by Edwin McArthur in Norway—Sept.-Oct., 1946

It has been brought to my attention that Kirsten Flagstad has been bitterly criticized for not having sung Scandinavian, and in particular Norwegian songs, on her recital programs during her American career.

As I personally arranged all of Madame Flagstad programs, naturally after consultations with her, I would like to express myself on this subject.

From the very beginning of her concert career in America, Madame Flagstad, to my knowledge, never sang a single recital program without at least one group of Scandinavian songs on the program.

It is important to state at once that on one occasion (her first Chicago appearance) she sang an all-Wagner program as a joint recital with the tenor, Lauritz Melchior. It is also necessary to state that when Kirsten Flagstad appeared as soloist on many occasions with orchestra, the programs were, because of public insistence and demand, all Wagnerian.

It would perhaps be interesting to state that Kirsten Flagstad's unrivaled fame as a singer in the world is as a Wagnerian soprano and not as a singer of Scandinavian songs.

Nevertheless, she always sang Norwegian and other Scandinavian songs on her programs and was even successful in popularizing such unknown songs as the "Haugtussa" Cycle of Grieg to an extent that her recording of this cycle had a most unusual sale for such an unknown set of songs.

On one occasion in New York City, Madame Flagstad arranged a program entirely of Norwegian songs. It had been her thought that her Norwegian country men in the area of New York might be glad to avail themselves of an opportunity to hear an evening of just their songs. But it soon became apparent to Madame Flagstad's management and to myself that it was the Americans, and not the Norwegians, who were buying tickets to this concert, and as a result we had made and printed a special book of words so that the public would have a clearer understanding of the songs. My recollection is that this concert took place in either 1939 or 1940, and I mention this lest someone might foolishly wish to state that the Norwegians were "boycotting" their most famous singer.

In regard to programs, a most interesting situation took place. As is well known, in the north-middle-western part of America there are a great many Scandinavians. With the exception of one or two cities like Minneapolis, St. Paul, etc. these people live in much smaller towns and therefore had never been able financially to engage a concert in their community of an expensive singer like Kirsten Flagstad.

Madame Flagstad had oft expressed a desire to visit some of these places, but the demands on her time, and at her regular high fees, made such a desire impossible to fulfill.

At the time Norway was invaded in 1940, Madame Flagstad had already decided that she would be returning to America for a very short season the following year, and this being the case, her time had been completely booked. Also, by that time of the year (April) concert courses and plans for the following season were completed for most of the big cities in America, and even though she was available, it was too late for many local managers who would have liked to have had her, to arrange appearances. It was then that Mr. Levine, then Madame Flagstad's concert manager, suggested that perhaps she could take three weeks of the fall of 1940 when she was not otherwise booked and do a tour of these very Scandinavian populated towns who had so oft expressed the desire to have her in their midst.

This special tour was therefore arranged and took place during October, 1940. The towns visited were: Duluth, St. Cloud, Fargo, Minot, Fergus Falls, Aberdeen, Northfield, etc. A comparison of the fees Mme. Flagstad received on this tour with her fees from other tours will show clearly what special favors these towns were getting.

The tour having been especially arranged for Madame Flagstad's Scandinavian compatriots, the very special program for just these cities was especially arranged. And instead of the usual *one* group of five or six Scandinavian songs, she put on *two* groups.

When we returned to New York, Madame Flagstad's management told me that in every case on this Scandinavian concert tour, there had been complaints from the local managements that the public had been bitterly disappointed. They had wanted to hear Kirsten Flagstad sing *Wagner* and demanded an explanation of why so many Norwegian, Swedish, Danish songs had been put on her programs in their cities. Rather than being criticized for *not* singing Scandinavian songs, she was being censured for doing too many.

I wish now to speak specifically of Washington, D. C. as it has been reported to me that Mr. Morgenstierne has complained that Madame Flagstad sang an all-German program in the National capital, and that she had invited the German Ambassador to be her guest.

I will speak first about the German Ambassador. At no time

during her stay in America did Madame Flagstad have any contact whatsoever with a representative of the German Government. She did not even know who were the representatives of the German Government in America. She never met them, she never accepted hospitality from them nor did she offer any. Even when her trip was being arranged to Europe in 1941, she herself had no contact with German authorities. Her transit visa across Germany was arranged through the offices of her management, the NBC, and a specially engaged agent in these affairs. Especially I can testify as to Washington, for except on the occasion of the visit of Madame Flagstad's mother and sister to Washington in 1938, when I myself arranged with the local concert manager for their seats at the concert, Madame Flagstad at no time asked, or even purchased, any tickets for her concerts there. This accusation is entirely false and without a single thread of justification.

On January 23, 1940 Madame Flagstad sang a recital in Constitution Hall with piano accompaniment. The program was of the usual type with several Scandinavian songs included.

On February 14, 1940 Madame Flagstad appeared with the National Symphony Orchestra in Constitution Hall. I conducted the orchestra. Her part of the program was as follows:

Ah, Perfido! *Beethoven*

___

Vaaren *Grieg*
En Svane *Grieg*
En Drøm *Grieg*

___

Immolation Scene
    "Die Götterdämmerung" *Wagner*

324

Appendix A

During the summer of 1940, Madame Flagstad sang at all the large open air concert series with the great orchestras of America. She received the highest fees of any artist in the profession at that time, and drew the biggest crowds. In each case, the request by management and public alike was for an *all-Wagner* program. Such a concert took place in Washington with the National Symphony Orchestra on July 31, 1940.

On November 27, 1940 Madame Flagstad again appeared in Constitution Hall with the National Symphony Orchestra. I again conducted. It must be noted that this was her third orchestral appearance, with the same orchestra, and in the same City within the short space of ten months. A change of repertoire in such circumstances is imperative. The program on this occasion was as follows:

Aria: "Leise, leise"	*Weber*

Befreit	*Richard Strauss*
Allerseelen	*Richard Strauss*
Cäcilie	*Richard Strauss*

Elisabeth's "Gebet"	"Tannhäuser"	*Wagner*
"Du bist der Lenz"	"Walküre"	*Wagner*

On February 11, 1941 Madame Flagstad sang a recital in Constitution Hall with me at the piano. On this program she sang the "Haugtussa" Cycle by Grieg.

It is my understanding that Mr. Morgenstierne specifically objects to the program of November 27, 1940.

We have remained completely non-partisan regarding music, even throughout the war. Prominent political refugees like the great conductor, Dr. Bruno Walter, have repeatedly given programs in New York entirely of Brahms, Wagner, Strauss, etc.

It is ridiculous to me as an American and as a musician that any such question regarding programs should ever have come up. But I am sure it will be readily seen that in five programs between January 23, 1940 and February 11, 1941 Madame Flagstad sang a very fine representation of Norwegian songs in the American capital.

And further, if there is to be any more criticism on this point, I will request that it be directed at me and not at Madame Flagstad. Especially in the case of the orchestral concerts, I arranged the programs entirely myself, and will take full responsibility.

I believe Mr. Morgenstierne has stated further that he was present at the concert on November 27, 1940 and was embarrassed to be placed so close to the German Ambassador. If Mr. Morgenstierne was present at this particular concert, knowledge of it as the result of his testimony is the first information I have had that he was even there. And had he been so unfortunate as to have been in the box next the German Ambassador, he still was most unfair and completely out of order in accusing Mme. Flagstad of having invited the German Representative to her concert.

ARRANGEMENT OF CONCERTS
FOR NORWEGIAN RELIEF IN AMERICA

Written by Edwin McArthur in Norway—Sept.-Oct., 1946

In the summer of 1940 Madame Flagstad notified her management, the NBC Artists Service, that she would like to do some Norwegian Relief concerts if they could be arranged at convenient times and places to coincide with her regularly booked professional engagements.

Appendix A

Miss Elsie Illingworth of the NBC Artists Service took charge of making these arrangements.

It was tentatively planned to arrange three concerts—one in New York—one in Chicago—and one in San Francisco.

Miss Illingworth immediately communicated with a Mr. Rygg who apparently had an official position in the arrangement of such Norwegian concerts in America.

It was discovered that a concert in San Francisco was not possible because the only time at which it would have been possible to make arrangements in this city, Madame Flagstad was occupied elsewhere in America.

A concert was arranged for Chicago, and this concert did take place in the Chicago Civic Opera House on January 17, 1941 and something in the neighborhood of six thousand dollars was realized for Norwegian relief from this concert alone. The arrangements for this concert were personally supervised by Rev. Mr. Ingvolstad who was secretary of Norwegian Relief in America. The house was entirely sold out. Following the concert, a dinner took place in a private dining room in the Opera House building. The escaped Mayor of Narvik was among the guests, as was Mr. Rygg. There were speeches and Rev. Ingvolstad explained to Madame Flagstad, myself, and the other guests present that the money being raised for Norwegian relief in America could not reach Norway until after the war was over account of the British blockade making the sending of help impossible. I mention this here, as I will again in later testimony, because when Madame Flagstad reported this fact upon her return to Norway, she was called a "liar." Mr. Ingvolstad went further to state that there were thousands of dollars already then raised for help to Norway, and the minute the war was over this money would immediately be available for such needs in Norway as relief money would help. I wish to add that in the spring of 1942 I had lunch with Rev. Ingvolstad in New York and I asked him if he had made this statement, or if we had misunderstood. He stated then to me that what he had said was correct, that what Madame Flagstad had told in Norway was true, and he was sorry she had been accused falsely of being a liar, but account of war feelings, etc. there was nothing to be done about it.

In the case of the concert in New York, for which a date had been set in Carnegie Hall (March 3, 1941) most insulting and embarrassing difficulties arose from Mr. Rygg.

He made an insistence that the prices of tickets be reduced so that the poor Norwegians in the New York area could attend the concert. Mme. Flagstad sang annually either one or two concerts in Carnegie Hall and at the highest prices. It would have been most damaging to her professional standing to sing a concert at reduced prices, and further her desire was to give a concert to raise money, and not necessarily for the entertainment for an hour and a half of those poor Norwegians who might wish to attend. Neither she nor her management were willing that any reduction of regular prices for tickets be made, and as a matter of fact, wished to insist that the prices be increased so that much more money could be raised.

Mr. Rygg countered with the suggestion that if he could persuade H.R.H. Princess Martha to attend the concert, it would be all right to raise the price of tickets. Madame Flagstad was herself sufficient of a star and box office favorite to sell out a house in New York at any price without the presence of anyone, even be she the Crown Princess of Norway.

The third and absolutely unacceptable condition set forth by Mr. Rygg was that she submit for approval the program she proposed to sing at this concert. When this last insulting demand was made, the concert was regretfully cancelled. It is interesting to note that the Metropolitan Opera Company availed themselves of this date, March 3, 1941, for an extra performance with Mme. Flagstad and that this performance was sold out within a couple of hours after it had been announced in the newspapers.

In collaboration with Karin Branzell, Lauritz Melchoir, Lawrence Tibbett, the NBC Symphony Orchestra with Eugene Goossens conducting, and myself as pianist, Madame Flagstad did sing a concert in Carnegie Hall for Finnish Relief at which concert close to twenty-five thousand dollars was raised. A similar amount could have been raised for Norway by a concert of Madame Flagstad herself had it not been for the interference herein explained in the person of Mr. Rygg.

DINNER HONORING WENDELL WILLKIE

Written by Edwin McArthur in Norway—Sept.-Oct., 1946

On April 25, 1940 the Association of Newspaper Publishers from all over the United States met in annual convention in New York City.

At the official dinner for this convention, the honor guest and speaker was Wendell Willkie, who was later that same year to be the Republican Candidate for the President of the United States.

Mrs. Ogden Reid, the executive director of the New York Herald Tribune, telephoned me and expressed a desire to have Madame Flagstad appear as soloist at this dinner. Mrs. Reid explained that at that time particularly, with the entire world in the throes of war-fare, it was important to have an outstanding and beloved personality to appear at this dinner and they would consider it a great honor if Madame Flagstad would so honor them.

Madame Flagstad did sing at this dinner. I played for her. When she came on the platform, the entire audience rose to its feet, as much a tribute to Norway as to Madame Flagstad herself.

Regardless of the accusations of Norwegians themselves, I as an American and thousands of other Americans feel that in Kirsten Flagstad Norway had, and still has, one of the finest representatives that any country could pray for.

OF TELEPHONE CALLS

Written by Edwin McArthur in Norway—Sept.-Oct., 1946

There have been repeated reports that because of his alleged connection with the Nazis, Mr. Henry Johansen was able to telephone his wife on many occasions while he was still in Norway and she in the United States. One book, by Howard Taubman, goes so far as to say he made a regular weekly telephone call.

This report is absolutely false. I will swear to it. And if it should be necessary, I am sure the Overseas Telephone Service can produce records to show that no calls were received by Kirsten Flagstad from Norway during the course of the War.

It is true that on two occasions she telephoned her husband from the United States. One of these telephone calls took place on the morning of Thanksgiving Day, 1940 from the Waldorf-Astoria Hotel in New York City.

The second call took place from the Blackstone Hotel in Chicago either the night of January 15, 1941 or the night of January 16th of the same year.

A third, but unsuccessful attempt to reach Norway was made from the Hotel Waldorf-Astoria in New York in the night of March 1, 1941.

Appendix A

This is a complete record of telephone communications between Kirsten Flagstad in the United States and Europe during the years of the war.

AMERICAN SOCIAL LIFE AND PARTIES

Written by Edwin McArthur in Norway—Sept.-Oct., 1946

It has been reported that Madame Flagstad was very lavish in the spending of her money on parties in order to get engagements in America and led a very active social life.

Actually, Kirsten Flagstad would never have had to do anything to get an engagement in America except sing. And certainly at no time did she have to entertain anyone or spend her money on a party with the idea of promoting her business.

On two occasions she entertained for her colleagues and close friends.

One was on October 22, 1939 in San Francisco. This was a large cocktail party given in the Mark Hopkins Hotel in San Francisco for her colleagues in the San Francisco Opera Company and the Directors and their wives. The party was partly in my honor as I had made my operatic debut in San Francisco two evenings before.

The other party to which I refer took place on December 12, 1938. This date Madame Flagstad celebrated her twenty-fifth year on the operatic stage and she gave a supper following a performance of "Die Götterdämmerung" for the entire Metropolitan Opera Company. When I say entire, I mean everyone from the biggest star to the cleaning woman was invited. And as I ran the details of the party, I alone, was the only person present who was not officially connected with the Opera company in some way.

Except for these two parties, Madame Flagstad never entertained except in the most casual way of having one or two friends very rarely for tea or a drink.

As far as her leading a social life, the only objection that Americans ever had about Kirsten Flagstad was that she consistently refused invitations to social functions. And I can testify that she would never have been able to give of her glorious voice and art had she been occupied with a social schedule.

ARRANGEMENT OF TRIP TO NORWAY IN 1941

Written by Edwin McArthur in Norway—Sept.-Oct., 1946

So much controversial discussion has taken place over Kirsten Flagstad's arrangement for and the actual trip to Europe in 1941. As I, more than anyone else in the world know more of the details in the arrangement of this trip, at long last I would like to tell the straight of the story.

It is a false conception that anyone forced Kirsten Flagstad to return to Europe. This she did of her own free will, and I always insisted that she had the right to make her own decision. Personally I felt that she should be with her husband, the same as I would expect my wife to be with me, and knowing her love of Norway, despite the horrors of war and the dangers of making such a journey, I could well understand the impossibility of her situation being away from home.

I wish to state clearly and frankly here and now that when she flew from LaGuardia Field in New York on April 19, 1941 she had every full intention of returning to the United States the following September.

Contrary to published reports, except for four thousand dollars in Travelers checks and about three hundred dollars in currency, *all* of her money which she possessed at that time in America was left in the bank in New York, and the account is still there.

Her personal belongings are in storage in New York.

She permitted her management, the NBC Artists Service to book her a season of concerts for 1941–1942, a thing she would not have permitted had she thought it possible she would not be returning to the United States.

It was clearly understood by the NBC that if upon her return to Norway she decided it better not to return, she would not be held either morally or financially responsible.

Upon Kirsten Flagstad's arrival, and after a short stay in Norway, she decided not to risk the return to America. She remained at home, and she is frank in stating that she was better satisfied, regardless of the war, to be in her own home-land and with her own family and people.

In the fall of 1940 she decided that she would like to return to Norway. She was entirely booked for that musical season, with her last engagement scheduled for Cleveland, Ohio on April 17th.

I investigated the possibility of sailing via Swedish boats to Europe. This turned out not to be practical. I then investigated the possibility of a trip across the Pacific, thence across Siberia and Russia, etc. and the rigors of such a trip were almost forbidding.

I then discussed with her the possibility of her flying home. Two things were plainly discussed—first her fear of flying, and second the necessity of crossing Germany. Regardless of the difficulties, she was determined to make the trip.

The NBC Artists Service, Madame Flagstad's management in America, was instructed to make plane reservations *to* and *from* Europe. The reservation was made for a possible flight in April, but they were informed that there might be a postponement.

I wish to make clear that I directed all of the plans and negotiations.

When I learned from NBC that there might be a delay, I

reported this to Madame Flagstad. As there were no engagements following her last appearance on April 17th in Cleveland, Ohio, she was anxious to start her journey homeward as early as possible.

NBC pressed the Pan-American Airways for a confirmation of an April flight. This was not difficult in peace times, but during war, such confirmations were often a problem.

On February 16, 1941 Mme. Flagstad went to the house of Mr. Sloan in New York for dinner. Mr. Sloan was then, as he is now, the president of the Metropolitan Opera Company in New York. In the course of dinner conversation, Madame Flagstad discussed the difficulty she was having in securing a definite flying schedule from New York to Portugal. Mr. Sloan offered to help her. A few days later he personally brought Mr. Juan Trippe, who is president of Pan-American, to Madam Flagstad's apartment in the Waldorf-Astoria. There Mr. Sloan and Mr. Trippe discussed her trip with Madame Flagstad and it is a fact that Mr. Trippe himself personally arranged and confirmed Madame Flagstad's flight from New York.

The NBC arranged with Mr. Stephen Spiegel, who is an expert immigration and customs broker in New York, to handle the obtaining of necessary travel papers.

Madame Flagstad delivered to Mr. Spiegel her *Norwegian* passport and Mr. Spiegel's office, together with the NBC arranged her various visae. At no time, did Madame Flagstad personally see an ambassador, a consul, or any representative of any foreign country in the arrangement of this trip. Particularly I mention that she had no contact whatsoever with the German representatives in America, although it has been publicly stated that she traveled on a German passport.

The German representatives in America granted her a transit visa to cross Germany enroute to Norway as well as one for return. There was no pressure brought to bear on anyone in the securing of this visa.

For reasons of communication, which were never explained except the general wartime condition, the transit visa from Portugal was delayed. A representative of Mr. Spiegel's office visited the Norwegian Embassy in Washington and requested the Embassy to ask the Portuguese Ambassador to stamp Madame Flagstad's passport with the necessary transit visa. Subsequently word came from the Norwegian Embassy that they had no objections to Madame Flagstad's returning to Norway, but acting upon instructions from the Norwegian Government in London, they were not to assist her in making this trip if she proposed to cross enemy territory.

Eventually the Portuguese visa was granted, and Madame Flagstad flew as scheduled the morning of April 19, 1941 on the "Dixie Clipper" of Pan-American Airways, bound for Lisbon, where she landed the next day.

It is interesting, especially in view of the fact that she is supposed to have been in such bad repute especially with the Norwegians in America at the time of her leaving, that Mr. Rolf Christensen, Consul General for Norway in New York, was at the Airport to wish his friend and country-woman "bon voyage."

OF PUBLICATIONS

Written by Edwin McArthur in Norway—Sept.-Oct., 1946

The articles in newspapers, pamphlets and books which have been written about Kirsten Flagstad since she returned to Norway in 1941 are too numerous to mention in full. The majority of these articles are completely false and in most instances the contents are shockingly legitimate ground for libel suits.

A consistent offender has been Nordisk Tidende, the Norwegian newspaper printed in Brooklyn, New York. The articles appearing in this publication have been consistently false. In June 1945, an American music journal of questionable repute called "The Musician" printed an editorial accusing Madame Flagstad, among other things, of having been an open Nazi in the United States, and having left the United States with all of her American Dollars, and of having travelled on a German Passport. These are only a few of the scurrilous lies in this article. Nordisk Tidende had the effrontery to reprint this article in its columns.

A great many of the articles which appeared in Nordisk Tidende were naturally in Norwegian, and for lack of having them here at hand and not having available translations, I am unwilling to make quotations. Suffice it to say a complete file of these libelous articles is in existence for future reference and use.

The Agency in America which has been responsible for the printing of the pamphlet "News of Norway" should also be sued for libel. On the 2nd of May, 1941, an account of the interview given by Kirsten Flagstad upon her return to Norway is printed. It is completely false. The statements, which Madame Flagstad made to a general press conference in Oslo, and not to a private interview with "Fritt Folk" as the "News of Norway" would lead us to believe, were merely repetitions of valid information she had received in the United States personally from such prominent citizens as former President Herbert Hoover. Mr. Hoover and his late wife entertained Madame Flagstad privately at tea in the Waldorf-Astoria Hotel in New York during the winter of 1941 and he personally told her then of his unsuccessful attempts to persuade the British to lift their blockade. Nor was this private information. Everyone who read the newspapers in the United States knew that Mr. Hoover was working in this direction. Nevertheless, when Madame Flagstad quoted this information in Oslo, she was branded in the "News from Norway" as a liar. When she told of information given her by Rev. Mr. Ingvolstad to the effect that money being raised for Norway could not reach Norway until after the war, she was called a still further liar.

On May 26, 1941 "Newsweek," apparently quoting "News from Norway" reprinted some of the above mentioned article of May 2nd. On October 29, 1945 Mr. W. Munthe, the Director of Universitetsbibliotsket in Oslo, wrote in response to Miss Edith Faigman of New York City as follows:

"Fritt Folk was the official newspaper of the Quisling regime. It was as far as possible boycotted by press colleagues and the public, but of course it was impossible to exclude it from open press conference. The newspaper stopped its issue with the Number of May 7, this year.

"The paragraph of the first number (April 28, 1941) relates that Mrs. Flagstad had returned to Norway, but declined to give any interview to Fritt Folk. Her secretary, however, answered some questions about the journey, but declared that Mrs. Flagstad would not give any public concert during her stay in her native country, which was intended purely as a vacation.

"The second article of April 30 is an interview on the ground of a general press conference. How much the reporter of Fritt Folk has added of his own to her announcements is impossible to say. Personally I cannot see how Mrs. Flagstad should have been able to shut out a member of the Staff of Fritt Folk.

"In the interview there is neither propaganda nor declaration in favour of the Quisling-regime. The notice in Newsweek cited in your letter is not correct. She has neither praised the conditions in Germany nor criticized the British blockade, but only stated the fact that no relief goods from America could be delivered to Norway till the war was ended.

"To the last question, I can only say that it was possible to send letters to America, but the connection was very slow.

"I wish to add that I am not a relative and have not the slightest connection with Mrs. Flagstad or personal interest in this matter. I am only glad to give these facts and thereby do my part to prevent any injustice being done to our most famous opera singer."

There have been repeated reports in the American newspapers to the effect that Kirsten Flagstad sang in Germany during the war.

In a book entitled "Europe in Revolt" by Rene Kraus, and published in 1942 by the MacMillan Company, I quote from page 236:

"Not even the nightingale of Nazism could lure Norwegians into the Russian deathtrap. In vain Kirsten Flagstad of faded Metropolitan fame appeared at a gala performance in the Royal Opera in Oslo for the benefit of potential crusaders. Very few were interested in benefiting. Equally few availed themselves of a promise made by Mr. Henry Johansen, who happens to be Madame Flagstad's husband, and by the same token, Quisling's chief financial backer, that he would give a job to every hero who returned alive from the Russian front."

This foregoing article from "Europe in Revolt" regarding Kirsten Flagstad is a complete lie—every word.

Howard Taubman, associate music critic of the New York Times states in a book printed since 1941, that Kirsten Flagstad received a weekly telephone call from her husband in occupied Norway. Such a statement as this can be proven entirely false as well. In time, it will along with all the others, so be proven.

There has seemingly been a concerted campaign of information of a false nature regarding Kirsten Flagstad, and I am sorry as an American that some of our newspaper correspondents in this country seem to have been influenced themselves.

I arrived in Norway on this trip on Sunday, September 8, 1946 after a twenty-four hour flight from New York. That afternoon, I dined in the dining room of the Grand Hotel in Oslo with Madame Flagstad, her sister, and a friend. She herself told me that that day, September 8, 1946 was the first day she had appeared publicly in a dining room in Norway since the end of the war in May, 1945. The next evening, September 9, 1946, Madame Flagstad and I dined alone about ten-thirty at night in the same dining room of the Grand Hotel in Oslo. Since that date she has not been in a public dining room.

It is strange then to understand how an article under date-line of September 21, 1946 and with the city of Kristiansand, Norway as its origin and Ned Nordness its writer can appear on September 22, 1946 in the New York Journal-American and read:

"Kirsten Flagstad sits in a restaurant ignored by other diners as completely as if she were not there."

I say it is strange to understand, when I state that on the two occasions we publicly dined together, and described above, she was visited, I mean Kirsten Flagstad was visited, by so many people in the dining room that I was continually forced to stand up to greet her many friends and admirers and had great difficulty in getting the opportunity to eat my food.

Appendix B

KIRSTEN FLAGSTAD'S APPEARANCE IN OPERA

OPERA	HER ROLE	HER FIRST PERFORMANCE OF THE ROLE	TOTAL NUMBER OF HER PERFORMANCES OF THE ROLE
Tiefland (d'Albert)	Nuri	Dec. 12, 1913	20
Les Cloches de Corneville (The Chimes of Normandy) (Planquette)	Serpolette	1914	7
En hellig Aften (Schjelderup)	Engel	1915	8
Vaarnat (Schjelderup)	Emilie	1915	8
Der Evangelimann (Kienzl)	Marta	Jan. 16, 1919	6
I Pagliacci (Leoncavallo)	Nedda	March 23, 1919	13
Der Zigeunerbaron (Strauss)	Saffi	1919	10
Die schöne Galathee (Suppé)	Ganymed	March 25, 1919	17
Die Nürnberger Puppe (Suppé)	Bertha	April 1, 1919	7
Abu Hassan (Weber)	Die Frau	April 1, 1919	5
La Belle Hélène (Offenbach)	Oreste	1919	5
Die Lustigen Weiber von Windsor (Nicolai)	Anna	May 10, 1919	7
Die Zauberflöte (Mozart)	First Lady	Jan. 18, 1921	6
Otello (Verdi)	Desdemona	Jan. 26, 1921	19

Appendix B
KIRSTEN FLAGSTAD'S APPEARANCE IN OPERA

OPERA	HER ROLE	HER FIRST PERFORM- ANCE OF THE ROLE	TOTAL NUMBER OF HER PERFORM- ANCES OF THE ROLE
Un Ballo in maschera (Verdi)	Amelia	Feb. 20, 1921	9
Das höllisch Gold (Bittner)	Die Frau	April 17, 1921	3
La Fanciulla del West (Puccini)	Minnie	May 5, 1921	18
Orphée aux enfers (Offenbach)	Euridice	1922	?
Boccaccio (Suppé)	Fiametta	1923	?
Carmen (Bizet)	Micaëla	Nov. 22, 1924	47
Die Fledermaus (Strauss)	Rosalinda	1924	10
Les Brigands (Offenbach)	Fiorella	1925	?
Sjömandsbruden (Aspestrand)	Ragnhild	Dec. 12, 1925	4
Faust (Gounod)	Marguérite	Dec. 12, 1926	41
Orfeo ed Euridice (Gluck)	Euridice	July 6, 1927	11
Der Freischütz (Weber)	Agathe	Oct. 4, 1928	28
Saul og David (Nielsen)	Mikal	Nov. 29, 1928	15
Aïda (Verdi)	Aïda	March 7, 1929	27
La Bohème (Puccini)	Mimi	April 11, 1929	6
Tosca (Puccini)	Tosca	April 19, 1929	21
Lohengrin (Wagner)	Elsa	June 14, 1929	40
La Rondine (Puccini)	Magda	Oct. 4, 1929	7
Die Meistersinger (Wagner)	Eva	Feb. 18, 1930	21
Jonny spielt auf (Křenek)	Anita	April 10, 1930	6

KIRSTEN FLAGSTAD'S APPEARANCE IN OPERA

OPERA	HER ROLE	HER FIRST PERFORMANCE OF THE ROLE	TOTAL NUMBER OF HER PERFORMANCES OF THE ROLE
Schwanda der Dudel-sackpfeifer (Wein-berger)	Dorota	Dec. 3, 1931	14
Rodelinda (Handel)	Rodelinda	Feb. 16, 1932	7
Tristan und Isolde (Wagner)	Isolde	June 29, 1932	182
Die Walküre (Wagner)	Ortlinde	July 25, 1933	2
Götterdämmerung (Wagner)	Third Norn	July 28, 1933	2
Die Walküre (Wagner)	Sieglinde	May 24, 1934	14
Götterdämmerung (Wagner)	Gutrune	July 6, 1934	3
Tannhauser (Wagner)	Elisabeth	Oct. 5, 1934	35
Fidelio (Beethoven)	Leonore	Dec. 10, 1934	37
Die Walküre (Wagner)	Brünnhilde	Feb. 15, 1935	78
Götterdämmerung (Wagner)	Brünnhilde	Feb. 28, 1935	47
Parsifal (Wagner)	Kundry	April 17, 1935	39
Siegfried (Wagner)	Brünnhilde	Nov. 6, 1935	30
Der fliegende Holländer (Wagner)	Senta	Jan. 7, 1937	11
Oberon (Weber)	Rezia	May 30, 1942	2
Alceste (Gluck)	Alcestis	May 29, 1943	8
Dido and Aeneas (Purcell)	Dido	Sept. 9, 1951	111

Flagstad also sang the part of Lia in Debussy's *L'Enfant prodigue:* first time, October 4, 1929; 7 performances. According to *The Flagstad Manuscript*, edited by Louis Biancolli (New York, 1952), Flagstad recalled having sung also in the following modern operettas and musical comedies: *The Little Lark* (1919); *Zigeunerliebe* (1921); *Phi-Phi* (1922); *The Lady in Ermine* (1922); *The Cousin from Batavia* (so played in Denmark in 1922; known also as *The Girl from Holland*); *Die Bajadere* (1922); *The Dollar Princess* (1923); *The Queen of the Movies* (1923); *Lucullus* (1923); *Wenn Liebe erwirbt* (1923); *The Circus Princess* (1925? 1926?); *Der Orloff* (1925); *Gräfin Maritza* (Finland, 1928); *Her Excellency* (Finland, 1928); *La Teresina* (Göteborg, 1929).

The same source states that Flagstad also appeared as soloist in the following oratorios and choral works:

Bach various cantatas
Beethoven *Missa Solemnis;* Ninth Symphony
Handel *Joshua; Alexander's Feast; Judas Maccabaeus; Solomon; Messiah*
Haydn *The Creation*
Mendelssohn *St. Paul*
Rossini *Stabat Mater*

INDEX

i

Index

Index

Index

Index

viii

A NOTE ON THE TYPE

THE TEXT of this book is set in Caledonia, a typeface designed by W(illiam) A(ddison) Dwiggins for the Mergenthaler Linotype Company in 1939. Dwiggins chose to call his new typeface Caledonia, the Roman name for Scotland, because it was inspired by the Scotch types cast about 1833 by Alexander Wilson & Son, Glasgow type founders. However, there is a calligraphic quality about this face that is totally lacking in the Wilson types. Dwiggins referred to an even earlier typeface for this "liveliness of action"—one cut around 1790 by William Martin for the printer William Bulmer. Caledonia has more weight than the Martin letters, and the bottom finishing strokes (serifs) of the letters are cut straight across, without brackets, to make sharp angles with the upright stems, thus giving a "modern face" appearance.

W. A. Dwiggins (1880-1956) was born in Martinsville, Ohio, and studied art in Chicago. In 1904 he moved to Hingham, Massachusetts, where he built a solid reputation as a designer of advertisements and as a calligrapher. He began an association with the Mergenthaler Linotype Company in 1929, and over the next twenty-seven years designed a number of book types for that firm. Of especial interest are the Metro series, Electra, Caledonia, Eldorado, and Falcon. In 1930, Dwiggins first became interested in marionettes, and through the years made many important contributions to the art of puppetry and the design of marionettes.